Multinationality— Earnings, Efficiency, and Market Considerations

Multinationality— Earnings, Efficiency, and Market Considerations

Ahmed Riahi-Belkaoui

QUORUM BOOKS
Westport, Connecticut • London

Library of Congress Cataloging-in-Publication Data

Riahi-Belkaoui, Ahmed, 1943–
    Multinationality : earnings, efficiency, and market considerations / Ahmed Riahi-Belkaoui.
        p.   cm.
    Includes index.
    ISBN 1–56720–471–6 (alk. paper)
    1. International business enterprises.   2. International business
enterprises—Management.   3. Investments, Foreign.   I. Title.
    HD2755.5.R53   2002
    658'.049—dc21   2001019868

British Library Cataloguing in Publication Data is available.

Library of Congress Catalog Card Number: 2001019868
ISBN: 1–56720–471–6

First published in 2002

Quorum Books, 88 Post Road West, Westport, CT 06881
An imprint of Greenwood Publishing Group, Inc.
www.quorumbooks.com

Printed in the United States of America

The paper used in this book complies with the
Permanent Paper Standard issued by the National
Information Standards Organization (Z39.48–1984).

10 9 8 7 6 5 4 3 2 1

Copyright Acknowledgments

The author and publisher gratefully acknowledge permission for use of the following material:

Chapter 23 adapted from *Research in Accounting* 3, Ahmed Riahi-Belkaoui, "Prediction Performance of Earnings Forecasts of U.S. Multinational Firms Active in Developed and Developing Countries," pp. 85–97, Copyright 1995, with permission from Elsevier Science.

Chapter 18 has been adapted with permission of the editor from: Riahi-Belkaoui, Ahmed, and E. Pavlik, "Effects of Ownership Structure, Firm Performance, Size and Diversification Strategy on CEO Compensation: A Path Analysis," *Managerial Finance*, Vol. 19, No. 2, 1993, pp. 33–54.

Chapter 19 has been adapted with the permission of the editor from: Riahi-Belkaoui, Ahmed, and E. Pavlik, "Determinants of Executive Tenure in Large U.S. Firms," *Managerial Finance*, Vol. 19, No. 2, 1993, pp. 12–19.

Chapter 20 has been adapted with permission of the editor from: Riahi-Belkaoui, Ahmed, and R. Picur, "An Analysis of the Use of Accounting and Market Measures of Performance, CEO Experience and Nature of the Deviation from the Analysts' Forecasts in CEO Compensation Contracts," *Managerial Finance*, Vol. 19, No. 2, 1993, pp. 20–32.

Chapter 21 has been adapted with permission of the editor from: Riahi-Belkaoui, Ahmed, and J. Monti-Belkaoui, "Effects of Personal Attributes and Performance on the Level of CEO Compensation: Direct and Interaction Effects," *Managerial Finance*, Vol. 19, No. 2, 1993, pp. 3–11.

Chapter 22 has been adapted with permission of the editor from: Riahi-Belkaoui, Ahmed, and R. Picur, "Explaining Market Reactions: Earnings Versus Value Added Data," *Managerial Finance*, Vol. 20, 9, 1994, pp. 44–55.

Chapter 15 has been adapted with permission of the editor from Riahi-Belkaoui, Ahmed, and R. Picur, "Multidivisional Structure and Productivity: The Contingency of Diversification Strategy," *Journal of Business Finance and Accounting*, June 1997, pp. 615–27.

Chapter 17 has been adapted with permission of the editor from: Riahi-Belkaoui, Ahmed, "Executive Compensation, Organizational Effectiveness, Social Performance and Firm Performance: An Empirical Investigation," *Journal of Business Finance and Accounting*, January 1992, pp. 25–38.

To Dimitra

Contents

Illustrations

TABLES

FIGURES

Preface

Multinationality has an impact on the conduct of operations. As a result, it has an impact on the magnitude and properties of earnings, efficiency, and the consequent market valuation. The thesis of this book is that multinationality affects the known relationships between earnings, efficiency, disclosure, and market valuation by playing a major role as dependent, moderating, antecedent, and consequent variables. Known relationships and phenomenon as the timeliness of earnings, the informativeness of earnings, the security analyst underreaction, the post-earnings-announcement drifts, and the level and quality of disclosure are shown to be better explained by the consideration of the impact of multinationality as a dependent, moderating, intervening, antecedent or consequent variable. An understanding of this particular role of multinationality in the earnings-disclosure-efficiency-market valuation relationships is useful for the conduct of a more inclusive research process by accountants and researchers, and for a better management of multinational firms by managers, who will be aware that it is crucial. This thesis is examined in the following chapters:

Chapter 1: The Impact of Multinationality on the Informativeness of Earnings and Accounting Choices. This chapter hypothesizes that the level of multinationality affects both the informativeness of earnings and the magnitude of discretionary accounting accrual adjustments. The hypothesis draws on multinationality theories and exploits: (1) the international diversifications opportunities provided by multinational firms; (2) managers' incentives in using discretionary accrual adjustments. Results show that multinationality is positively associated with earnings' explanatory power for returns and related to the magnitude of accounting accrual adjustments.

Chapter 2: The Timeliness of Accounting Earnings as an Antecedent of Disclosure Informativeness. The objective of this chapter is to investigate how disclosure informativeness of U.S. multinational corporations vary with information properties of numbers produced by their financial accounting systems. We predict that firms whose current accounting numbers do not capture well the effects of the firm's current activities and outcomes on shareholder value will institute better disclosure systems and improve their disclosure informativeness to compensate for their less-useful accounting data. Disclosure informativeness is measured by analyst ratings of corporate disclosures provided in the annual volumes of the *Report of the Financial Analysts Federation Corporate Information Committee.* We investigate whether these ratings vary with the timeliness of earnings by examining the cross-sectional relation between process for earnings timeliness and subsequent analyst ratings of corporate disclosure of one hundred firms included in *Forbes*'s survey of the largest U.S. multinationals. The results support a significant negative relation between the timeliness metrics and subsequent values of disclosure informativeness after controlling for the firm characteristics.

Chapter 3: Level of Multinationality as an Explanation for Post-Announcement Drift. This chapter tests whether the observed patterns in stock returns after quarterly earnings announcements are related to the level of multinationality, a variable used to proxy for firm complexity. Our findings show that the level of multinationality is negatively correlated with the observed post-announcement abnormal returns. The findings suggest that the level of multinationality as a proxy for firm complexity underlies the predictability of stock returns after earnings announcements.

Chapter 4: The Effect of Multinationality on Security Analyst Underreaction. Previous research presented evidence of bias and serial correlation in forecast errors suggesting that analysts do not properly recognize the time-series properties of earnings when setting expectations of future earnings. A reason for the security analyst underreaction is the level of multinationality of the firm's activities. Using a time-series research design, we find that analysts underreact to prior information more as the level of multinationality of the firm examined increases.

Chapter 5: Growth Opportunities, Internalization, and Market Valuation of Multinational Firms. This chapter examines the role of the investment opportunity set as an encompassing intangible to explain the relative market value compared to the accounting value for a multinational firm. The results of this study are also consistent with internalization theory that greater multinationality corresponds to a higher valuation of the firm if growth opportunities are high, and the tenets of imperfect capital markets theory in that greater multinationality above does not correlate positively to a significantly greater market value. However, this chapter supports the hypothesis that greater multinationality above correlate negatively to a significantly greater market value, which confirms the views of managerial objectives theory. It implies that while investors and the market value highly the internalization of growth opportunities, they are less enthusiastic about the divergence of interests with management on the merits of international diversification.

Chapter 6: Level of Multinationality, Growth Opportunities, and Size as Determinants of Analyst Ratings of Corporate Disclosures. This chapter examines the cross-sectional variations in analysts' published evaluations of firms' disclosure practices and provides evidence that the analysts' ratings, as a measure of disclosure informativeness, are positively related to size, growth opportunities, and the degree of multinationality. The larger the firm and the higher its growth opportunities and its degree of internationalization, the more informative are its corporate disclosures.

Chapter 7: The Effects of Multinationality on Earnings Response Coefficients. This chapter investigates the effects of multinationality on the relation between unexpected returns and unexpected earnings of U.S. multinational firms. The findings indicate a systematic relation between multinationality and the information content of earnings. Firms with relatively more (less) multinationality appeared to have smaller (larger), less significant (more significant) earnings response coefficients.

Chapter 8: The Effects of Multinationality on Earnings Persistence. This chapter tests the relationship between multinationality and earnings persistence produced by Autoregressive, Integrated, Moving-Average (ARIMA) models. When higher-order ARIMA models are used, this study shows earnings persistence to be positively related to size and negatively related to multinationality.

Chapter 9: The Association between Performance Plan Adoption and Organizational Slack. This chapter investigates the potential impact of the adoption of performance plans on absorbed and unabsorbed organizational slack. The empirical results indicate that U.S. multinational firms adopting performance plans (relative to similar nonadopting firms) decrease the amount of unabsorbed slack they were holding.

Chapter 10: Corporate Disclosure Quality and Corporate Reputation of U.S. Multinational Firms. This chapter extends the investigation of both the determination of corporate reputation and the consequences of disclosure quality of multinational firms by showing evidence of a link between disclosure quality and corporate reputation of large U.S. multinational firms. Although the signals used in previous studies show attendance by corporate audiences to market and accounting cues, the results suggest that disclosure quality also influences reputation building for large U.S. multinational firms.

Chapter 11: Growth Opportunities, Multinationality, and Reputation Building. This chapter provides empirical evidence supporting the general hypothesis that corporate audiences construct reputations of U.S. multinational firms based on information regarding a firm's asset management performance, specially using market and accounting signals that indicate the size of the firm, the level of the investment opportunity set, and the level of multinationality.

Chapter 12: Net Value Added and Earnings Determination for U.S. Multi-

national Firms. This chapter posits that earnings determination is a response to the net wealth generated by the firm or net value added and as an adjustment to the previous level of earnings. The empirical evidence is consistent with the role of net value added and the previous level of earnings in the determination of earnings by U.S. multinational firms.

Chapter 13: The Substitution of Net Value Added for Earnings in Equity Valuation. This chapter provides evidence that the substitution of net value added for earnings in equity valuation models results in a better association with the equity value of U.S. multinational firms.

Chapter 14: Implementation of the M-Form Organizational Structure and Shareholders' Wealth of Multinational Firms. This chapter investigates the impact of the implementation of the M-form organizational structure by U.S. multinational firms on the shareholders' wealth. The evidence suggests that both price effects and risk changes are contingent on the multinational firms' existing type of diversification strategy (unrelated, related, or vertical).

Chapter 15: Implementation of the M-Form Organizational Structure and Productivity of Multinational Firms. This chapter investigates the proposition that the implementation of the M-form structure affects productivity differently, depending upon which diversification strategy existed prior to the implementation of the M-form, by comparing a value added-based measure of productivity of large multinational, multiproduct firms before and after their reorganization. The results confirm the thesis of a contingency of diversification strategy.

Chapter 16: Implementation of the M-Form Organizational Structure and Capital Structure of Multinational Firms. The central proposition of the chapter is that the implementation of the M-form structure affects the capital structure decision differently depending on which diversification strategy exists prior to M-form implementation. A comparison of the capital structure of large U.S. multinational firms before and after their reorganization supported the contingency view of the relationship between capital structure and the implementation of the M-form for multinational firms.

Chapter 17: Executive Compensation, Organizational Effectiveness, Social Performance, and Firm Performance: An Empirical Investigation. This chapter presents evidence on the determinants of executive compensation of U.S. multinational firms. The results show that executive compensation is related to various measures of firm performance, social performance, and organizational effectiveness.

Chapter 18: Effects of Ownership Structure, Firm Performance, Size, and Diversification Strategy on CEO Compensation in U.S. Multinational Firms: A Path Analysis. This chapter develops and tests a model that attempts to describe the influence of ownership structure, diversification strategy, firm size, and firm performance on CEO compensation of multinational firms. The results, based on data from a cross-sectional set of 216 Fortune 500 multinational firms, suggested that size, ownership structure, and diversification strategy affect CEO compensation through the mediating effects of firm performance.

Chapter 19: Determinants of Executive Tenure in Large U.S. Multinational

Firms. This chapter examines the relationship between executive tenure and selected company characteristics for 196 U.S. corporations. Tenure was found to be negatively related to both related and unrelated diversification strategies, and positively related to firm performance and both types of ownership structure: stock concentration and management stockholdings.

Chapter 20: An Analysis of the Use of Accounting and Market Measures of Performance, CEO Experience, and Nature of the Deviation from the Analysts' Forecasts in CEO Compensation Contracts of Multinational Firms. This chapter develops and tests a model that attempts to describe the influence of CEO experience, nature of the deviation from the analysts' forecasts, and measures of firm performance on executive compensation. Results based on data from a cross-sectional set of 247 multinational firms from twenty-two industries verified the model.

Chapter 21: Effects of Personal Attributes and Performance on the Level of CEO Compensation in Multinational Firms: Direct and Interaction Effects. CEO compensation in multinational firms is shown to be not only related to size and performance, but also to personal attributes. CEO compensation is found to be positively related to the number of years as a CEO and to the interaction of age and tenure, and negatively related to tenure and to the interaction of age and number of years as a CEO of a multinational firm.

Chapter 22: Explaining Market Returns of U.S. Multinational Firms: Earnings Versus Value-Added Data. The objective of the chapter is to determine whether value-added data variables possess incremental information beyond accrual earnings in the context of explaining security returns of U.S. firms that disclose data needed for the computation of net value added. A case can be made for the voluntary or mandated disclosure of value-added reports for U.S. multinational firms.

Chapter 23: Prediction Performance of Earnings Forecasts of U.S. Firms Active in Developed and Developing Countries. This chapter investigates the accuracy and dispersion among analysts' earnings forecasts for three groups of U.S. firms: those with no significant international operations, those with significant international operations in developed countries, and those with significant international operations in developing countries. The results indicate that domestic firms and firms with significant international operations in developed countries have more accurate earnings forecasts than firms with significant international operations in developing countries.

This book should be of interest to according academics; managers of multinational firms; and students of international business, accounting, and finance interested in the role of multinationality in the different relationships between earnings, efficiency, and market valuation.

Many people helped in the development of this book. I received considerable assistance from the University of Illinois research assistants, especially Shahrzad Ghatan, Ewa Tomaszewska, and Vivian Au. I also thank Eric Valentine, Frank Saunders, and the entire production team at Quorum for their continuous and intelligent support.

CHAPTER 1

The Impact of Multinationality on the Informativeness of Earnings and Accounting Choices

INTRODUCTION

This chapter reports the results of an investigation in how the degree of multinationality affects the informativeness of accounting and the accounting choices of managers. Three theories link multinationality to investment value, predicting either a higher or lower value (Morck and Yeung, 1991, 1992; Mishra and Gobelli, 1998). They are the internalization theory, the imperfect world capital markets theory, and the managerial objectives theory.

The internalization theory maintains that direct foreign investment occurs when a firm can increase its value by internalizing markets for certain of its intangibles (Rugman, 1980, 1981).

The imperfect world capital markets theory maintains that because of the imperfect world markets, multinational firms offer shareholders international diversification opportunities, which as a result enhance their share prices (Agmon and Lessard, 1977).

Finally, the managerial objectives theory predicts that the existence of divergence of objectives between managers and shareholders, with top management favoring international diversification, may reduce the value of multinationals relative to uninationals.

The three theories are silent on the role of earnings in the relationship between multinationality and investment value. Earnings is known to be informative in explaining stock returns; therefore, the first hypothesis predicts the informativeness of earnings in explaining stock returns varies systematically with the level of multinationality in the corporation.

The second hypothesis derives from the managerial objectives theory and postulates that managers' accounting choices are systematically related to the level of multinationality. The managerial objectives theory recognizes divergence of objectives between management and shareholders of multinational firms regarding the merits of international diversification. Accordingly, contracts must be written, often containing accounting-based constraints, to restrict managers' value-changing behavior when multinationality is high. These same accounting-based constraints may lead managers to exploit the latitude available in accepted accounting procedures to alleviate the same constraints. For multinational firms, therefore, the magnitude of discretionary accounting accrual adjustment is positively related to the level of multinationality.

The results of this study using U.S. multinational firms shows that (a) the level of multinationality is positively associated with the informativeness of accounting earnings, and (b) the magnitude of discretionary accounting accrual adjustments is significantly higher when the level of multinationality is high. These results are robust in the presence of endogenous and exogenous determinants of accounting choices and earnings' explanatory power for returns, including firm size, systematic risk, growth opportunities, and the variability and persistence of accounting earnings.

MULTINATIONALITY, CONTRACTS, AND ACCOUNTING

The Impact of Multinationality on the Informativeness of Earnings

Both the internalization theory and the imperfect capital markets theory predict a positive association between multinationality and firm value.

The internalization theory maintains that foreign direct investment will cause the increase of the market value of the firm relative to its accounting value only if the firm can internalize markets for certain of its intangibles.[1] Examples of these firm-specific intangible assets include: production skills, managerial skills, patent, marketing abilities, consumer goodwill, research and development, advertising spending, managerial incentives alignment, and corporate reputation, to name a few (Mishra and Gobelli, 1998; Morck and Yeung, 1991). These information-based proprietary intangible assets cannot be copied or exchanged at arm's length, but can only be transferred to subsidiaries, thereby internationalizing the markets for such assets. As a result, the market value of a multinational firm, possessing these intangibles and engaging in foreign direct investment will be directly proportional to the firm's degree of multinationality.

The imperfect capital markets theory suggests that investors, confined by institutional constraints on international capital flows and the information asymmetries that exist in global capital markets, invest in multinational firms to gain from the international diversification opportunities they provide.[2] This direct valuation of multinational firms by investors as a means of diversifying their portfolios internationally is assumed to enhance the share prices of multinational firms, independently of the information-based proprietary intangible assets possessed by these firms.

Accounting research has, however, consistently showed earning's explanatory power for returns, without explicitly examining the contingent role of multinationality. What has appeared in the international business literature, with regards to the association between firm value and multinationality, may be an association between earnings and firm value that is more pronounced with increased multinationality (Bodnar and Weintrop, 1997). This argumentation leads to the first testable hypothesis: *The informativeness of accounting earnings as an explanatory variable for returns is systematically related to the level of multinationality.*

The Impact of Multinationality on the Behavior of Discretionary Accounting Accruals

The managerial objectives theory rests on the assumption of the differences of motives between management and shareholders. The complexity of the multinational firm and the resulting difficulty for shareholders in monitoring management's decisions allows management to act in their self-interest. They may favor international diversification because it reduces firm-specific risk. The situation is assumed to potentially reduce the market value of multinational firms (Morck and Yeung, 1991). It can be predicted that when multinationality is high, incentives arise for managers to pursue non-value-maximization behavior. The situation calls for the writing of contracts, often containing accounting-based constraints, to monitor managers' decisions. Most likely, managers will exploit the latitude offered in available accepted accounting techniques to manage these constraints to their own interest. Their accounting choices, as reflected by the behavior of the discretionary portion of total accruals, will be a positive function of the level of multinationality. These arguments lead to the second hypothesis: *The magnitude of adjustments in managers' accounting choices is systematically related to the level of multinationality.*

Other Considerations Affecting Accounting Choices

Based on contracting theory and economic theories of the political process that govern managers' incentives in the selection and reporting of accounting numbers, other endogenous and exogenous determinants of accounting choices and earnings' explanatory power for returns are also examined. They include six additional factors: firm size, systematic risk, leverage, growth opportunities, earnings variability, and earnings persistence (Warfield et al., 1995).

SAMPLE SELECTION AND DATA

Multinationality was measured as foreign sales over total sales for the most international one hundred American manufacturing and service firms, a list of which *Forbes* publishes every year. To be included in the sample, a firm must meet the following selection criteria:

1. The firm must be included in *Forbes*'s most international one hundred American manufacturing and service firms from 1994 to 1998.
2. Annual earnings-per-share and dividends are available from *Standard and Poor's Compustat primary, secondary, tertiary, and full coverage* database.
3. Data necessary to compute stock returns (including dividends) are available from *Compustat Price, Dividends, and Earnings* database. Both price-per-share and earnings-per-share were adjusted for stock splits and stock dividends.
4. Annual data necessary to compute discretionary accruals are available from *Standard and Poor's Compustat primary, secondary, tertiary, and full coverage* database.

The complete sample consists of 404 for the first hypothesis, and 368 firm-year observations for the second hypothesis.

Descriptive statistics and correlation analysis of the data used in both hypotheses are shown in tables 1.1 and 1.2.

INFORMATIVENESS OF EARNINGS CONDITIONAL ON MULTINATIONALITY

Multinationality as a Determinant of Earnings' Explanatory Power

Table 1.3 presents the correlation between earnings and returns (column 3) and the earnings coefficients (column 4) for the different ranges of multinationality measured as foreign sales over total sales (column 3). The correlation between returns and earnings is positive and significantly greater than zero for the total sample with a level of multinationality ranging from 0% to 75%, and for each of the other multinationality ranges. These correlations range from a minimum of 0.42 for the 0–25% level of multinationality, to a high of 0.65 for the 50–75% level of multinationality. In addition, the Pearson (Spearman) correlation between the level of multinationality (column 1), and the correlation between earnings and returns (column 3) for the three multinationality levels equals 0.67 (0.75), which is significantly greater than zero at the 0.05 level. The evidence from this first test points to multinationality as a determinant of the informativeness of earnings.

The second test of the informativeness of earnings conditional on multinationality levels examines the cross-sectional variation of the earnings coefficient conditional on multinationality. The following pooled cross-sectional regression model, with a multinationality interaction term, is used:

$$(R_{i,t}) = \alpha_0 + \alpha_1 \cdot E_{i,t} / P_{i,t-1} + \alpha_2 E_{i,t} \, MULTY_i / P_{i,t-1} + \varepsilon_{i,t} \tag{1}$$

Table 1.1
Summary for the Variables

Panel A : Descriptive Statistics

Variable	Mean	Standard deviation	Median	First quartile	Third quartile
Stock return $(R_{i,t})$	0.0952	0.0552	0.0897	0.0602	0.1286
Accounting earning $(E_{i,t} / P_{i,t-1})$	0.0570	0.0854	0.0649	0.0369	0.0847
Earnings interacted with :					
a. Multinationality $(E_{i,t} . MULTY_i / P_{i,t-1})$	0.0193	0.0514	0.0189	0.0081	0.0332
b. Size $(E_{i,t} . SIZE_i / P_{i,t-1})$	0.5309	0.6125	0.5689	0.3171	0.7832
c. Growth opportunities $(E_{i,t} . GROWTH_i / P_{i,t-1})$	0.0881	0.2349	0.0508	0.0331	0.0774
d. Systematic risk $(E_{i,t} . RISK_i / P_{i,t-1})$	0.0072	0.0134	0.0028	0.0008	0.0083
e. Leverage $(E_{i,t} . DEBT_i / P_{i,t-1})$	0.0087	0.0119	0.0072	0.0023	0.0139
f. Earnings variability $(E_{i,t} . VAR_i / P_{i,t-1})$	0.1269	0.099	0.1028	0.0601	0.1653
g. Earnings persistence $(E_{i,t} . PERS_i / P_{i,t-1})$	-0.0082	0.1686	-0.0010	-0.0018	0.0005

Panel B : Pearson correlation matrix (using variables from Panel A)

Variable	E	MULTY	SIZE	GROWTH	RISK	DEBT	VAR	PERS
Accounting earnings (E)	1.00	0.281	0.2633	0.2320	0.2030	0.3496	0.3328	-0.3856
Multinationality (MULTY)		1.00	0.3588	0.3727	0.1652	0.2814	0.3685	-0.4813
Size (SIZE)			1.00	0.3670	0.3489	0.2051	0.2586	-0.4788
Growth opportunities (GROWTH)				1.00	0.0690	0.0067	0.3351	0.0103
Systematic risk (RISK)					1.00	0.1172	0.3417	0.0158
Leverage (DEBT)						1.00	0.1557	-0.0596
Earnings variability (VAR)							1.00	-0.2069
Earnings persistence (PERS)								1.00

Stock returns (R) are measured for the twelve-month period from nine months prior to the fiscal year-end through three months after the fiscal year-end, earnings (E) is the accounting earnings-per-share, multinationality (MULTY) is measured as foreign sales/total sales, size (SIZE) is measured as the company's market value of equity (in 000s), systematic risk (RISK) is measured by the market model beta, growth opportunities (GROWTH) are measured by the market-to-book ratio for common equity, leverage (DEBT) is measured by the ratio of total debt to total assets, earnings variability (VAR) is measured by the standard deviation of earnings for the 20 quarters 1994–98, earnings persistence (PERS) is the first-order autocorrelation in earnings for the 20 quarters 1994–98, and price (P) is the stock price at the beginning of the period. The sample size is 404 firm-year observations.

Table 1.2
Summary Statistics for the Variables

Panel A : Descriptive Statistics

Variable	Mean	Standard deviation	Median	First quartile	Third quartile
Absolute Abnormal Accrual (/AAC/)	0.0190	0.0110	0.0179	0.0120	0.0092
Multinationality (MULTY)	0.3492	0.142	0.3345	0.2360	0.4520
Size (SIZE)	8.782	0.9284	8.6983	8.1616	9.4140
Systematic risk (RISK)	0.090	0.131	0.044	0.016	0.124
Leverage (DEBT)	0.1583	0.1428	0.1384	0.0541	0.2277
Growth opportunities (GROWTH)	35.893	52.129	2.460	1.5881	4.2165
Earnings variability (VAR)	0.1673	0.0789	0.1374	0.1164	0.1930
Earnings persistence (PERS)	-0.1618	0.1316	-0.015	-0.023	-0.0097

Panel B : Pearson correlation matrix

Variable	MULTY	SIZE	RISK	DEBT	GROWTH	VAR	PERS
Multinationality (MULTY)	1.00	0.0136	0.1642	-0.1576	0.0544	0..2448	0.0326
Size (SIZE)		1.00	0.1083	-0.1312	-0.0613	0.3006	0.1590
Systematic risk (RISK)			1.00	-0.1341	-0.0704	0.1606	0.0818
Leverage (DEBT)				1.00	-0.2428	-0.2193	0.1183
Growth opportunities (GROWTH)					1.00	-0.1521	-0.0651
Earnings variability (VAR)						1.00	0.0808
Earnings persistence (PERS)							1.00

Abnormal accrual, AAC, is defined as the current-period accrual less the expected normal accrual, where the difference is standardized by the beginning period stock price. Absolute abnormal accrual, /AAC/ is measured as the absolute value of abnormal accruals (AAC). All other variables are as defined in table 1.1.

where $(R_{i,t})$ is the return of firm i for annual period t, extending from nine months prior to fiscal year-end through three months after fiscal year-end; $E_{i,t}$ is earnings-per-share; $P_{i,t-1}$ is the price-per-share at the end of period $t - 1$; and $MULTY_i$ is the level of multinationality as measured by foreign sales over total sales for the year. The joint relation between earnings and multinationality is measured by α_2, showing the extent to which the informativeness of earnings is affected by the level of multinationality. The regression results in table 1.4 indicate that the informativeness is affected by the level of multinationality as both the regression coefficient (0.575) and the earnings-multinationality coefficient (0.865) are both significantly greater than zero at the 0.0001 level.

Given that the results in table 1.3 imply nonlinearity with the data, the same regression was run separately for each of the three categories of multinationality levels in table 1.3, thereby not imposing a constant residual assumption across multinationality categories. The earnings coefficients from these regressions, re-

Table 1.3
Relation between Earnings and Returns Depending on the Level of
Multinationality

Level of Multinationality	Number of firm-period observations	Correlation between earnings and returns	Earnings coefficient
0-75	404	0.07	0.06
0-25	108	0.42	0.57
25-50	232	0.53	0.58
50-75	64	0.65	0.71

Stock returns are measured for the twelve-month period extending from nine months prior to the fiscal year-end through three months after the fiscal year-end, earnings-per-share is scaled by the beginning-of-period stock price per share, and multinationality is equal to foreign sales/ total sales. The sample of annual earnings reports are drawn from the five-year period corresponding to the 1994–98 calendar years. All correlation (Pearson) between annual accounting earnings-per-share and stock returns, and the earnings coefficients from the regression of stock returns, and the earnings coefficients from the regression of stock returns on accounting earnings-per-share, are significant at the 0.01 level or better.

ported in column 3 of table 1.3, imply a monotonic increase in the regression coefficients. The increase of these coefficients from 0.52 for the 0–25 range of multinationality to 0.71 for the 50–75 range of multinationality verifies the results of hypothesis 1 in table 1.4.

Multinationality and Other Determinants of Earnings' Explanatory Power

As stated earlier, additional considerations are recognized regarding both the informativeness of earnings and managerial incentives determining accounting choices. These considerations, in addition to multinationality include firm size, systematic risk, leverage, growth opportunities, earnings variability, and earning persistence. Accordingly, the following pooled cross-sectional regression model is formulated:

$$R_{i,t} = \alpha_0 + \alpha_1 \cdot E_{i,t} / P_{i,t-1} + \alpha_2 E_{i,t} MULTY_i / P_{i,t-1}$$
$$+ \alpha_3 E_{i,t} SIZE_i / P_{i,t-1} + \alpha_4 E_{i,t} GROWTH_i / P_{i,t-1}$$
$$+ \alpha_5 E_{i,t} RISK_i / P_{i,t-1} + \alpha_6 E_{i,t} DEBT_i / P_{i,t-1}$$
$$+ \alpha_7 E_{i,t} VAR_i / P_{i,t-1} + \alpha_8 E_{i,t} PERS + \varepsilon_{i,t} \qquad (2)$$

The new variables are defined as follows: SIZE is the natural logarithm of a firm's market value of equity, RISK is a firm's systematic risk,[3] DEBT is the firm's ratio of total debt to total assets, GROWTH is measured as the market value of equity scaled by book value, VAR is the variability of earnings for all the quarters of the period of analysis, and PERS is persistence of earnings as measured by the first-order autocorrelation in earnings for the same period.

Table 1.4
Regression in Stock Return on Both Earnings and Earnings-Multinationality Interaction

$(R_{i,t}) = \alpha_0 + \alpha_1 . E_{i,t} / P_{i,t-1} + \alpha_2 E_{i,t} MULTY_i / P_{i,t-1} + \varepsilon_{i,t}$

Parameter estimates

α_0	α_1	α_2	Sample size	Adjusted $R^2\%$	F-value (sig.level)
0.077	0.575	0.865	404	7.47	17.30
(18.57)*	(5.882)*	(5.57)*			(0.001)

Stock returns (R) are measured for the twelve-month period extending from nine months prior to the fiscal year-end through three months after the fiscal year-end. Earnings (E) is the accounting earnings-per-share, multinationality (MULTY) is equal to foreign sales/total sales, and price (P) is the stock price per share. Parameter estimates and t-statistics (in parentheses) are presented for the regression. An asterisk (*) designates statistical significance at the 0.01 level. The sample is comprised of firm-year observations from the 1994–98 calendar years.

The results, shown in table 1.5, verify again the relation between multinationality and earnings' informativeness after the inclusion of these additional considerations. As expected, the market reaction to earnings was negatively related to systematic risk [α_5 (−0.532) is significant at the 0.01 level], and to variability of earnings [α_7 (−0.338) is significant at the 0.01 level]. It is also positively related to firm size [α_3 (0.08) is significant at the 0.01 level], growth opportunities [α_4 (0.351) is significant at the 0.01 level], leverage [α_6 (0.199) is significant at the 0.01 level], and earnings persistence [α_8 (0.057) is significant at the 0.01 level].[4]

EARNINGS MANAGEMENT CONDITIONAL ON MULTINATIONALITY

The second hypothesis states that the magnitude of adjustments in managers' accounting choices is systematically related to multinationality. The higher the level of multinationality, the higher is managers' reliance on discretionary accruals, as measured by the magnitude of discretionary accrual adjustments.

An abnormal accruals research design will be used to test the hypothesis of managers' accounting choices conditional on multinationality.[5] Basically, the abnormal accounting accrual (AAC) is computed as the current period accrual (AC) minus the expected normal accrual [E(AC)], and then standardized by beginning-of-year stock price (P):

$$AAC_{i,t} = [AC_{i,t} - E(AC)_{i,t}]/P_{i,t-1} \qquad (3)$$

The accounting accrual (AC) is defined as the change in non-cash working capital (i.e., change in non-cash current assets less current liabilities) less depreciation expense.[6]

An accruals prediction model, suggested by Jones (1991), is used to estimate normal accruals. It is specified as:

$$AC_{i,t} = \beta_o / P_{i,t-1} + \beta_1 \cdot \Delta REV_{i,t} / P_{i,t-1} + \beta_2 \cdot PPE_{i,t} / + \varepsilon_{it} \tag{4}$$

where the new variables are defined as follows:

$\Delta REV_{i,t}$ = Changes in revenues from year t to t − 1 for firm i.

$PPE_{i,t}$ = Gross property plant, and equipment in year t.

A time-series regression using available prior-year data for seven years, generated firm-specific and time-period-specific predictions of $E(AC_{i,t})$ which are then used in equation (3) to generate estimate of abnormal accruals ($AAC_{i,t}$).

Because the interest in this study is with the magnitude of the accrual adjustments, rather than the direction of the accrual, the absolute value of the abnormal accrual ($/AAC_{i,t} /$) is used as a department variable in the following model:[7]

$$/AAC_{i,t} / = \delta_0 + \delta_1 \cdot MULTY_i + \delta_2 \cdot SIZE_i + \delta_3 \cdot GROWTH_i + \\ \delta_4 \cdot RISK_i + \delta_5 \cdot DEBT_i + \delta_6 \cdot VAR_i + \delta_7 \cdot PERS_I + \varepsilon_{it} \tag{5}$$

Equation (5) is a multivariate-pooled cross-sectional regression model to be used to investigate the joint interaction of multinationality and the level of abnormal accounting accruals.

The model includes, in addition to the multinationality variable, other factors that have been shown in previous research to affect the magnitude of abnormal accruals (Warfield et al., 1995). These factors include size of the firm, growth, systematic risk, leverage, earnings variability, and earnings persistence. Consistent with the second hypothesis, a positive relation between the level of multinationality and the magnitude of abnormal accruals is predicted (i.e., $\delta_1 > 0$). The evidence in table 1.6 supports the hypothesis that the magnitude of abnormal accruals is positively related to the level of multinationality, i.e., δ_1 equals 0.00002, which is significantly greater than zero at the 0.01 level.[8]

SUMMARY AND CONCLUSIONS

This chapter presented two hypotheses linking the level of multinationality to both the informativeness of earnings and the magnitude of discretionary accounting accrual adjustments. The hypotheses draw on multinationality theories and exploits (a) the internalization and the international diversification opportunities provided by multinational firms, and (b) managers' incentives in using discretionary accounting accrual adjustments. Based on both the internalization

Table 1.5
Regression of Returns on Earnings, Earnings-Multinationality Interaction, and Earnings Interaction with Other Determinants of Earnings Explanatory Power

$$(R_{i,t}) = \alpha_0 + \alpha_1 \cdot E_{i,t}/P_{i,t-1} + \alpha_2\, E_{i,t} \cdot MULTY_i/P_{i,t-1} + \alpha_3\, E_{i,t} \cdot SIZE_i/P_{i,t-1} + \alpha_4\, E_{i,t} \cdot GROWTH_i/P_{i,t-1} \cdot$$
$$RISK_i/P_{i,t-1} + \alpha_6\, E_{i,t} \cdot DEBT_i/P_{i,t-1} + \alpha_7\, E_{i,t} \cdot VAR_i/P_{i,t-1} + \alpha_8\, E_{i,t} \cdot PERS + \varepsilon_{i,t} \quad (2)$$

Parameter estimates											
α_0	α_1	α_2	α_3	α_4	α_5	α_6	α_7	α_8	Sample size	Adjusted R 2%	F
0.024	0.139	0.019	0.08	0.351	-0.532	0.199	-0.338	0.057	3.91	23.52%	248.70*
(9.84)*	(5.09)*	(5.18)*	(2.73)*	(15.77)*	(-3.39)*	(3.48)*	(17.07)*	(4.20)*			

Stock returns (R) are measured for the twelve-month period from nine months prior to the fiscal year-end through three months after the fiscal year-end, earnings (E) is the accounting earnings-per-share, multinationality (MULTY) is the foreign sales/total sales, size (SIZE) is measured as the company's natural logarithm of the market value of equity, systematic risk (RISK) is measured by the market model beta, growth opportunities (GROWTH) are measured by the market-to-book ratio for common equity, leverage (DEBT) is measured by the ratio of total debt to total assets, earnings variability (VAR) is measured by the standard deviation of earnings, earnings persistence (PERS) is the first-order autocorrelation in earnings, and price (P) is the stock price at the beginning of the period. The sample size is comprised of firm-year observations drawn from the 1994–98 calendar years.

Table 1.6

Regression of Absolute Abnormal Accruals on Multinationality and Other Determinants of the Magnitude of Discretionary Accruals

$$|AAC_{i,t}| = \delta_0 + \delta_1 . MULTY_i + \delta_2 . SIZE_i + \delta_3 . GROWTH_i + \delta_4 . RISK_i + \delta_5 . DEBT_i + \delta_6 . VAR_i + \delta_7 PERS_i + \varepsilon_{it}$$

Parameter estimates

δ_0	δ_1	δ_2	δ_3	δ_4	δ_5	δ_6	δ_7
-0.077	0.00002	0.0003	0.01	0.00001	0.08	0.008	-0.00001
(-1.13)	(8.52)*	(7.48)*	(7.39)*	(4.52)*	(5.62)*	(17.68)*	(0.51)*

Sample size	Adjusted	F-Value
368	28.55%	75.26*

Absolute abnormal accruals, $/AAC_{i,t}/$, is defined as the current-period accrual loss of the expected normal accruals, where the difference is standardized by the beginning-period stock price. All other variables are as defined in table 1.3. An asterisk (*) designates statistical significance at the 0.01 level, two-tailed tests. The sample size is comprised of firm-year observations drawn from the 1994–98 calendar years.

theory and the imperfect world capital markets theory, the first hypothesis postulates that the informativeness of earnings in explaining stock returns varies systematically with the level of multinationality in the corporation. Based on the managerial objectives theory, the second hypothesis postulates that managers' accounting choices are systematically related to the level of multinationality. The results on a sample of U.S. multinational firms show a significantly greater earnings coefficient for firms with higher multinationality, and a positive relation between the magnitude of discretionary accruals and the level of multinationality.

NOTES

1. The internalization theory is developed in Coase (1937), Caves (1974), Hymer (1976), Buckley and Casson (1976), Rugman (1980, 1981), Casson (1987), Buckley (1988), Dunning (1980, 1988), Morck and Yeung (1991, 1992), and Mishra and Gobelli (1998).

2. See Agmon and Lessard (1977), Brewer (1981), Errunza and Senbet (1981), Adler and Dumas (1983), Fatemi (1984), Kim and Lyn (1986), Doukas and Travlos (1988), and others.

3. Systematic risk is measured by the market model beta using the most recent sixty months' stock returns prior to the test period.

4. To measure the degree of collinearity among the regression variables, condition indexes are calculated. The condition index shows the regression was 23.6 which is between the 30 level, considered by Belsley et al. (1980) as indicative of moderate to strong multicollinearity. Similarly, to assess the effect of cross-correlation in the residuals for the estimation of parameters, bootstrapping analyses were conducted using the techniques described in Kross et al. (1990). The results showed bootstrapping estimates qualitatively identical to the estimates reported in table 1.5.

5. The abnormal accruals research design was pioneered by Healey (1985), DeAngelo (1986, 1988), Liberty and Zimmerman (1986), and others.

6. Specifically, the accounting per share is calculated as follows (*Compustat* data item numbers are in parentheses);

$$AC_{i,t} = [\cap \text{ Accounts Receivable}_{i,t} (2) + \cap \text{ Inventories}_{i,t} (3) + \cap \text{ Other Current Assets}_{i,t} (68)] - [\cap \text{ Current Liabilities}_{i,t} (5)] - [\text{Depreciation and Amortization Expense}_{i,t} (14)]$$

where the change $(\cap)$ is the difference between years (t and t-1). The *Compustat* data item number for Stock Price, $P_{i,t-1}$, is (24).

7. A similar methodology is used by Warfield et al. (1995).

8. Similar results were obtained when the Jones model (1991) was replaced by either the modified Jones model (Dechow et al., 1995) or the cross-sectional Jones model (Defond and Jiambalvo, 1994).

REFERENCES

Adler, M., and B. Dumas. 1983. International portfolio choice and corporation finance: A synthesis. *Journal of Finance* 38: 925–84.

Agmon, J., and D. Lessard. 1977. Investor recognition of corporate international diversification. *Journal of Finance* 32: 1049–55.

Belsley, D.A., E. Kuh, and R.E. Welsh. 1980. *Regression diagnostics: Identifying influential data and sources of collinearity.* New York: Wiley.

Bodnar, Gordon M., and Joseph Weintrop. 1997. The valuation of the foreign income of U.S. multinational firms: A growth opportunities perspective. *Journal of Accounting and Economics* 24: 69–97.

Brewer, H.L. 1981. Investor benefits from corporate international diversification. *Journal of Financial and Quantitative Analysis* 16: 113–26.

Buckley, P. 1988. The limits of explanation: Testing the internalization theory of the multinational enterprise. *Journal of International Business Studies* 19: 113–26.

Buckley, P. and M. Casson. 1976. *The Future of Multinational Enterprises.* London: Macmillian.

Casson, M. 1987. *The Firm and the Market.* London: Basil Blackwell.

Caves, R.E. 1974. Causes of direct investment: Foreign firms' shares in Canadian and United Kingdom manufacturing industries. *Review of Economics and Statistics* 56: 273–93.

Coase, R.H. 1937. The nature of the firm. *Economics* 4: 386–405.

DeAngelo, L.F. 1986. Accounting numbers as market valuation substitutes: A study of management buyouts of public stockholders. *The Accounting Review* 41: 400–420.

———. 1988. Managerial competition, information costs, and corporate governance: The use of accounting performance measures in proxy contests. *Journal of Accounting and Economics* 10: 3–36.

Dechow, P.M., R.G. Sloan, and A.P. Sloan. 1995. Detecting earnings management. *The Accounting Review* 70: 193–225.

Defond, M.L., and J. Jiambalvo. 1994. Debt covenant violations and manipulation of accruals. *Journal of Accounting and Economics* 17: 145–76.

Doukas, J., and N.G. Travlos. 1988. The effect of corporate multinationalism on shareholders' wealth: Evidence from international acquisitions. *Journal of Finance* 43: 1161–75.

Dunning, J.H. 1980. Toward an eclectic theory of international production: Some empirical tests. *Journal of International Business Studies.* 11: 9–31.

———. 1988. The eclectic paradigm of international production: A restatement and some possible extensions. *Journal of International Business.* 19: 1–31.

Errunza, V.R., and L.W. Senbet. 1981. The effects of international operations on the market values of the firm: Theory and evidence. *Journal of Finance* 36: 401–17.

Fatemi, A.M. 1984. Shareholders benefits from corporate international diversification. *Journal of Finance* 39: 1325–44.

Healey, P. 1985. The effects of bonus schemes on accounting decisions. *Journal of Accounting and Economics* 7: 85–107.

Hymer, S. 1976. *The International Operations of National Firms: A Study of Direct Foreign Investment.* Cambridge: MIT Press.

Jones, J. 1991. Earnings management during import relief investigations. *Journal of Accounting Research* 29: 193–228.

Kim, W.S., and E.O. Lyn. 1986. Excess market value, the multinational corporation, and Tobin's Q ratio. *Journal of International Business Studies* 17: 119–26.

Kross, W., B. Ro, and D. Schroeder. 1990. Earnings expectations: The analyst's information advantage. *The Accounting Review* 65 (April): 461–76.

Liberty, S.F., and J.I. Zimmerman. 1986. Labor union contract negotiations accounting choices. *The Accounting Review* 61: 692–712.

Mishra, C., and D.H. Gobelli. 1998. Managerial incentives, internalization, and market valuation of multinational firms. *Journal of International Business Studies* 29, 3: 583–98.

Morck, R., and B. Yeung. 1991. Why investors value multinationality. *Journal of Business* 64: 165–87.

———. 1992. Internationalization: An event study test. *Journal of International Economics* 33: 41–56.

Rugman, A.M. 1980. Internalization as a general theory of foreign direct investment: A re-appraisal of the literature. *Journal of Economic Literature* 116: 365–75.

———. 1981. *Inside the Multinationals: The Economics of Internal Markets*. New York: Columbia University Press.

Warfield, T.D., J.J. Wild, and K.L. Wild. 1995. Managerial ownership, accounting choices, and informativeness of earnings. *Journal of Accounting and Economics* 20: 61–91.

CHAPTER 2

The Timeliness of Accounting Earnings as an Antecedent of Disclosure Informativeness

INTRODUCTION AND MOTIVATION

Disclosure policy is partly at the discretion of management, given that disclosures include both mandatory and voluntary ones. The quality of disclosure is the overall informativeness of a firm's discretionary disclosures. It measures the firm's effectiveness in communicating with investors and the extent to which the firm provides information so that investors have the data necessary to make informed judgments across all types of disclosures (FAF, 1986–1990). Disclosure informativeness is considered to be important to users and analysts and the efficient functioning of capital markets. The purpose of this chapter is to investigate how disclosure informativeness varies with the information properties of numbers produced by their financial accounting systems.

We argue that differences in the ability of information systems to portray the financial structure, performance, and conduct across firms will lead to differential disclosure informativeness. The financial accounting system relies on generally accepted accounting principles (GAAP) to produce accounting numbers deemed useful for the existence of well-functioning capital markets, as well as satisfying the information needs of such users as the shareholders, analysts, directors, and executives.

The various users need accounting information in order to comprehend changes in equity value. This chapter maintains that in firms whose current accounting numbers do not capture well the effects of a firm's current activities and outcomes on shareholder value, the financial accounting system is less effective in providing adequate disclosure informativeness. We predict that such firms will subsequently improve their disclosure informativeness to correct the present inadequacies in financial accounting information.[1]

The "changes in disclosure informativeness" argument is based on (a) the evidence that prior accounting representations may lead firms to opt for non-accounting performance measures in managerial incentive plans (Bushman et al., 1996; Ittner et al., 1997) and capital market participants to rely on costly, private information gathering (e.g., Verrecchia, 1982, 1983), and (b) the thesis that firms will opt for improving their disclosure informativeness to limit the usefulness of these costly alternative mechanisms. The basic question is whether cross-firm differences in the ability of GAAP to capture value relevant information drive real differences in subsequent disclosure informativeness mechanisms.

Our analysis extends existing research on disclosure informativeness in one important way. We focus on the properties of a firm's financial system as an antecedent variable that is the cause of the independent variable (see figure 2.1). For example, the quality of disclosure is viewed as important to an efficient functioning of the capital markets. It is considered in the estimate of default risk with, for example, Standard & Poor's Corporation stating that accounting quality is a factor in establishing the rating of an industrial bond issue (Standard & Poor's, 1982, 1985). It makes up a large part of the information analysts use in their evaluations and provisions of earnings forecasts, buy/sell recommendations, and other information to brokers, money managers, and institutional investors (Lang and Lundholm, 1993, 1996). In addition, a growing body of empirical studies demonstrates that informative disclosures can increase the market price and liquidity of a firm's securities (Healy et al., 1999; Coller and Yohn, 1997; Botosan, 1997; Byrd et al., 1995; Piotroski, 1999; and Bloomfield and Wilks, 2000). As figure 2.1 shows, this study complements previous research by considering differences across firms in capturing current value-relevant information, or differences in timeliness of accounting earnings as an antecedent variable causing subsequent disclosure informativeness.

The timeliness of information, used to capture the information property of earnings, is defined by Ball, Kothari, and Robin (2000) as the extent to which current earnings incorporate current economic increase or value-relevant information. Traditional and reverse regression of stock prices and changes in earnings are used in this study to develop several metrics for earnings timeliness.

We explore whether disclosure informativeness varies with earnings timeliness by examining the cross-sectional relation between our timeliness metrics computed for five years ending in 1986 and a proxy for *subsequent* disclosure informativeness of one hundred U.S. multinational firms in 1986 and 1986–90. Our results support a significant and negative relation between the timeliness metrics used and subsequent disclosure informativeness after controlling for other firm characteristics considered in the international and disclosure literature. We interpret this result as support for the view that firms whose earnings do not explain well the effects of a firm's current activities and outcomes on share-

Figure 2.1
Nomological Network in Which Disclosure Informativeness is the Independent Variable

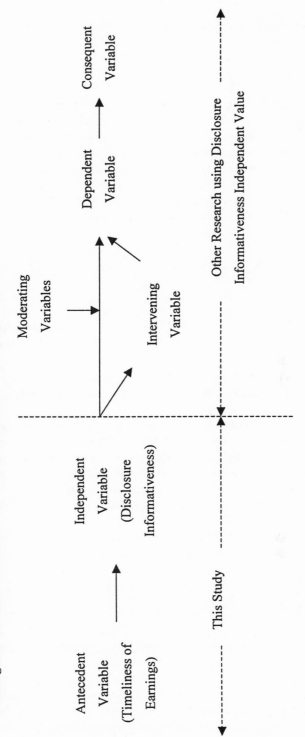

holder value will institute better disclosure systems and improve their disclosure informativeness.

MEASURING TIMELINESS OF EARNINGS

As defined in Ball, Kothari, and Robin (2000), the timeliness of earnings means the extent to which current earnings incorporate current economic value or income. By capturing current changes in values, the accounting numbers will appear to be useful and relevant to users in general and to analysts in particular. Timeliness of earnings may be considered a major determinant of the usefulness of earnings. It may be operationalized by three possible metrics.

The first two timeliness metrics result from firm specific regressions between annual earnings and contemporary stock returns over a period of at least five years ending in 1986.

$$EARN_t = a_0 + a_1 NEG_t + a_2 RET_t + a_3 NEG_t \times RET_t + e_t \tag{1}$$

where

$EARN_t$ = Earnings before extraordinary items, discontinued operations, and special items, deflated by the beginnings of year market value of equity of a given firm in year t.

RET_t = Annual stock return for year t.

NEG_t = Dummy variable equal to 1 if RET is negative and 0 otherwise.

Both Basu (1997) and Ball, Kothari, and Robin (2000) maintain that a_2 captures the speed with which good news reflected in a firm's stock returns is reflected in accounting earnings and $a_1 + a_3$ captures the same phenomena for bad news. As in previous research (Ball, Kothari, and Robin, 2000; Bushman et al., 2000), both a_2 and R_1^2 from equation (1) will be used as a measure of the timeliness and usefulness of earnings. Firms with timing problems will have lower a_2 and R^2.

The third timeliness metric, depicting the usefulness of earnings, is the R_2^2 from the following equation:

$$RET_t = a_0 + a_1 EARN_t + a_2 \Delta EARN_t + e_t \tag{2}$$

where

$\Delta EARN$ = Changes in earnings from year t–1 to year t deflated by the market value of equity at the beginning of year t.

Equation (2) allows the determination of the power of both levels and changes in earnings in explaining market return.

The three metrics are therefore TOE1, the slope (a_2); TOE2, the R^2 from equation (2); and TOE3, the R^2 from equation (2).[2]

DEVELOPMENT OF THE HYPOTHESIS AND DESCRIPTION OF THE DISCLOSURE INFORMATIVENESS VARIABLE

Hypothesis

Our prediction concerns the relation between the timeliness of accounting numbers and the subsequent disclosure informativeness. We predict that the lower the timeliness of earnings, the higher the consequent disclosure informativeness in response to the benefits from users' positive responses. This prediction is based on:

a. findings made by Lang and Lundholm (1996), who provide evidence that firms with more informative disclosure policies have a larger analyst following, more accurate analyst earnings forecasts, less dispersion among individual analyst forecasts, and less volatility in forecast revisions, and

b. findings on how discretionary disclosure affects analysts' forecasts (Baginski and Hassell, 1990; Jennings, 1987; Williams, 1996; Waymire, 1986; Kross et al., 1990; Knutson, 1992),[3] and the prediction that the total benefits of disclosure increase with the volatility of a firm's environment (SRI, 1987).

It is, therefore, expected that the timeliness of earnings is an antecedent to and will be negatively related to disclosure informativeness.

Measurement of Disclosure Informativeness

To measure disclosure, this study relies on data from the annual volumes of the *Report of the Financial Analysts Federation Corporate Information Committee* (FAF, 1986–1990). It is generally considered a comprehensive measure of the informativeness of a firm's disclosure policy (Lang and Lundholm, 1993, 1996; Farragher et al., 1994; Welker, 1995; Sengupta, 1998; Botosan, 1997). The data measure the firm's effectiveness in communicating with investors and the extent to which the firm provides information, so that investors have the data necessary to make informed judgment across all types of disclosures. The disclosures provided through annual reports, quarterly reports, proxy statements, published information in the form of press releases and fact books, and direct disclosures to and communication with analysts are used for the evaluation of the firm's disclosures, summarizing their evaluations by a score (out of one hundred possible points) on the firm's total disclosure efforts and separate scores for the different disclosure categories. Although these scores are based on analysts' perception of corporate disclosure practices, any potential biases or errors are minimized by a procedure that (a) requires the reporting of average scores (across industry analysts), and (b) rests on the use of detailed guidelines and a comprehensive checklist of a criteria that allows a standardization of the rating process both within and across industries. The disclosure informativeness variable will be labeled DISI for the 1986 and 1986–90 period.

CONTROL VARIABLES

Based on a survey of the theoretical and empirical literatures on the determinants of disclosure informativeness, three potential control variables are considered and grouped into three categories—*growth variable* (growth opportunities), *structural variable* (firm size), and a *multinationality variable* (the degree of internationalization or foreign involvement) (Lang and Lundholm, 1993). The growth opportunities are measured by the market value of equity to book value of equity (MTB). Firm size is measured by the logarithm of revenues (LR). The level of multinationality is measured by foreign profits over total profits (FPTP). The motivation for the three control variables follows.

Disclosure and Growth Opportunities

The firm may be viewed as a combination of assets-in-place and future investment options. Assets-in-place refer to the actual assets recognized in the balance sheet. Future investment options refer to the unobservable growth opportunities or options. The lower the proportion of firm value represented by assets-in-place, the higher are the growth opportunities. Myers (1977) describes these potential investment opportunities as call options whose values depend on the likelihood that management will exercise them. Like call options, the growth options represent value to the firm (Kester, 1984). These growth options are intangible assets or ownership advantages that represent the investment opportunity set (IOS). The higher these growth options, the more likely there will be a good firm performance. In fact, theoretical models developed by Bushman and Indjejikian (1993) and Kim and Suh (1993) suggest that as a firm's IOS increases, stock price becomes relatively more informative about firm performance. One implication is that firms that have experienced an expansion in investment opportunities will increase their disclosures to match their market performance. In addition, the expansion of new investment opportunities or product markets may adversely impact accounting earnings in the short term (Abbott, 1999). The development of investment opportunities requires immediate outlays of capital, while the payoffs may not be immediately reflected in accounting earnings. This is generally consistent with Yermack (1995), who finds evidence of an unexpectedly negative relationship between a firm's market-to-book ratios (a known IOS proxy) and the granting of stock options. The implication is that firms experiencing an expansion in investment opportunities with no present payoffs should increase their disclosures to counteract any adverse effect to the accounting earnings in the short run. This is generally consistent with Skinner (1993), who finds evidence suggesting that the IOS affects the "accepted set" of accounting procedures.

Taken as a whole, the results from both theoretical and empirical research suggest disclosure could be positively related to firm growth opportunities as measured by the investment opportunities set.

Disclosure and Firm Size

There are a number of reasons why we might expect a positive association between disclosure and firm size. One main reason is provided by *agency theory*. The proportion of outside capital tends to be higher for larger firms (Leftwich, Watts, and Zimmerman, 1981). Similarly, agency costs increase with the amount of outside capital (Jensen and Meckling, 1976). Accordingly, the potential benefits from shareholder-debtholder-manager contracting—including the extent of financial disclosure—would also increase with firm size (Chow and Wang-Borem, 1987).

Other reasons include:

a. *the disclosure cost hypothesis*, which maintains that the decreasing costs associated with larger firm size leads to more affordable disclosure (Lang and Lundholm, 1993),

b. *the transaction cost hypothesis*, which maintains that the incentives for private information acquisitions are greater for large firms, resulting in disclosure increasing with firm size, and

c. *the legal cost hypothesis*, which maintains that the dollar values of damages in securities litigations are a function of firm size leading to higher disclosure with larger size (Skinner, 1992).

Disclosure and Multinationality

There are basically two main reasons why we might expect a positive association between disclosure and multinationality.

A first reason is provided by *the capital-need hypothesis* whereby much of the impetus for voluntary disclosure by multinational firms surrounds the need to raise capital at the lowest possible cost (Choi, 1973; Spero, 1979). The pressure for information associated with global competition for capital manifests itself in the supplementary voluntary disclosures that multinational firms have been found to make (Meek, Roberts, and Gray, 1995).

A second reason is provided by *the multiple listing hypothesis* (Cooke, 1989). Multinational firms are generally listed in more than one stock exchange. The firms with multiple listings are more likely to have a greater number of shareholders, thereby making monitoring costs more significant. One way of reducing shareholders' monitoring costs and of alleviating the moral hazard problem is through disclosure in corporate annual reports.

MODEL

This study examines the cross-sectional variations in analysts' published evaluation of a firm's disclosure practices, as a measure of disclosure informativeness, and hypotheses that the analysts' ratings are negatively related to the previous timeliness of accounting earnings, and increasing in the degree of multinationality, the level of growth opportunities and size. The model to be tested is as follows:

$$DISI = a_0 + a_1 \, TOE + a_2 \, FPTP + a_3 \, MTB + a_4 \, LR + e \qquad (3)$$

where

DISI = Disclosure informativeness as measured by the FAF disclosure score for the year 1986.

TOE = Timeliness of earnings computed over a period of five years ending in 1986.

FTPT = Degree of multinationality as measured by foreign profits/total profits for the year 1986.

MTB = Growth opportunities as measured by the market value of equity are book value of equity for the year 1986.

LR = Size of the firm as measured by the logarithm of revenues for the year 1986.

The timeliness of earnings, TOE, is to be measured by the three metrics discussed previously, namely: TOE 1, the slope from equation (1); TOE 2, the R^2 from equation (1); and TOE 3, the R^2 from equation (2).

SAMPLE AND DATA

To ensure the greatest sample of firms for which data would be available for all variables, the initial sample chosen was for all firms included in *Forbes*'s 1986 survey of the largest U.S. multinationals and in the annual volumes of the *Report of the Financial Analysts Federation of Corporate Information Committee* (FAF, 1986–1990). A sample of one hundred firms was obtained.

Table 2.1 summarizes the sample distribution of our metrics for the timeliness of earnings. The mean and median levels of TOE 1, the slope on positive returns in equation (2), are 0.037 and 0.026 respectively, while the mean and median levels of TOE 3, the R^2 from equation (2), are 0.34 and 0.26 respectively. Table 2.2 also summarizes the sample distribution of the control variables used in equation (3), including the level of multinationality (FPTP), the level of the growth opportunities (MTB), and the size (LR). Finally, table 2.1 summarizes

Table 2.1
Sample Distribution of Model Variables

Variables	MEAN	STD. DEV	Q_1	MEDIAN	Q_3
Earnings timeliness metrics					
TOE1	0.037	0.13	-0.02	0.026	0.08
TOE2	0.29	0.22	0.15	0.31	0.45
TOE3	0.34	0.25	0.18	0.26	0.52
Control Variables					
FPTP	48.26	56.32	32.52	38.23	51.52
MTB	2.56	2.82	2.32	1.51	1.28
TR (Total Revenues)	1,512.62	18,752.53	8,230	8,531	18,752
Disclosure Informativeness					
DISI	77.56	6.725	42.32	66.32	68.20

Variable Definitions:
TOE1=Slope of equation (1)
TOE2=R^2 from equation (1)
TOE3=R^2 from equation (2)
FPTP=Foreign profits/Total profits
MTB=Market value of equity over total value of equity
TR=Total revenues
DISI=FAF disclosure score

the sample distribution of disclosure informativeness (DISI), with a mean of 77.56 and a median of 66.32.

EMPIRICAL DESIGN AND RESULTS

Table 2.2 reports the Spearman rank correlations between the independent and control variables used in equation (3). As expected, the correlations between the three individual timeliness metrics are positive and highly significant.

The results in table 2.3 indicate that the estimated coefficients in the timeliness of earnings have the predictive negative sign and are significant at the 1% level for disclosure informativeness. Adjusted R^2 levels for the three sets of regression range from 30.28% to 42.52%.[4] The estimated coefficients in the three control variables—growth opportunities, size, and multinationality—have also the predicted positive sign and are significant at the 1% level. F-test for the joint significance of the control variables (FPTP, MTB, and LR) reject the null

Table 2.2
Spearman Rank Correlation Table

	TOE1	TOE2	TOE3	FPTP	MTB	TR
TOE1	1.00	0.19*	0.14*	0.02	0.05	0.21
TOE2		1.00	0.46*	0.01	0.06	0.23
TOE3			1.00	0.07	0.09	0.27
FPTP				1.00	-0.16	0.031
MTB					1.00	0.018
TR						1.00

*Correlations with asterisk (*) denote significance at 1% level *variable definition.*
Variables are defined in table 2.1.

hypothesis in the estimation of disclosure informativeness (p-values of 0.01 or less). We examined several sensitivity issues. First, we estimated equation (3) using (a) timeliness of earnings metrics where equations (1) and (2) are based on quarterly earnings, (b) average disclosure score for the 1986–90 period, and (c) multinationality measured by either foreign assets, total assets, or foreign revenues/total revenues. Second, we reestimate equation (3) using interindustry and intraindustry variation in both the timeliness metrics and the disclosure informativeness measure using either industry means of those variables or firm deviations from industry means for each variable. Overall, the results of these sensitivity tests verified our initial results of (a) a negative relation between timeliness of earnings and subsequent disclosure informativeness, and (b) a positive relationship for the control variables.

SUMMARY AND IMPLICATIONS

This study predicts that the disclosure informativeness of large U.S. multinational firms is a function of the timeliness of firms' accounting numbers. We examine the usefulness of accounting numbers by how well they capture the effects of the firms' current activities and outcomes on shareholder values. The differences in the resulting timeliness of earnings are the results of differences in the production function and investment and market opportunities of these firms. A consequence of this timeliness is the need for firms to adjust their disclosure informativeness to compensate for their less useful accounting numbers. Therefore, we predict that firms whose current accounting numbers do not capture well the effects of the firms' current activities and outcomes on share-

Table 2.3
Summary Statistics from Regressions of Disclosure Informativeness on Timeliness of Earnings and Various Control Variables[1]

$$DIS\ I = a_0 + a_1 TOE + a_2 FPTP + a_3 MTB + a_4 LR + e$$

Regression	a_0	a_1	a_2	a_3	a_4	$a_2+a_3+a_4=0$	Adjusted R
1. TOE as TOE1	-9.832 (-3.292)*	-11.823 (2.327)*	0.020 (2.342)*	1.032 (4.028)*	7.223 (25.628)*	0.001	42.52
2. TOE as TOE2	-6.628 (-3.426)*	-2.135 (2.527)*	0.011 (2.351)*	1.022 (4.321)*	7.321 (24.252)*	0.001	41.28
3. TOE as TOE3	-6.515 (-3.232)*	-1.856 (2.358)*	0.013 (2.652)*	1.501 (3.926)*	7.820 (23.282)*	0.001	30.28

1. Notes

a. For variable definitions, see table 2.1.

b. Summary statistics include coefficient estimates until statistics in parentheses (after correcting for heteroscedascity in the manner described by White, 1980).

c. Significant at $\alpha=0.01$.

holder value will institute better disclosure systems and improve their disclosure informativeness.

To test a prediction concerning the timeliness of earnings as an antecedent and cause of disclosure informativeness, we estimate proxies of the timeliness of earnings for the one hundred largest U.S. multinationals for five years ending in 1986. We estimate the cross-sectional relation between disclosure informativeness as measured by the FAF disclosure score in the periods 1986 and 1986–90, and three metrics for the timeliness of earnings—controlling for size, growth opportunities, and multinationality.

Our results largely support the thesis that disclosure informativeness is one of the responses to the timeliness of earnings situation. The timeliness of earnings acts as an antecedent to the firms' effort to improve disclosure in general, and disclosure informativeness in particular. The main implication is that the effect of accounting numbers on equity value is one of the signals to be used by management to correct for the limitations of their accounting systems and provide for the kind of disclosure that may improve the timeliness metrics. Disclosure informativeness indicates the improvement in these disclosures and the perceptions of financial analysts on their usefulness. The firm-specific timeliness metrics captured differences across U.S. multinational firms in the information properties of their accounting numbers and were taken with consideration in the subsequent firms' disclosure policies.

NOTES

1. Bushman at al. (2000) predict instead that such firms will substitute costly governance mechanisms to compensate for their less-useful accounting numbers.

2. The study relied also on a composite index of the three measures a_2, R_1^2, and R_2^2 by computing a percentile rank for each firm in the sample for each of the three metrics and computing an average of the three percentile rank values for each firm. The results using the composite index were similar to those obtained with the individual metrics.

3. The choice of analysts in the discussion is motivated by the suggestions that the behavior of analysts provide insight with the activities and beliefs of investors that cannot be observed directly (Nichols, 1989; Schipper, 1991).

4. The adjusted R^2 levels from the three sets of regression were slightly lower when the regressions did not include the control variables.

REFERENCES

Abbott, L.J. 1999. *Executive Compensation Subsequent to a Split in IOS*. Tennessee: University of Memphis.

Baginski, S., and J. Hassell. 1990. The market interpretation of management earnings forecasts as a predictor of subsequent financial analyst forecast revision. *The Accounting Review* 65 (January): 175–90.

Ball, R., S.P. Kothari, and A. Robin. 2000. The effect of international institutional factors on properties of accounting earnings. *Journal of Accounting and Economics* (forthcoming).

Basu, S. 1997. The conservatism principle and the asymmetric timeliness of earnings. *Journal of Accounting and Economics* 24: 3–37.

Bloomfield, R.J., and T.J. Wilks. 2000. Disclosure effects in the laboratory: Liquidity, depth, and the cost of capital. *The Accounting Review* 75: 13–42.

Botosan, C.A. 1997. Disclosure level of the cost of equity capital. *The Accounting Review* 72 (July): 323–49.

Bushman, R., and R. Indjejikian. 1993. Accounting income, stock price, and managerial compensation. *Journal of Accounting and Economics* 16: 3–24.

Bushman, R., R. Indjejikian, and A. Smith. 1996. CEO compensation: The role of individual performance evaluation. *Journal of Accounting and Economics* 21: 161–93.

Bushman, R., Q. Chen, E. Engel, and A. Smith. 2000. The sensitivity of corporate governance systems to the timeliness of accounting earnings. Working paper, University of Chicago.

Byrd, J., M. Johnson, and M. Johnson. 1995. Investor relations and the cost of capital. Working paper, University of Michigan.

Choi, F.D.S. 1973. Financial disclosure and entry to the European capital market. *Journal of Accounting Research* (Autumn).

Chow, C.W., and A. Wang-Borem. 1987. Voluntary financial disclosure by Mexican corporations. *The Accounting Review* (July): 533–41.

Coller, M. 1996. Information, noise, and asset prices: An experimental study. *Review of Accounting Studies* 1: 35–50.

Coller, M., and T. Yohn. 1997. Management forecasts and information asymmetry: An examination of bid-ask spreads. *Journal of Accounting Research* 35 (2): 181–91.

Cooke, T.E. 1989. Voluntary corporate disclosure by Swedish companies. *Journal of International Financial Management and Accounting* (Summer): 171–95.

Farragher, E., R. Kleiman, and M. Baza. 1994. Do investor relations make a difference? *Quarterly Review of Economics and Finance* 34 (Winter): 403–12.

Financial Analysts Federation (FAF). 1986–90. *Report of the Financial Analysts Federation Corporate Information Committee.* New York: FAF.

Healy, P., A. Hutton, and K. Palepu. 1999. Stock performance and intermediation changes surrounding sustained increases in disclosure. *Contemporary Accounting Research* (forthcoming).

Ittner, C., D. Larcker, and M. Rajan. 1997. The choice of performance measures in annual bonus contracts. *The Accounting Review* 72: 231–55.

Jennings, R. 1987. Unsystematic security price movements, managerial earnings forecasts, and revisions in consensus analyst earnings forecasts. *Journal of Accounting Research* 25 (Spring): 90–110.

Jensen, H., and W. Meckling. 1976. Theory of the firm: Managerial behavior, agency costs and ownership structure. *Journal of Financial Economics* (October): 305–60.

Kester, W.C. 1984. Today's options for tomorrow's growth. *Harvard Business Review* (March–April) 153–60.

Kim, O., and Y. Suh. 1993. Incentive efficiency of compensation based on accounting and market performance. *Journal of Accounting and Economics* 16: 25–53.

Knutson, P. 1992. Financial reporting in the 1990s and beyond: A position paper of the

Association for Investment Management and Research. Working paper, University of Pennsylvania, Philadelphia.

Kross, W., B. Ro, and D. Schroeder. 1990. Earnings expectations: The analysts' information advantage. *The Accounting Review* 65 (April): 461–76.

Lang, M., and R. Lundholm. 1993. Cross-sectional determinants of analyst ratings of corporate disclosure. *Journal of Accounting Research* 31 (Autumn): 246–71.

———. 1996. Corporate disclosure policy and analyst behavior. *The Accounting Review* 71 (October): 467–92.

Leftwich, R., R. Watts, and J. Zimmerman. 1981. Voluntary corporate disclosure: The case of interim reporting. *Journal of Accounting Research* (Supplement): 50–77.

Meek, G.M., C.B. Roberts, and S.J. Gray. 1995. Facts influencing voluntary annual report disclosures by U.S., U.K. and continental European multinational corporations. *Journal of International Business Studies* 96, 3: 555–72.

Myers, S. 1977. Determinants of corporate borrowing. *Journal of Financial Economics*: 147–75.

Nichols, D. 1989. *The Handbook of Investor Relations*. Homewood, IL: Dow Jones-Irwin.

Piotroski, J.D. 1999. The impact of newly reported segment information on market expectations and stock prices. Working paper, University of Michigan.

Schipper, K. 1991. Analysts' forecasts. *Accounting Horizons* 4 (December): 105–21.

Sengupta, P. 1998. Corporate disclosure quality and the cost of debt. *The Accounting Review* 4 (October): 459–74.

Skinner, D.J. 1992. *Why firms voluntarily disclose bad news*. Working paper, University of Michigan.

———. 1993. The investment opportunity set and accounting procedure choice: Preliminary evidence. *Journal of Accounting and Economics* 160: 407–46.

Spero, L.L. 1979. The extent and cases of voluntary disclosure of financial information in three European capital markets: An exploratory study. Unpublished Doctoral Dissertation, Harvard University.

SRI International. 1987. *Investor Information Needs and the Annual Report*. Morristown, NJ: Financial Executives Research Foundation.

Standard & Poor's Corporation. 1982. *Credit Overview: Corporate and International Ratings*. New York: Standard & Poor's Corporation.

Verrecchia, R. 1982. The use of mathematical models in financial accounting. *Journal of Accounting Research* 20: 1–55.

———. 1983. Discretionary disclosure. *Journal of Accounting and Economics* 5: 179–94.

Waymire, G. 1986. Additional evidence on the accuracy of analyst forecasts before and after voluntary management earnings forecasts. *The Accounting Review* 59 (January): 129–42.

Welker, M. 1995. Disclosure policy, information asymmetry and liquidity in equity markets. *Contemporary Accounting Research* 11 (Spring): 801–27.

White, H. 1980. A heteroscedasticity. *Econometrica* 48: 817–38.

Williams, P. 1996. The relation between a prior earnings forecast by management and analyst response to a current management forecast. *The Accounting Review* 71 (January): 103–15.

Yermack, D. 1995. Do corporations award CEO stock options effectively? *Journal of Financial Economics* 39: 23.

CHAPTER 3

Level of Multinationality as an Explanation for Post-Announcement Drift

INTRODUCTION

The predictability of stock returns after earnings announcements (i.e., the post-earnings announcement drift) was first noted by Ball and Brown (1968). They reported that even after earnings are announced, estimated cumulative "abnormal" returns continue to drift up for "good news" firms and down for "bad news" firms. Explanations offered for the phenomenon include: (a) the inadequacy of the Capital Asset Pricing Model (CAPM) as a model of asset pricing (Holthausen, 1983; Foster et al., 1984); (b) the market's failure to fully reflect the attributes of the stochastic process underlying earnings (Rendleman et al., 1987; Freeman and Tse, 1989; Bernard and Thomas, 1990; and Bartov, 1992); (c) the transaction costs (Bhushan, 1994); (d) investor sophistication (Bartov et al., 2000); and (e) analyst experience (Mikhail et al., 2000).

Our study further investigates whether drift is a manifestation of the complexity of the firm issuing the quarterly earnings by examining the relation between drift and the level of multinationality. The position to be discussed in detail in the next section, is that post-earnings announcements drift in stock prices will be most pronounced for firms with a low level of multinationality whose earnings are more difficult to predict. An intuition for this result is that stock prices reflect the performance of both domestic and international activities, and consequently, the greater the level of a firm's multinationality, the greater the predictability of its price (Choi et al., 1999; Agmon and Lessard, 1977; Errunza and Senbet, 1981; Yang et al., 1985). The foreign profit/total profits variable is used as a proxy for the level of multinationality.

We find that the level of multinationality variable is important in explaining both the drift and the stock price responses to subsequent earnings announcements. Drift is found to be positively related to an earnings-surprise variable and negatively related to the multinationality variable after controlling and firm size (e.g., Foster et al., 1984).

The findings show that the magnitude of the postearnings announcement drift is firms with a low level of multinationality. The level of multinationality appears to be a cause of the predictability of stock returns after earnings announcement.

A MULTINATIONALITY PERSPECTIVE ON DRIFT

The predictability of abnormal stock returns was found in early work to last up to two months after annual earnings announcements (e.g., Foster et al., 1984). Misperception of the time-series properties of earnings (Freeman and Tse, 1989); misperception of quarterly earnings to be a seasonal variable random walk, while the actual process is a seasonally differenced first-order autoregressive process with a seasonal moving-average term (Bernard and Thomas, 1990); and market misperception of the process underlying earnings (Ball and Bartov, 1996) are some of the cited conjectures and evidence of the cause of the postearnings announcement drift in abnormal returns. The primary purpose of the current study is to evaluate and test the conjecture that multinationality is a leading cause of the postearnings announcement drift in abnormal returns. The idea that the drift is negatively related to the level of multinationality can be supported by:

a. Findings that drift is inversely related to size (Bhushan, 1999), and bigger multinationality is characteristic of large firms (Errunza and Senbet, 1981).

b. Findings that drift is a result of misperception of the earnings process by holding of unsophisticated investors (Bartov et al., 2000), and high multinationality firms are largely sought by sophisticated investors in general and fund managers who specialize in large capitalization stocks (Choi et al., 1999).

c. Findings that drift is inversely related to share price and annual dollar trading volume as proxy for the inverse of direct and indirect cost of trading (Bhushan, 1994) and the growth of institutional holdings in large, multinational firms (Choi, et al., 1999).

d. Findings consistent with investors anchoring on the more efficient and accurate earnings expectations of high multinationality firms, mitigating any resulting postearnings announcement drift. (Bodnar and Weintrop, 1997; Rugman, 1977; Rivera, 1991).

DESCRIPTION OF THE SAMPLE AND THE VARIABLES

The sample used in this study is comprised of all the firms included in the 1990–99 *Forbes* one hundred largest U.S. multinationals. It consists of 3,972 firm-quarter observations.

To test the hypothesis, we examine the association between postearnings announcement drift and the level of multinationality, controlling for the firm's standardized unexpected earnings and for size shown in prior research to affect the drift. Those variables are defined as follows:

For each observation, we calculate the firm's daily abnormal return as the firm's raw return minus the return on the size decile portfolio to which the firm belongs as of the beginning of the year. Those daily returns are compounded from $t = 0$ to $t = +59$ (where $t = 0$ is the quarterly announcement data from *Compustat* to obtain the cumulative abnormal return (CAR60) for firm at quarter t. The choice of the sixty-day window reflects Bernard and Thomas's (1990) finding that most of the drift occurs during this time period.

Standardized unexpected earnings is computed as in previous research on drift (e.g., Bernard and Thomas, 1990). First, standardized unexpected earnings (SUE) are measured as the difference between reported and expected earnings, where expected earnings are estimated using a seasonal random walk deflated by the standard deviation of forecast errors from this model over the most recent twenty quarters of data, beginning in the quarter $t - 21$ and going through quarter $t - 1$ (the estimation period). Second, SUE_{it} is classified into deciles ($DSUE_{it}$), based on the sample distribution of SUE each calendar year, with zero representing the smallest decile of the level of multinationality and nine representing the largest, and then scaled to range between zero and one.

Multinationality (MULTY) for firm j at quarter$_t$ is defined by the yearly foreign profits/total profits. Our results are unchanged if multinationality was defined by either foreign sales/total sales or foreign assets/total assets. Similarly to SUE, MULTY was categorically classified as DMULTY.

Size is measured by MU_{it}, the market value of equity for firm; and year t. DMB is the ranked market value of equity.

REGRESSION RESULTS

The relation between drift and multinationality is analyzed using regression analysis with CAR60 as the dependent variable. A first regression is used to replicate the documented inverse relationship between drift and size as follows:

$$CAR60 = b_0 + b_1DSUE_{it} + b_2DMV_{it} + b_3DSUE_{it} * DMV_{it} + E_{it} \qquad (1)$$

A second regression is used to estimate the relationship between multinationality and drift after controlling for firm size as follows:

$$CAR60 = b_0 + b_1DSUE_{it} + b_2DMV_{it} + b_3DSUE_{it} * DMV_{it} \\ + b_4DMULTY_{it} + b_5DSUE_{it} * DMULTY_{it} + E_{it} \qquad (2)$$

In estimating both equations (1) and (2), observations with studentized residuals greater than two or Cook's D greater than one, are eliminated. The results are

Table 3.1
Variable Descriptive Statistics and Correlations

A. Descriptive Statistics			
	Mean	Median	Standard Deviation
CAR60	0.0023	-0.0011	0.1321
SUE	-0.7232	0.0532	15.265
Market Value of			
Common Equity (MV)	14081.50	12290.51	6232.50
MULTY	0.5321	0.4132	0.2232

B. Correlation Table				
	CAR60	DSUE	DMV	DMULTY
CAR60	_____	0.0523	-0.0326	0.0321
		(0.000)	(0.013)	(0.000)
DSUE		_____	0.0821	0.0812
			(0.000)	(0.000)
DMV			_____	0.1325
				(0.000)
DMULTY				_____

Panel A provides descriptive statistics on the sixty-day cumulative abnormal return following the quarterly earnings announcement date (CAR60), the standardized unexpected earnings (SUE), market value of consumer equity (MV), and the level of multinationality (MULTY), measured as the yearly foreign profits/total profits. Panel B provides Pearson correlations. DSUE, DMV, and DMULTY represent the ranked values of SUE, MV, and MULTY, respectively.

insensitive to this elimination. If the drift is less for high multinationality firms, we expect the coefficient estimate associated in the DSUE*DMULTY to be reliably negative.

Table 3.1 provides the variable descriptive statistics and correlations. Table 3.2 provides the results of the regressions. The first column shows the results of regressing CAR60 on unexpected earnings. The magnitude of the postearnings announcement drift in our sample of large firms is 2.32% (t = 7.235, one-tailed p<.001).

The second column is used to document the inverse relationship between drift and size. As in prior research, the estimated coefficient in DSUE remains significantly positive (0.0354, t = 8.232, one-tailed p<0.01). As predicted, the estimated coefficient on DSUE*DMV is negative and statistically significant (−0.0026, t = −4.252, p<0.01).

The third column is used to investigate the relation between drift and multinationality. As predicted, the estimated coefficient on DSUE*DMULTY is neg-

Table 3.2

The Association between Postearnings Announcement Drift and Level of Multinationality

Equation (2): $b_0 + b_1 DSUE_{it} + b_2 DMV_{it} + b_3 DSUE_{it} * DMV_{it} + b_4 DMULTY_{it} +$

$b_5 DSUE_{it} * DMULTY_{it} + E_{it}$

Variable	Predicted sign		Model		
		1	2	3	4
Intercept	?	-0.0131	-0.0134	-0.0134	-0.0242
		(-8.023)*	(-8.263)*	(-8.123)*	(-8.212)*
DSUE	+	0.0232	0.0354	0.0344	0.0362
		(7.235)*	(8.232)*	(6.321)*	(5.231)*
DMV	?		0.0102		0.0121
			(2.321)**		(2.425)**
DSUE*DMV	-		-0.0026		-0.0015
			(-4.252)*		(-2.119)**
DMULTY	0			0.0126	0.0135
				(2.852)**	(2.721)**
DSUE*DMULTY	-			-0.0087	-0.0013
				(-3.251)*	(-3.521)**
Adjusted R^2		0.42%	0.44%	0.62%	0.73%
		(72.320)	(28.520)	(25.321)	(14.256)

The variables are defined in table 3.1. The t statistic is provided in parentheses below the estimated coefficient; the model F statistic is presented below the adjusted R^2. Single asterisk (*) denotes one-tailed probability <0.01; double asterisk (**) denotes one-tailed probability <0.05.

ative and statistically significant (-0.0087, $t = -3.251$, one-tailed $p<0.01$). The results indicate the magnitude of the drift is reduced as the level of multinationality increases. The fourth column shows that the negative association between CAR60 and level of multinationality holds after including interaction terms for size. Overall, those results show a negative association between the postearnings announcement drift and the level of multinationality.

CONCLUDING REMARKS

This study is another empirical examination of a potential explanation of observed post-announcement drift in stock prices. Does the level of multinationality, a variable used for firm complexity, relate to postearnings announcement drift? The findings are that postearnings announcement drift is negatively related to the level of multinationality and that this relation exists when firm size is controlled.

The findings may be related to prior research by stating that the misperception of the time-series properties of earnings observed by Freeman and Tse (1989), the misperception of quarterly earnings to be a seasonal random walk observed by Bernard and Thomas (1990), and the market misperception of the process underlying earnings (Ball and Bartov, 1996) are *possibly* reflecting the low level of multinationality causing the post-announcement drift in general.

REFERENCES

Agmon, T., and D. Lessard. 1977. Investor recognition of corporate international diversification. *Journal of Finance* 5: 1049–55.

Ball, R., and E. Bartov. 1996. How naive is the stock market's use of earnings information? *Journal of Accounting and Economics* 21: 319–37.

Ball, R., and P. Brown. 1968. An empirical evaluation of accounting income numbers. *Journal of Accounting Research* 6: 159–78.

Bartov, E., S. Radhakrishnan, and I. Krinsky. 2000. Investor sophistication and patterns in stock returns after earnings announcements. *The Accounting Review* (January): 43–63.

Bartov, E. 1992. Patterns in unexpected earnings as an explanation for post-announcement drift. *The Accounting Review* 67: 610–22.

Bernard, V.L., and J. Thomas. 1990. Evidence that stock prices do not fully reflect the implications of current earnings for future earnings. *Journal of Accounting and Economics* 13: 305–40.

Bhushan, R. 1994. An informational efficiency perspective on the post-earnings-announcement drift. *Journal of Accounting and Economics* 18: 45–65.

Bhushan, R. 1999. An informational efficiency perspective on the post-earnings announcement drift. *Journal of Accounting and Economics* (July): 45–65.

Bodnar, G.N., and J. Weintrop. 1997. The valuation of the foreign income of U.S. multinational firms: A growth opportunities perspective. *Journal of Accounting and Economics* 94: 69–97.

Choi, F.D.S., C.A. Frost, and G.K. Meek. 1999. *International Accounting*. Upper Saddle River, NJ: Prentice Hall.

Errunza, V., and L. Senbet. 1981. The effects of international corporate diversification, market valuation and size adjusted evidence. *Journal of Finance* 11: 717–43.

Foster, G., C. Olsen, and T. Shevlin. 1984. Earnings releases, anomalies, and the behavior of securities returns. *The Accounting Review* 59: 574–603.

Freeman, R.N., and S.Y. Tse. 1989. The multiperiod information content of accounting earnings: Confirmations and contradictions of previous earnings reports. *Journal of Accounting Research* 27 (Supplement): 49–79.

Holthausen, R. 1983. Abnormal returns following quarterly earnings announcements. In *Proceedings of the CRSP Seminar on the Analysis of Security Prices*, 37–59. Chicago, IL: University of Chicago.

Mikhail, M.B., B.R. Walter, and R.H. Willis. 2000. The effect of experience on security analyst underreaction and post-earnings announcement drift. Working paper, Duke University.

Rendleman, R.J., C.P. Jones, and H.A. Latane. 1987. Further insight into the standardized unexpected earnings anomaly: Size and serial correlation effects. *Financial Review* 22: 131–44.

Rivera, J.M. 1991. Prediction performance of earnings forecasts: The case of U.S. multinationals. *Journal of International Business Studies* 22.

Rugman, A.R. 1977. Foreign operations and the stability of U.S. corporate earnings: Risk reduction by international diversification. *Journal of Finance* 5: 223–34.

Tsetsekos, G.P. 1991. Multinationality and common stock offering. *Journal of International Financial Management and Accounting* 3: 1–16.

Yang, H., J. Wansley, and W. Lane. 1985. Stock market recognition of multinationality of a firm and international events. *Journal of Business, Finance, and Accounting* 12: 263–74.

CHAPTER 4

The Effect of Multinationality on Security Analyst Underreaction

INTRODUCTION

Evidence of bias and positive correlation in forecast errors suggest that analysts do not properly recognize the time-series properties of earnings and return information when setting expectations of future returns (Abarbanell, 1991; Abarbanell and Bernard, 1992). Prior work has investigated firm-and horizon-related cross-sectional variations in analysts underreaction to publicly available information focusing on the explanatory power of permanent or transitory earnings (Ali, Klein, and Rosenfeld, 1992), the forecast horizon (Raedy and Shane, 1999), the firm's information environment (Jacob and Lys, 1999), and analyst-specific characteristics, such as analyst experience (Mikhail, Walther, and Willis, 2000). We focus instead on the complexity provided by the firms being analyzed in general and the level of multinationality in particular. We examine whether analysts underreact to prior earnings and returns information more as the level of multinationality increases. Using a time-series research design, we examine if there is variation in underreaction correlated with the level of multinationality.

Using a sample of five hundred firm-year observations from the firms included in *Forbes*'s one hundred largest U.S. multinationals, our results indicate that analysts underreact to prior earnings information more as the level of multinationality increases. The results of a regression of current forecast error on prior forecast error, prior return, prior forecast error interacted with the level of multinationality, and prior return interacted with the level of multinationality show a significantly positive mean estimated coefficient in the prior forecast error and multinationality interaction term.

This chapter makes an important contribution by showing that analyst's efficient use of earnings and return information varies with the level of multinationality. The higher the level of multinationality, the higher the analyst's underreaction to prior earnings and returns information. The study suggests that in addition to other factors, found in prior work, to impact the level of underreaction, the complexity of the firm in general and the level of multinationality in particular affect the analyst's efficient use of public information. This finding is consistent with analysts relying on sources of information other than prior earnings and returns, to gain a better grasp of the factors and conditions affecting multinational firms. In addition to or instead of prior earnings and returns, analysts may be focusing on specific factors that affect the financial performance of multinational firms, such as economic transaction and translation and political risk exposures, to name a few (Choi, Frost, and Meek, 1999).

DEVELOPMENT OF THE HYPOTHESIS AND DESCRIPTION OF THE MULTINATIONALITY VARIABLE

Prior research provides ample evidence that analysts appear to underreact to prior returns (Abarbanell, 1991; Lys and Sohn, 1990; Ali, Klein, and Rosenfeld, 1992; Brown, Griffin, Hageeman, and Zmijewski, 1987; and Klein, 1990) and prior earnings (Abarbanell and Bernard, 1992; Mendenhall, 1991; Ali, Klein, and Rosenfeld, 1992; Easterwood and Nutt, 1999; and Elliot, Philbrick, and Wiedman, 1995). Explanations for this phenomenon included (a) the positive effect of predominantly prior permanent earnings (Ali, Klein, and Rosenfeld, 1992); (b) the positive effect of the forecast horizon (Raedy and Shane, 1999); (c) the positive effect of forecast horizon, firm size, the extent to which other analysts following the same firm have serially correlated forecast errors, and the extent to which seasonal random walls forecast errors for the firm are serially correlated (Jacob and Lys, 1999); and (d) the negative impact of the analyst's experience (Mikhail, Walther, and Willis, 2000).

The prediction in this study concerns the positive relationship between multinationality and the level of analysts' underreaction. We predict that the higher the level of multinationality, the higher the level of underreaction. The prediction is based on:

1. Findings on bias in forecasting earnings and/or decrease in forecasting accuracy in complex firm environments such as: (a) firm's cost structure, strikes, start-up and break-in problems with new products and processes (Barefield and Comiskey, 1975); (b) low-quality management discussion and analysis (Barron, Kile, and O'Keefe, 1999); (c) uncertainty about firm's future economic performance (Barron and Stuerkse, 1998); (d) differential information (Barry and Brown, 1985); (e) auditor conservatism (Basu, Hwang, and Jan, 1999); (f) large capitalization firms (Branson, Lorek, and Pagach, 1995); (g) optimism concerning the future of negative earnings firms (Dowen, 1996); (h) level of industry diversification (Dunn and Siva, 2000); (i) future earnings

uncertainty (Han, Manry, and Shaw, 1996); (j) degree of corporate seasonality (Luttman and Silhan, 1993); (k) earnings variability (Luttman and Silhan, 1995); (l) earnings forecast for failing firms (Moses, 1990); (m) earnings management (Pae, 1998); and (n) business risk, financial risk, and information availability (Parkash and Salatka, 1999).

2. Findings on bias in forecasting earnings and/or decrease in greatest accuracy in specific international and country contexts (Calalv and Druvefors, 1997; Capstaff, Paudyal, and Rees, 1995, 1998; Chan, Hamao, and Lakonishok, 1993; Claus and Thomas, 1999; Conroy and Harris, 1995; Conroy, Harris, and Park, 1994, 1998; Darrough and Harris, 1991; DeBondt and Forbes, 1998; Dimson and Marsh 1984; Erickson and Cunniff, 1995; Hennessey, 1995; Higgins, 1999; Ho, 1996; Land and Neidermeyer 1998; L'Her and Suret, 1991; Moller and Hufner, 1998; Moksnes and Ytterhus, 1998; Lynn, Schreuder and Klaassen, 1984; and Speidell and Ramos, 1998).

3. Findings on difficulty of forecasting earnings of multinational firms due to specific international problems such as cultural, transaction, economic, translation, and political risk exposures (Choi, Frost, and Meek, 1999; Chen, Comiskey, and Mulford, 1990; Frankel and Lee, 1996; Jacques and Rie, 1994; Katz, Zarzaeski, and Hall, 1998; Riahi-Belkaoui, 1995; Riahi-Belkaoui and Alvertos, 1993; Riahi-Belkaoui and Picur, 1993; Rivera, 1991; Zarzeski and Roberts, 1999; and Das and Saudagaran, 1998, 1999).

DATA AND VARIABLE DEFINITIONS

Analysts' forecast errors for firm i for year t, $FEPR_{it}$, is defined as:

$$FEPR_{it} = (EPS_{it} - F_{it})/P_{it} \tag{1}$$

When EPS_{it} is reported annual earnings-per-share for firm i for year t, F_{it}, is the median analysts' forecast for annual EPS of year t, and P_{it} is the market price of the stock at the beginning of the month in which analysts' forecasts are released. The median is used as the measure of the analysts' consensus. The initial sample of analysts' forecasts of annual earnings consists of firms from *Forbes*'s list of the largest one hundred U.S. multinationals from 1995 to 1999 for which the IBES database contains forecasts of annual earnings. The procedure yielded a sample of five hundred firm-year observations over the 1995–99 period. For each firm-year observation, the firms' prior return RET_{it} is defined as the firms' one-year stock return. Multinational (MULTY) is measured by the firm's yearly foreign profits over total profits.

Table 4.1 presents descriptive statistics on the sample used in the study.

MULTINATIONALITY AND UNDERREACTION

The analysis in this study includes both a replication of prior research on serial correlation and bias in analysts' forecast errors and an investigation of whether the underreaction varies with the level of multinationality of the firm.

Table 4.1
Sample Descriptive Statistics

	Mean	Median	Standard Deviation	
MULTY	31.82	41.7	13.5	
RET	0.0062	0.0065	0.1827	
FEPR	-0.0042	.00000	0.0623	

Variable Definitions:
1. MULTY: Level of multinationality as measured by foreign profits/total profits.
2. RET: The firm's raw return from the prior earnings announcement date until the date on which the analyst issued the yearly forecast.
3. FEPR: Actual earnings-per-share minus the analyst forecast, deflated by the end of the year price.

To test for the bias and serial correlation in analysts' forecast errors, the following regression is used:[1]

$$FEPR_{it} = a_0 + a_1 FEPR_{it-1} + a_2 RET_{it-1} + e_{it}t \qquad (2)$$

where $FEPR_{it}$ ($FEPR_{it-1}$) is the analysts' yearly forecast error for firm i in year t (t−1) and RET_{it-1} is the one-year stock return.[2]

A rejection of the null hypothesis that a_0 equals zero and a_1 equals zero indicates that the analysts' forecasts do not incorporate the information contained in past errors and the information contained in the past stock returns. The pooled cross-sectional time-series regression results for equation (2), estimated with or without RET_{it-1} are shown in table 4.2. The statistical significance of the OLS coefficients is presented after the White (1980) adjustment for heteroscedasticity.[3]

Consistent with prior research, the coefficient on $FEPR_{it-1}$ is significantly positive at the 0.05 level, regardless of whether RET_{it-1} is included as an independent variable in the equation (2). It indicates that forecast errors of annual earnings are correlated in adjacent years. The overestimation of earnings, shown in other studies (Stober, 1991; Barefield and Comiskey, 1975; Fried and Givoly, 1982; and Ali, Klein, and Rosenfeld, 1992), is again supported by the significantly negative intercept term.[4]

The results in table 4.2 support prior findings that analysts, on the average, underreact to the information in prior earnings surprises or prior stock returns when stating their earnings forecasts.

The second step is to test whether the underreaction, a bias and positive

Table 4.2
Bias and Serial Correlation in Yearly Forecast Errors

(Dependent variable = FEPR $_{it}$)

Independent Variable	Predicted Sign	OLS Coefficient	t Statistic	Adjusted R2
Intercept	-	-0.0003	0.823	
FEPR $_{it-1}$	+	0.2231	9.632*	
RET $_{it-1}$	+	0.0063	10.831*	
Adj. R ^{2}				0.10

1. Variable Definitions: See table 4.1.
2. Asterisk (*) denotes one-tailed probability <0.01.

correlation, found in table 4.2, is conditional on the level of multinationality. To examine this question, the following equation is estimated:

$$FEPR_{it} = B_0 + B_1 \, MULTY_{it} + B_2 \, FEPR_{it-1} + B_3 \, MULTY_{it} * FEPR_{it-1}$$
$$+ B_4 \, RET_{it-1} + B_5 \, RET_{it-1} * MULTY_{it} + E_{it} \qquad (3)$$

The results of the estimation of the equation (3) are shown in table 4.3. Similarly to the results in table 4.2, the coefficients in $FEPR_{it-1}$ and RET_{it-1} are positively significant after inclusion of the MULTY variable and interaction variables. As predicted, the explanatory power of the model in table 4.3 is 14%, 40% higher than in table 4.2, an increase due to the effect of multinationality on the variation in analyst forecast efficiency. Similarly, the effect of multinationality is more evident in the positive and significant coefficient on MULTY * FEPR. The coefficient in RET * MULTY is also positive and significant, indicating that analysts fail to incorporate the information in prior returns as the level of multinationality increases.

The results show that analysts' underreaction varies with the level of multinationality in the sense that analysts fail to incorporate the information in prior earnings and prior return as the level of multinationality increases.

CONCLUSIONS

This study examines whether analysts' underreaction to prior earnings and return information varies with the level of multinationality. The results support prior research by documenting significant positive serial correlation in the one-year forecast errors for U.S. multinational companies and support our thesis that

Table 4.3

The Efficiency of Analyst Forecasts Conditional on the Firm's Level of Multinationality

Equation (3): $FERP_{it} = B_0 + B_1 MULTY_{it} + B_2 FEPR_{it-1} + B_3 MULTY_{it}*FEFPR_{it-1}$

$$+ B_4 RET_{it-1} + B_5 RET_{it-1} + B_5 RET_{it-1} * MULTY_{it} + E_{it}$$

Variable	Predicted Sign	OLS Coefficient	t Statistic	Adjusted R2
Intercept	-	-0.0002	(-6.252)*	
MULTY	+	0.0232	(5.256)*	
FEPR	+	0.1838	(8.232)*	
MULTY*FEPR	+	0.0032	(8.325)*	
RET	+	0.0093	(6.257)*	
RET*MULTY	+	0.0003	(4.852)*	
Adj. R^2				0.14

1. Variable Definitions: See table 4.1.
2. Asterisk (*) denotes one-tailed probability <0.01.

analysts' underreaction increases with the level of multinationality, suggesting that the complexities associated with increased multinationality call for the use of alternative sources of information.

NOTES

1. The regression was estimated after eliminating observations with studentized residuals greater than two or Cook's D greater than one; this elimination did not affect the results. The estimation of equation (2) using rank regression techniques yielded comparable results.

2. The results remained unchanged when the firms' market-adjusted return was used in lieu of the firms' raw return.

3. A bootstrapping procedure is used (Noreen, 1989) to estimate the coefficients and their standard errors. The procedure controls for possible cross-sectional correlations in forecast errors.

4. Equation (2) was reestimated on a year-by-year basis. The results are similar to those reported in table 4.2 for every one of the five years examined.

REFERENCES

Abarbanell, J. 1991. Do analysts' earnings forecasts incorporate information in prior stock price changes? *Journal of Accounting and Economics*: 147–65.

Abarbanell, J., and V. Bernard. 1992. Tests of analysts' overreaction/underreaction to earnings information as an explanation for anomalous stock price behavior. *The Journal of Finance* 7: 1181–207.

Ali, A., C. Klein, and J. Rosenfeld. 1992. Analysts' use of information about permanent and transitory earnings components in forecasting annual EPS. *The Accounting Review*: 183–98.

Barefield, R.M., and E.E. Comiskey. 1975. The accuracy of analysts' forecasts of earnings per share. *Journal of Business Research* 3: 241–52.

Barron, O.E., C.O. Kile, and T.B. O'Keefe. 1999. MD&A quality as measured by the SEC and analysts' earning forecasts. *Contemporary Accounting Research*, Vol. 16, 1: 75–109.

Barron, O.E., and P.S. Stuerke. 1998. Dispersion in analysts' earnings forecasts as a measure of uncertainty. *Journal of Accounting, Auditing and Finance*, Vol. 13, 3: 245–70.

Barry, C.B., and S.J. Brown. 1985. Differential information and security market equilibrium. *Journal of Financial and Quantitative Analysis*, Vol. 20, 4: 407–22.

Basu, S., L.S. Hwang, and C.L. Jan. 1999. Auditor conservatism and analysts' fourth quarter earnings forecasts. Working paper.

Branson, B.C., K.S. Lorek, and D.P. Pagach. 1995. Evidence on the superiority of analysts' quarterly earnings forecasts for small capitalization firms. *Decision Sciences* 2: 243–63.

Brown, L., P. Griffin, L. Hageeman, and M. Zmijewski. 1987. An evaluation of alternative proxies for the market's assessment of unexpected earnings. *Journal of Accounting and Economics* 2: 159–93.

Calalv, R., and F. Druvefors. 1997. An empirical study of earnings forecast for companies listed in Sweden. Working paper.

Capstaff, J., K. Paudyal, and W. Rees. 1995. The accuracy and rationality of earnings forecasts by UK analysts. *Journal of Business Finance & Accounting* 1: 67–85.

———. 1998. Analysts' forecasts of German firms' earnings: A comparative analysis. *Journal of International Financial Management & Accounting* 2: 83–116.

Chan, L.K.C., Y. Hamao, and J. Lakonishok. 1993. Can fundamentals predict Japanese stock returns? *Financial Analysts Journal* 4: 63–69.

Chen, A.Y.S., E.E. Comiskey, and C.W. Mulford. 1990. Foreign currency translation and analyst forecast dispersion: Examining the effects of statement of financial accounting standards no. 52. *Journal of Accounting and Public Policy* 4: 239–56.

Choi, F.D.S., C.A. Frost, and G.K. Meek. 1999. *International Accounting*. Upper Saddle River, NJ: Prentice Hall.

Claus, J., and J.K. Thomas. 1999. Measuring risk premia using earnings forecasts: An international analysis. Working paper.

Conroy, R.M., and R.S. Harris. 1995. Analysts' earnings forecasts in Japan: Accuracy and sell-side optimism. *Pacific-Basin Finance Journal* 4: 393–408.

Conroy, R.M., R.S. Harris, and Y.S. Park. 1994. Analysts' earnings forecast accuracy in

Japan and the United States. *Research Foundation of Chartered Financial Analysts* 5, 33: 50.

———. 1998. Fundamental information and share prices in Japan: Evidence from earnings surprises and management predictions. *International Journal of Forecasting* 2: 227–44.

Darrough, M.N., and T.S. Harris. 1991. Do management forecasts of earnings affect stock prices in Japan? *Japanese Financial Market Research*, edited by W.T. Ziemba, W. Bailey, and Y. Hamao. New York: Elsevier Science Publishers B.V.

Das, S., and S.M. Saudagaran. 1998. Accuracy, bias, and dispersion in analysts' earnings forecasts: The case of cross-listed foreign firms. *Journal of International Financial Management & Accounting* 1: 16–33.

———. 1999. Predictive accuracy of analysts' earnings forecasts: A comparison of non-U.S. cross-listed firms and U.S. multinationals. Working paper, University of Illinois at Chicago.

DeBondt, W.F., and W.P. Forbes. 1998. Herding in analyst earnings forecasts: Evidence from the United Kingdom. Working paper.

Dimson, E., and P. Marsh. 1984. An analysis of brokers' and analysts' unpublished forecasts of U.K. stock returns. *Journal of Finance* 5: 1257–92.

Dowen, R.J. 1996. Analyst reaction to negative earnings for large well known firms. *Journal of Portfolio Management* 1: 49–55.

Dunn, K., and N. Siva. 2000. The effect of industry diversification on analysts' earnings forecast. Working paper.

Easterwood, J., and S. Nutt. 1999. Inefficiency in analysts' earnings forecasts: systematic misreaction or systematic optimism? *The Journal of Finance*: 1777–97.

Elliot, J., D. Philbrick, and C. Wiedman. 1995. Evidence from archival data on the relation between security analysts' forecast errors and prior forecast revisions. *Contemporary Accounting Research*: 919–38.

Erickson, H.L., and J.F. Cunniff. 1995. A comparative look at consensus earnings in world markets. *Journal of Investing*, Vol. 4, 1: 19–28.

Frankel, R., and C.M.C. Lee. 1996. Accounting diversity and international valuation. Working paper.

Fried, D., and D. Givoly. 1982. Financial analysts' forecasts of earnings—A better surrogate for market expectations. *Journal of Accounting and Economics* 4: 85–107.

Han, B.H., D. Manry, and W. Shaw. 1996. Predicting analysts' forecast bias with proxies for future earnings uncertainty. Working paper.

Hennessey, S.M. 1995. Earnings forecasts revisions and security returns: Canadian evidence. *Accounting & Business Research* 25: 240–52.

Higgins, H.N. 1999. Analysts' forecasts of Japanese firms' earnings: Additional evidence. Working paper.

Ho, L.J. 1996. Bias and accuracy of analysts' forecasts: Evidence from Australia. *International Journal of Investment* 13: 306–13.

Jacob, J., and T. Lys. 1999. Determinants and implications of the serial-correlation in analysts' earnings forecast errors. Working paper, University of Colorado and Northwestern University.

Jacques, W., and D. Rie. 1994. Valuation factors across countries. *The Handbook of Corporate Earnings Analysis*, New York: Probus Publishing.

Katz, J.P., M.T. Zarzaeski, and H.J. Hall. 1998. Analysts' earnings forecasts across countries: The impact of strategy, industry and culture. Working paper.

Klein, A. 1990. A direct test of the cognitive bias theory of share price reversals. *Journal of Accounting and Economics* 8: 155–66.

Land, R.T., and P.E. Neidermeyer. 1998. An examination of security analysts' consensus earnings forecasts for German companies. Working paper.

L'Her, J.S., and J.M. Suret. 1991. The reaction of Canadian securities to revisions of earnings forecasts. *Contemporary Accounting Research* 2: 378–406.

Luttman, S.M., and P.A. Silhan. 1993. Corporate seasonality as a potential determinant of earnings forecast accuracy. *Advances in Accounting* 11: 139–58.

———. 1995. Identifying factors consistently related to value line earnings predictability. *Financial Review* 30: 445–68.

Lys, T., and S. Sohn. 1990. The association between revisions of financial analysts' earnings forecasts and security-price changes. *Journal of Accounting and Economics* 10: 341–63.

Mendenhall, R. 1991. Evidence on the possible underweighting of earnings-related information. *Journal of Accounting Research* 11: 170–79.

Mikhail, M., B. Walther, and R. Willis. 1997. Do security analysts improve their performance with experience? *Journal of Accounting Research* 5: 131–57.

———. 1999. Does forecast accuracy matter to security analysts? *The Accounting Review* 3: 185–200.

———. 2000. The effect of experience on security analyst underreaction and post earnings announcement drift. Working paper, Duke University.

Moksnes, K., and O. Ytterhus. 1998. Consensus earnings forecasts and financial profits in the Norwegian stock market. Working paper.

Moller, H.P., and B. Hufner. 1998. The value relevance of German financial analysts' earnings. Working paper.

Moses, D.O. 1990. On analysts' earnings forecasts for failing firms. *Journal of Business Finance & Accounting* 17: 101–18.

Noreen, E. 1989. *Computer-intensive methods for testing hypotheses: An introduction.* New York: John Wiley & Sons.

O'Brien, P. 1988. Analysts' forecasts as earnings expectations. *Journal of Accounting and Economics* 8: 53–83.

Pae, J. 1998. The impact of earnings management on the properties of analysts forecasts. Working paper.

Parkash, M., and W.K. Salatka. 1999. The relation of analysts' forecast dispersion with business risk, and information availability. Working paper.

Raedy, J., and P. Shane. 1999. Analysts and investor underreaction to information about future earnings: Tests for a horizon effect. Working paper, University of North Carolina and University of Colorado, September.

Rees, L., E.P. Swanson, and M.B. Clement. 1999. The influence of experience, resources, and portfolio complexity on analyst forecast accuracy in the U.K. Germany, Japan, and Canada. Working paper.

Riahi-Belkaoui, A. 1995. Prediction performance of earnings forecasts of U.S. firms active in developed and developing countries. *Research in Accounting in Emerging Economies* 3: 85–97.

Riahi-Belkaoui, A., and D.K. Alvertos. 1993. The effects of country return and risk differences on prediction performance of earnings forecasts. *Managerial Finance* 6: 3–9.

Riahi-Belkaoui, A., and R.D. Picur. 1993. An analysis of the use of accounting and market measures of performance, CEO experience and nature of the deviation from the analysts' forecasts in CEO compensation contracts. *Managerial Finance* 2: 20–32.

Rivera, J.M. 1991. Prediction performance of earnings forecasts: The case of U.S. multinationals. *Journal of International Business Studies* 2: 265–88.

Schreuder, H., and J. Klaassen. 1984. Confidential revenue and profit forecasts by management and financial analysts: Evidence from the Netherlands. *The Accounting Review* 1: 64–77.

Speidell, L.S., and E. Ramos. 1998. Do international earnings estimates matter? *Journal of Investing* 7: 23–31.

Stober, T.L. 1991. Summary financial statement measures and analysts' forecasts of earnings. Working paper, Indiana University, Bloomington.

White, W.H. 1980. A heteroscedasticity-consistent covariance matrix estimation and a direct test for heteroscedasticity. *Econometrica* 48: 817–38.

Zarzeski, M.T., and R. Roberts. 1999. The impact of strategy, industry and culture on forecasting the performance of global competitors: A strategic perspective. Working paper.

CHAPTER 5

Growth Opportunities, Internalization, and Market Valuation of Multinational Firms

INTRODUCTION

With the increased level of business activities conducted by multinational firms, the international business literature raises the empirical question of whether multinationality does in fact add to share value (Morck and Yeung, 1991; Mishra and Gobeli, 1998). Three theories are commonly used to link multinationality to investment value, namely: (a) the internalization theory, (b) the imperfect capital markets theory, and (c) the managerial objectives theory.

The internalization theory maintains that foreign direct investment will cause the increase of the market value of the firm relative to its accounting value only if the firm can internalize markets for certain of its intangibles. Examples of these firm specific intangible assets include production skills, managerial skills, patents, market abilities, and consumer goodwills.[1] These information-based proprietary intangible assets cannot be copied or exchanged at arm's length, but can only be transferred to subsidiaries, thereby internalizing the markets for such assets. As a result, the market value of a multinational firm, possessing these intangibles and engaging in foreign direct investment, will be directly proportional to the firm's degree of multinationality.

The imperfect capital markets theory suggests that investors, confined by institutional constraints on international capital flows and the information asymmetries that exist in global capital markets, invest in multinational firms to gain from the international diversification opportunities they provide. This direct valuation of multinational firms by investors as a means of diversifying their portfolios internationally is assumed to enhance the share price of multinational firms, independently of the information-based, proprietary intangible assets possessed by these firms.[2]

The managerial objectives theory rests on the assumption of the differences of motives between management and shareholders. The complexity of the multinational firm and the resulting difficulty for shareholders to monitor management's decisions allow management to act in their own self-interest. Management may favor international diversification because it reduces firm-specific risk. The situation may reduce the market value of multinational firms (Morck and Yeung, 1991).

This chapter addresses the issues by extending internalization theory to include the role of growth opportunities on the market value of multinationals relative to the accounting value, or q-Value. It tests the implications of internalization, imperfect capital markets, and managerial objectives theories, considering the effects of growth opportunities, to explain the q-Value of a multinational firm.

The results of the study support the implications of internalization theory, and corroborate the results of Morck and Yeung (1991, 1992) and Mishra and Gobeli (1998). A higher level of growth opportunities leads to a higher firm q-Value as firms increase their multinationality. Conversely, while the results do not support the imperfect capital market theories that shareholders value multinationals as a means of diversifying their portfolios, they support the managerial objectives theory that the divergence of interest between management and shareholders reduces the firm q-Value with greater multinationality.

RELATED RESEARCH

As reported earlier, various empirical studies examined the implication of either internalization, imperfect capital markets, or managerial objective theories. Of interest to this study are two studies that examined simultaneously the implication of each of these theories and relied on firm-level data. The first study by Morck and Yeung (1991) showed that the positive impact of research and development and advertising spending on a firm's Tobin q is enhanced by multinationality, but multinationality itself has no significant impact. Their results support the internalization theory in that intangible assets are necessary to justify the direct foreign investment, and do not support the imperfect capital market theory in that investors value multinational firms as a means of diversifying their portfolios internationally. The second study by Mishra and Gobeli (1998) examines the same issues as Morck and Yeung (1991) and adds a managerial incentives alignment variable. Their results are also consistent with internalization theory in that greater multinationality corresponds to a higher valuation of the firm if technology investment is high, and the impact is even greater if managerial incentives alignment is high as well. The results do not also support the imperfect capital markets theory. The intangible assets examined in both studies includes research and development, as well as advertising spending in the case of Morck and Yeung (1991) and research and development spending and managerial incentives alignment in the case of Mishra and Gobeli (1998). While these variables may act as proxies for intangible assets whose value might be enhanced by multinational expansion, a more encompassing intangible that needs to be tested is the construct of growth opportunities.

HYPOTHESES AND METHODOLOGY

Hypotheses

The first hypothesis addresses the relationship between the q-Value of the multinational firm and the level of multinationality as follows:

H_1: the q-Value of the multinational firm will be higher with a higher level of multinationality.

The market value relative to the accounting value, denoted "q-Value," is computed as the ratio of the market value of the firm to the book value of its assets.[3] The market value of the firm is the sum of the market value of its outstanding common shares plus the book values of preferred stock and debt (both current and long-term).

The second hypothesis addresses the role of growth opportunities to explain the q-Value of a multinational firm. The growth opportunities of a firm are for various decisions ranging from resource allocation and career decisions to product choices, to name a few. The concept is an important signal of the firm's organizational effectiveness. Growth opportunities can create favorable situations for a firm that include: (1) the generation of excess returns by inhibiting the mobility of rivals in an industry; (2) the capability of charging premium prices to consumers; and (3) the creation of a better image in the capital markets and to investors. These growth opportunities have become established and constitute signals that may affect the activities of firm's stakeholders, including their shareholders. Good growth opportunities can be constructed as a competitive advantage within an industry. Specifically, the investment opportunity set of a firm encompasses the firm-specific intangible assets that can only be transferred to subsidiaries, local or foreign, thereby internalizing the markets for such assets. Accordingly, the following hypothesis is proposed:

H_2: The higher the growth opportunities, the greater the impact of multinationality on the q-Value of the multinational firm.

Method

To test the international investment hypothesis, the following regression model adopted from both Morck and Yeung (1991) and Mishra and Gobeli

(1998) show the independent variables expected to have an effect on the q-Value:

$$\text{q-Value} = b_0 + b_1\text{MNC} + b_2\text{IOS} + b_3\text{SIZE} + b_4\text{leverage} + \Sigma \, b_{5t} \, \text{Industry}_t \quad (1)$$

The variable MNC is the degree of multinationality. It is measured by foreign sales as a percentage of total sales. The growth opportunities concept is measured by the level of the investment opportunity set, IOS. To control for possible scale effects, a size variable measured by the logarithm of sales is included. Similarly, to control for changes in the firm's capital structure, a leverage variable, measured by higher debt over total assets, is also included in equation (1). A two-digit SIC dummy variable (industry) is used to control for growth effects and general industry effects.

Given the assumption that the value enhancement due to multinationality (b_1) is a function of corporate reputation, the following equation (2) is introduced:

$$b_1 = a_0 + a_1\text{CRS} \quad\quad\quad (2)$$

The public good property of corporate reputation is assumed to make it more valuable as the firm increases its foreign direct investment. As a result, the internalization theory predicts that a_1 should be positive, while a_0 should be zero. The imperfect capital markets theory, as well as theories based on taxes or input costs, predicts that a_0 should be positive, while a_1 should be zero. Finally, the managerial objectives theory predicts that a_0 should be negative, while a_1 should be zero.

Substituting the equation (2) into (1) yields a new and more complete regression equation that includes cross-products of the level of multinationality with corporate reputation:

$$\text{q-Value} = b_0 + a_0\text{MNC} + a_1\text{MNC*IOS} + b_2\text{IOS} + b_3\text{SIZE} + b_4\text{leverage}$$
$$+ \Sigma \, b_{5t}\text{Industry}_t \quad\quad\quad (3)$$

Sample

The population consists of firms included in *Forbes*'s most international one hundred American manufacturing and services firms 1986 to 1990. The security data are collected from CRS return files. The accounting variables are collected from *Compustat*. The derivation of the sample includes 362 firm-year observations that have all the accounting and nonaccounting variables over the period of analysis.

Table 5.1
Sample Statistics

Variables	Mean	Std. Error	Minimum	Median	Maximum
QV	0.897	0.792	0.014	0.665	5
LEV	0.645	0.187	0.120	0.625	1.25
SIZE	9.203	0.827	7.748	9.037	11.751
FS / TS	0.349	0.149	0.066	0.334	0.761

QV is the q-Value computed as the ratio of the value of the firm to the book value of total assets. LEV is the leverage computed as long-term debt over total assets. SIZE is measured by the logarithm of total sales.

Measuring Growth Opportunity

Most studies have used proxies for the measurement of the investment opportunity set. This study relies on a factor analysis of three measures of the investment opportunity set, namely: market-to-book assets, market-to-book equity, and earnings/price ratio. One common factor appeared to explain the intercorrelations among the three individual measures. The factor scores were used as measures of the level of the investment opportunity set of the firms in the sample.

ANALYSIS AND RESULTS

Table 5.1 reports the descriptive statistics for the sample of multinational firms. Table 5.2 reports the ordinary least square (OLS) regression results for equation (1), using three different measures of multinationality: (a) foreign sales/total sales, (b) a dummy variables set to 1 if foreign sales/total sales > 0.30, and (c) a dummy variable set to 1 if foreign sales/total sales > 0.50. The control variables include the investment opportunity set level, size, and leverage. The results show that for each measure of the degree of multinationality, the q-Value is positively and significantly related to the degree of multinationality as advocated by the international investment hypothesis (H_1). In addition, all the control variables are significant, indicating: (a) a growth opportunity effect in the sense that the higher the investment opportunity set score, the higher the q-Value of the firm, (b) a size effect in the sense that the larger the firm size, the lower the q-Value of the firm, and (c) a leverage effect in the sense that the larger the debt constraints, the lower the q-Value.

Table 5.3 reports the OLS regression results for equation (3) using again the three different measures of the degree of multinationality. In all cases, the investment opportunity score has both significant independent (main) and interaction (with the MNC variable) effects as predicted in equation (3). It supports

Table 5.2
OLS Regression of q-Value on the Degree of Multinationality as Measured by Foreign Sales/Total Sales

Independent Variables	Variables used to Measure the Degree of Multinationality		
	Foreign Sales / Total Sales	Dummy set to 1 if FS / TS > 0.30	Dummy set to 1 if FS / TS > 0.50
Intercept	2.612 (5.835)*	2.167 (5.259)	2.385 (5.257)
Degree of multinationality	0.4221 (2.345)*	0.1325 (1.865)**	0.1600 (1.821)**
Investment Opportunity Set	0.3606 (10.548)*	0.3883 (10.347)*	0.3856 (10.340)*
Size	-0.2885 (-7.824)*	-0.2754 (-7.837)*	-0.3068 (-8.162)*
Leverage	-1.236 (-8.565)*	-1.852 (-8.926)*	-1.685 (-8.530)*
Adjusted R^2	0.51	0.48	0.47

*Significant at 5% level
**Significant at 10% level
Note: White's t-statistics are in parentheses. Variables defined as in table 5.1.

Table 5.3
OLS Regression of q-Value on the Degree of Multinationality as Measured by Foreign Sales/Total Sales and Its Interaction with Investment Opportunity Set

Independent Variables	Variables Used to Measure the Degree of Multinationality		
	Foreign Sales / Total Sales	Dummy set to 1 if FS /TS > 0.30	Dummy set 1 if FS / TS > 0.50
Intercept	4.6058 (6.324)*	3.897 (6.725)*	2.850 (2.761)*
Degree of Multinationality	-5.8725 (-3.873)*	-1.890 (-3.283)*	-0.2370 (3.815)
Investment Opportunity Set	0.0360 (3.526)*	0.1856 (3.523)*	0.3876 (9.368)*
Multinationality * Reputation	0.9157 (4.189)	0.3075 (4.338)*	0.0528 (3.895)*
Size	-0.3236 (-8.682)	-0.3054(-8.277)*	-0.3010 (-8.120)
Leverage	-1.6488 (-8.236)*	-1.8356 (-8.234)*	-1.8770 (-8.725)*
Adjusted R^2	0.53	0.53	0.50

*Significant at 5% level
Note: White's t-statistics are in parentheses. Variables defined as in table 5.1.

the basic tenet of internalization theory as examined in this study—that increased multinationality leads to a higher firm q-Value, only in the presence of higher growth opportunities.

Multinationality appears to have a significant negative value without the firm-specific intangible of growth opportunities, as indicated in Table 5.3. The results do not support the imperfect capital markets theory *but* support the managerial objectives theory, in the sense that the potential divergence of interest between management and shareholders lead to a lower firm q-Value with greater multinationality.

CONCLUSION

Previous empirical research by Morck and Yeung (1991) and Mishra and Gobeli (1998) found evidence to support the internalization theory that there is a positive relationship between the market value of the firm and its multinationality, and that the relationship is explained by firm-specific intangibles. The intangible assets examined in these studies included research and development, advertising spending, and managerial incentives alignment. In addition, their evidence supported the tenets of imperfect capital markets theory in that greater multinationality alone does not correlate positively to a significantly greater market valuation.

This study examines the role of growth opportunities as a more "encompassing" intangible to explain the relative market value compared to the accounting value for a multinational firm. The results of this study are also consistent with internalization theory in that greater multinationality corresponds to a higher valuation of the firm if corporate reputation is high, and the tenets of imperfect capital markets theory in that greater multinationality alone does not correlate positively to a significantly greater market value. *However*, this study supports the hypothesis that greater multinationality alone correlates negatively to a significantly greater market value, which confirms the views of the managerial objectives theory. It implies that while investors and the market value highly the internalization of the markets for corporate reputation, they are less enthusiastic about the divergence of interests with management on the merits of international diversification.

NOTES

1. The internalization theory is developed in Coase (1937), Caves (1974), Williamson (1975), Hymer (1976), Buckley and Casson (1976), Rugman (1980, 1981), Casson (1987), Buckley (1988), Dunning (1980, 1988), Morck and Yeung (1991, 1992), and Mishra and Gobeli (1998).

2. See Agmon and Lessard (1977), Brewer (1981), Errunza and Senbet (1981), Adler and Dumas (1983), Fatemi (1984), Kim and Lyn (1986), Doukas and Travlos (1988), and others.

3. The q-Value, also used in Mishra and Gobeli (1998) and Smith and Watts (1992), is highly correlated with Tobin's q as used by Morck and Yeung (1991).

REFERENCES

Adler, M., and B. Dumas. 1983. International portfolio choice and corporation finance: A synthesis. *Journal of Finance* 38: 925–84.

Agmon, T., and D. Lessard. 1977. Investor recognition of corporate international diversification. *Journal of Finance* 32: 1049–55.

Beatty, R.P., and J.R. Ritter. 1986. Investment banking, reputation, and underpricing of initial public offerings. *Journal of Financial Economics* 15: 213–32.

Belkaoui, A. 1992. Organizational effectiveness, social performance and economic performance. *Research in Corporate Social Performance and Policy* 12: 143–55.

Brewer, H.L. 1981. Investor benefits from corporate international diversification. *Journal of Financial and Quantitative Analysis* 16: 113–26.

Buckley, P. 1988. The limits of explanation: Testing the internalization theory of the multinational enterprise. *Journal of International Business Studies* 19 (2): 1–16.

Buckley, P., and M. Casson. 1976. *The Future of Multinational Enterprises*. London: Macmillan.

Casson, M. 1987. *The Firm and the Market*. London: Basil Blackwell.

Caves, R.E. 1974. Causes of direct investment: Foreign firms' shares in Canadian and United Kingdom manufacturing industries. *Review of Economics and Statistics* 56: 273–93.

Caves, R.E., and M.E. Porter. 1997. From entry barrier to nobility barriers. *Quarterly Journal of Economics* 91: 421–34.

Coase, R.H. 1937. The nature of the firm. *Economica* 4: 386–405.

Doukas, J., and N.G. Travlos. 1988. The effect of corporate multinationalism on shareholders' wealth: Evidence from international acquisitions. *Journal of Finance* 43: 1161–75.

Dowling, G.R. 1986. Managing your corporate image. *International Marketing Management* 15: 109–115.

Dunning, J.H. 1980. Toward an eclectic theory of international production: Some empirical tests. *Journal of International Business Studies* 11: 9–31.

———. 1988. The eclectic paradigm of international production: A restatement and some possible extensions. *Journal of International Business Studies* 19: 1–31.

Errunza, V.R., and L.W. Senbet. 1981. The effects of international operations on the market values of the firm: Theory and evidence. *Journal of Finance* 36: 401–17.

Fatemi, A.M. 1984. Shareholders benefits from corporate international diversification. *Journal of Finance* 39: 1325–44.

Forbrum, C., and M. Shanley. 1990. What's in a name? Reputational building and corporate strategy. *Academy of Management Journal* 33: 233–58.

Hymer, S. 1976. *The International Operations of National Firms: A Study of Direct Foreign Investment*. Cambridge: MIT Press.

Kim, W.S., and E.O. Lyn. 1986. Excess market value, the multinational corporation, and Tobin's q ratio. *Journal of International Business Studies* 17: 119–26.

Klein, B., and K. Leffler. 1981. The role of market forces in assuring constructural performance. *Journal of Political Economy*, Vol. 85: 615–41.

Mishra, C.S., and D.H. Gobeli. 1998. Managerial incentives, internalization and market valuation of multinational firms. *Journal of International Business Studies* 29, 3: 583–98.

Morck, R., and B. Yeung. 1991. Why investors value multinationality. *Journal of Business* 64: 165–87.

———. 1992. Internalization: An event study test. *Journal of International Economics* 33: 41–56.

Riahi-Belkaoui, A., and E. Pavlik. 1991. Asset management performance and reputation building for large U.S. firms. *British Journal of Management*, Vol. 2: 231–38.

Rugman, A.M. 1980. Internalization as a general theory of foreign direct investment: A re-appraisal of the literature. *Journal of Economic Literature* 116: 365–75.

———. 1981. *Inside the Multinationals: The Economics of Internal Markets*. New York: Columbia University Press.

Smith, C.W., and R. Watts. 1992. The investment opportunity set and corporate financing, dividend, and compensation policies. *Journal of Financial Economics* 263–92.

Spence, A.M. 1974. *Market Signaling: Information Transfer in Hiring and Related Screening Process*. Cambridge: Harvard University Press.

Williamson, O.E. 1975. *Market and Hierarchies*. New York: Free Press.

Wolf, B.M. 1977. Industrial diversification and internalization: Some empirical evidence. *Journal of Industrial Economics* 26: 177–91.

CHAPTER 6

Level of Multinationality, Growth Opportunities, and Size as Determinants of Analyst Ratings of Corporate Disclosures

INTRODUCTION

This chapter examines the cross-sectional variation in analysts' published evaluations of firms' disclosure practices and provides evidence that the analysts' ratings are increasing in firm size, growth opportunities as measured by the investment opportunity set, and the degree of multinationality.

The extent to which mandatory disclosure requirements are exceeded differs from firm to firm, with a great latitude existing for both voluntary and discretionary disclosures. The primary users of this information are the analysts. In fact, analyst ratings of these varied corporate disclosures are included in the *Report of Financial Analysts Federation Corporate Information Committee* (FAF reports), providing an overall measure of the firm's effectiveness in communicating with investors. The main objective of this study is to explain these analysts' ratings of firm disclosure, with the assumption that the analysts' ratings measure disclosure informativeness. Theoretical research on motivations for disclosure is used to link the analysts' ratings to firm characteristics. The study builds on previous research on cross-sectional determinants of analysts' ratings of corporate disclosure to add as potential determinants the variables of size, growth opportunities, and multinationality (Piotroski, 1999; Bloomfield and Wilks, 2000).

LITERATURE AND MOTIVATION

As in Lang and Lundholm (1993), the empirical analysis is based on a survey of the theoretical and empirical literatures rather than relying on any particular model. Three potential explanatory variables are considered and grouped into three categories—*growth* variables (growth opportunities), *structural* variable (firm size), and a *multinationality* variable (the degree of internationalization or foreign involvement).

Disclosure and Growth Opportunities

The firm may be viewed as a combination of assets-in-place and future investment options. Assets-in-place refer to the actual assets recognized in the balance sheet. Future investment options refers to the unobservable growth opportunities or options. The lower the proportion of firm value represented by assets-in-place, the higher the growth opportunities. Myers (1977) describes these potential investment opportunities as call options whose values depend on the likelihood that management will exercise them. Like call options, the growth options represent value to the firm (Kester, 1984). These growth options are intangible assets or ownership advantages that represent the investment opportunity set (IOS). The higher these growth options, the more likely there will be a good firm performance. In fact, theoretical models developed by Bushman and Indjejikian (1993) and Kim and Smith (1993) suggest that as a firm's IOS increases, stock price becomes relatively more informative about firm performance. One implication is that firms that have experienced an expansion in investment opportunities will increase their disclosures to match their market performance. In addition, the expansion of new investment opportunities or product markets may adversely impact accounting earnings in the short term (Abbott, 1999). The development of investment opportunities requires immediate outlays of capital, while the payoffs may not be immediately reflected in accounting earnings. This is generally consistent with Yermack (1995), who finds evidence of an unexpectedly negative relationship between a firm's market-to-book ratios (a known IOS proxy) and the granting of stock options. The implication is that firms experiencing an expansion in investment opportunities with no present payoffs should increase their disclosures to counteract any adverse effect to the accounting earnings in the short run. This is generally consistent with Skinner (1993), who finds evidence suggesting that the IOS affects the "accepted set" of accounting procedures.

Taken as a whole, the results from both theoretical and empirical research suggest disclosure could be positively related to firm growth opportunities as measured by the investment opportunities set.

Disclosure and Firm Size

There are a number of reasons why we might expect a positive association between disclosure and firm size. One main reason is provided by *agency theory*. The proportion of outside capital tends to be higher for larger firms (Leftwich, Watts, and Zimmerman, 1981). Similarly, agency costs increase with the amount of outside capital (Jensen and Meckling, 1976). Accordingly, the potential benefits from shareholder-debtholder-manager contracting—including the extent of financial disclosure—would also increase with firm size (Chow and Wang-Borem, 1987; Riahi-Belkaoui, 2000).

Other reasons include:

a. *the disclosure cost hypothesis*, which maintains that the decreasing costs associated with larger firm size leads to more affordable disclosure (Lang and Lundholm, 1993),

b. *the transactions cost hypothesis*, which maintains that the incentives for private information acquisitions are greater for large firms resulting in disclosure increasing with firm size (King et al., 1990), and,

c. *the legal cost hypothesis*, which maintains that the dollar values of damages in securities litigations are a function of firm size leading to higher disclosure with larger size (Skinner, 1992).

Disclosure and Multinationality

There are basically two main reasons why we might expect a positive association between disclosure and multinationality.

A first reason is provided by the *capital-need hypothesis*, whereby much of the impetus for voluntary disclosure by multinational firms surrounds the need to raise capital at the lowest possible cost (Choi, 1973; Spero, 1979). The pressure for information associated with global competition for capital manifests itself in the supplemental voluntary disclosures that multinational firms have been found to make (Meek, Roberts, and Gray, 1995; Riahi-Belkaoui, 1994).

A second reason is provided by the *multiple listing hypothesis* (Cooke, 1989). Multinational firms are generally listed in more than one stock exchange. The firms with multiple listings are more likely to have a greater number of shareholders, thereby making monitoring costs more significant. One way of reducing shareholders' monitoring costs and of alleviating the moral hazard problem is through disclosure in corporate annual reports.

METHOD

Model

This study examines the cross-sectional variations in analysts' published evaluation of firms' disclosure practices and hypothesizes that the analysts' ratings are increasing in the degree of multinationality, the level of growth opportunities as measured by the investment opportunity set, and size. The model to be tested is as follows:

$$DISC_{it} = a_{0t} + a_{1t} MULTY_{it} + a_{2t} IOS_{it} + a_{3t} LR_{it} + e_{it} \tag{1}$$

where:

$DISC_{it}$ = Average of total FAF disclosure score over the year t, t − 1, and t − 2.

$MULTY_{it}$ = Degree of multinationality of firm in year t as measured by foreign profit/ total profit.

IOS_{it} = Investment opportunity set of firm i in year t.

LR_{it} = logarithm of total revenues at the end of year t.

The model was run for the 1986–90 period and for each individual year in that period.

Sample

To ensure the greatest sample of firms for which data would be available for all variables, the initial sample chosen was for all firms included in *Forbes*'s 1986 to 1990 survey of the largest U.S. multinationals and in the annual volumes of the *Report of the Financial Analysts Federation Corporate Information Committee* (FAF, 1986–90). A sample of 313 observations was obtained. The disclosure scores for each firm were averaged over three consecutive years (year t, t − 1, t − 2) to obtain the disclosure metric (DISC) capturing a firm's current and past disclosure performance. Multinationality was measured by foreign profit/total profit. Size was measured by the logarithm of the total revenues at the end of the year. Both the measurement of corporate disclosure (DISC) and investment opportunity set (IOS) are explained in the next two sections.

The Disclosure Quality Measure (DISC)

To measure disclosure, this study uses data from the annual volumes of the *Report of the Financial Analysts Federation Corporate Information Committee* (FAF 1986–90). It is generally considered as a comprehensive measure of the informativeness of a firm's disclosure policy (Lang and Lundholm, 1993, 1996; Farragher et al., 1984; Welker, 1995; Sengupta, 1988; Botosan, 1997). The data measure the firm's effectiveness in communicating with investors and the extent to which the firm provides information so that investors have the data necessary to make informed judgments across all types of disclosures. The disclosures provided through annual reports, quarterly reports, proxy statements, published information in the form of press releases and fact books, and direct disclosures to and communication with analysts are used for the evaluation of the firm's disclosure practices. In the FAF report, analysts evaluate the complete range of a firm's disclosures, summarizing their evaluations by scoring (out of one hundred possible points) on the firm's total disclosure efforts and separate scores for the different disclosure categories. Although these scores are based on analysts' perceptions of corporate disclosure practices, any potential biases or errors are minimized by a procedure that (a) requires the reporting of average scores (across industry analysts), and (b) rests on the use of detailed guidelines and a comprehensive checklist of a criteria that allows a standardization of the rating process both within and across industries.

Because corporate audiences may be expected to consider both past and present disclosures in their reputation assessments, the disclosure metric, DISC, to be used in this study is the average of the total disclosure score of a firm over three consecutive years (years t, t − 1, t − 2).

Measuring the Investment Opportunity Set

There has not been a consensus on an appropriate proxy variable for the investment opportunity set. Similar to Smith and Watts (1992) and Gaver and Gaver (1993), we use an ensemble of variables to measure the investment opportunity set. The three measures of the investment opportunity set used are: market-to-book assets (MASS), market-to-book equity (MQV), and the earnings/ price ratio (EP). These variables are defined as follows:

MASS = [(Assets − Total Common Equity) + (Shares Outstanding * Share Closing Price)]/Assets

MQV = [Shares Outstanding * Share Closing Price/Total Common Equity]

EP = [Primary EPS before Extraordinary Items]/Share Closing Price

The results of a factor analysis of the three measures of the investment opportunity set are shown in table 6.1. One common factor appears to explain the intercorrelations among the three individual measures. The factor score for each firm is used as the measure of the investment opportunity set.

RESULTS

Descriptive Statistics and Correlation Analysis

Table 6.2 presents the descriptive statistics for all the variables used in the study. The median disclosure score is 56.31. A wide dispersion is present with a minimum of 47.31, a maximum of 76.73, and a standard deviation of 6.85. The median of the revenues of 15,012 (in millions) indicates a sample of large U.S. firms, with a wide variation as indicated by the minimum and maximum values. The investment opportunity set varies from a minimum of 0.187 to a maximum of 7.383. Finally, the multinationality variable, as measured by foreign profits/total profits varies widely from a minimum of 0.1 to a maximum of 7.5.

Table 6.3 presents the rank-order correlations for the variables used in this study. The low intercorrelations among the predictor variables used in the model

Table 6.1
Selected Statistics Related to a Common Factor Analysis of Three Measures of
the Investment Opportunity Set for *Forbes*'s "The Most International 100 U.S.
Firms"

1. Eigenvalues of the Correlation Matrix

Eigenvalue	1	2	3
	1.0540	0.9868	0.9592

2. Factor Pattern

Factor	MASS	MQV	EP
	0.62821	0.66411	0.46722

3. Final Communality Estimates: Total = 1.053994

MASS	MQV	EP
0.394651	0.441045	0.218299

4. Standardized Scoring Coefficients

Factor	MASS	MQV	EP
	0.59603	0.63009	0.44329

5. Descriptive Statistics of the Common Factor Extracted from the Three Measures of the Investment Opportunity

Maximum	Third Quartile	Median	First Quartile	Minimum	Mean
9.3595	3.2200	2.0450	1.5085	2.5209	1.9812

indicate no reasons to suspect multicollinearity, and various diagnostic tests run
on the derived regression models confirmed that it was not a problem.

Regression Analysis

To examine the incremental explanatory power of the variables expressed in
equation (1), multiple regressions were estimated. Table 6.4 presents the results
of the regression coefficients for all the independent variables, using measures
of corporate disclosure as dependent variables. The Breusch and Pagan (1979)
test for heteroscedasticity yielded an X^2 with a minimum of 133.82 and a maximum of 162.32 for all the regressions, indicating that heteroscedasticity could

Table 6.2
Summary Statistics

Variables	Number of Observa-tions	Mean	Standard Deviation	Median	Minimum	Maximum
MULTY	313	48.375	58.131	38	0.1	87.5
DISC	313	57.868	6.895	56.312	47.315	76.730
IOS	313	0.561	0.821	0.511	0.187	7.383
R	313	15,012.65	18,953.44	8,331	2,318	126,932

Variable Definitions:
MULTY: Multinationality measured as foreign profits/total profits
DISC: FAF disclosure scale
IOS: Investment opportunity set score
R: Total revenues

be a problem in these regressions. Accordingly, the reported t-statistics are based on White's (1980) heteroscedasticity corrected covariance matrix. The results, in all cases, corroborate the significance of size, multinationality, and investment opportunity set as determinants of voluntary disclosure choice measured by the disclosure scores prepared by the Financial Analysts Federation.

To test the validity of the model, OLS regressions were also run with current disclosure as dependent variable, and multinationality measured as either foreign revenues over total revenues or foreign assets over total assets. The results indicated again a positive relationship between disclosure quality on one hand and multinationality, size, and growth opportunities on the other hand.

CONCLUSION

The study investigated the determinants of voluntary disclosure choice, as measured by disclosure scores prepared by the Financial Analysts Federation. The empirical results are consistent with existing theories and theses on voluntary disclosure choice.

First, the result that the disclosure scores increase in firm size, as measured by the logarithm of revenues, is consistent with agency theory considerations, the disclosure cost hypothesis, the transaction costs hypothesis, and the legal cost hypothesis.

Second, the result that disclosure scores increase in growth opportunities, as measured by the investment opportunity set, is consistent with the role of the expansion of growth opportunities in leading firms to be more informative.

Finally, the result that disclosure scores increase in multinationality, as measured by foreign profits/total profits, is consistent with the capital-need hypothesis and the multiple-listing hypotheses.

Table 6.3
Correlation among Selected Variables*

	DISC	MULTY	IOS	R
DISC	1.000 (0.00)	0.019 (0.698)	0.1799 (0.0009)	0.674 (0.0001)
MULTY		1.000 (0.00)	-0.1657 (0.0032)	0.0319 (0.5195)
IOS			1.000 (0.00)	0.0181 (0.3385)
R				1.000 (0.00)

*p-Values for two-tailed tests are provided in parentheses. Variables are defined in table 6.2.

Table 6.4
Explaining Corporate Disclosure Quality

Independent / Dependent Variables	Intercept	MULTY	IOS	LR	F	Adjusted R^2
DISC (1986-1990)	-7.474 (-3.496)*	0.010 (2.348)*	1.026 (4.058)*	7.228 (26.203)*	240.24*	75.31
DISC 1986	-9.952 (-3.920)	0.011 (2.457)	1.026 (4.058)	7.228 (26.203)*	240.24*	70.66
DISC 1987	-10.112 (-3.878)*	0.011 (2.510)*	1.049 (4.147)*	7.242 (25.591)*	228.47*	69.60
DISC 1988	-10.761 (-4.187)*	0.011 (2.515)*	0.998 (3.935)*	7.319 (96.149)*	241.99*	70.81
DISC 1989	-11.275 (-4.463)*	0.011 (2.659*	1.007 (94.002)*	7.373 (26.925*	253.33*	71.75
DISC 1990	-10.684 (-4.211)*	0.011 (2.593)*	1.021 (4.048)*	7.307 (26.536)*	245.83*	71.21

Variables are defined in table 6.2.
*Absolute value of t-statistics in parentheses, significant at $\alpha=0.01$.

The results show that disclosure informativeness differs between firms as a result of growth, structural, and multinationality variables. Future research is needed to examine the use of different proxies for the variables as well as to expand the number of variables most likely to influence the analyst ratings of corporate disclosure, as a measure of disclosure informativeness.

REFERENCES

Abbott, L.J. 1999. *Executive Compensation Subsequent to a Split in IOS*. Tennessee: University of Memphis.

Bloomfield, R.J., and T.J. Wilks. 2000. Disclosure effects in the laboratory: Liquidity, depth, and the cost of capital. *The Accounting Review* 75 (January): 13–41.

Botosan, C. 1997. Disclosure level of the cost of equity capital. *The Accounting Review* 72 (July): 323–49.

Breusch, T., and A. Pagan. 1979. A simple test for the heteroscedasticity and random coefficient variation. *Econometrica* 47: 1287–94.

Bushman, R., and R. Indjejikian. 1993. Accounting income, stock price, and managerial compensation. *Journal of Accounting and Economics* 16: 3–24.

Choi, F.D.S. 1973. Financial disclosure and entry to the european capital market. *Journal of Accounting Research* (Autumn).

Chow, C.W., and A. Wang-Borem. 1987. Voluntary financial disclosure by Mexican corporations. *The Accounting Review* (July): 533–41.

Cooke, T.E. 1989. Voluntary corporate disclosure by Swedish companies. *Journal of International Financial Management and Accounting* (Summer): 171–95.

Farragher, E., R. Kleiman, and M. Baza. 1994. Do investors relations make a difference? *Quarterly Review of Economics and Finance* 34 (Winter): 403–12.

Financial Analysts Federation (FAF). 1986–90. *Report of the Financial Analysts Federation Corporate Information Committee*. New York: FAF.

Gaver, J.J., and K.M. Gaver. 1993. Additional evidence on the association between the independent opportunity set and corporate financing, dividend and compensation policies. *Journal of Accounting and Economics* 6: 125–60.

Jensen, H., and W. Meckling. 1976. Theory of the firm: Managerial behavior, agency costs and ownership structure. *Journal of Financial Economics* (October): 305–60.

Kester, W.C. 1984. Today's options for tomorrow's growth. *Harvard Business Review* (March–April): 153–60.

Kim, O., and Y. Smith. 1993. Incentive efficiency of compensation based on accounting and market performance. *Journal of Accounting and Economics* 16: 25–53.

King, R., G. Pownall, and G. Waymire. 1990. Expectations adjustments in timely management forecasts: Review, synthesis, and suggestions for further research. *Journal of Accounting Literature* 9: 113–44.

Lang, M., and R. Lundholm. 1993. Cross-sectional determinants of analysts' ratings of corporate disclosures. *Journal of Accounting Research* 31 (Autumn): 246–71.

———. 1996. Corporate disclosure policy and analyst behavior. *The Accounting Review* 71 (October): 467–92.

Leftwich, R., R. Watts, and J. Zimmerman. 1981. Voluntary corporate disclosure: The case of interim reporting. *Journal of Accounting Research* (Supplement): 50–77.

Meek, G.M., C.B. Roberts, and S.J. Gray. 1995. Facts influencing voluntary annual report disclosures by U.S., U.K. and continental European multinational corporations. *Journal of International Business Studies* 96, 3: 555–72.

Myers, S. 1977. Determinants of corporate borrowing. *Journal of Financial Economics*: 147–75.

Piotroski, J.D. 1999. The impact of newly reported segment information on market expectations and stock prices. Working paper, University of Michigan.

Riahi-Belkaoui, A. 1994. *International and Multinational Accounting*. London: International Thomson.

———. 2000. *Accounting Theory*. London: International Thomson.

Sengupta, P. 1988. Corporate disclosure quality and the cost of debt. *The Accounting Review* 4 (October): 459–74.

Skinner, D.J. 1992. Why firms voluntarily disclose bad news. Working paper, University of Michigan.

———. 1993. The investment opportunity set and accounting procedure choice: Preliminary evidence. *Journal of Accounting and Economics* 160: 407–46.

Smith, C.W., and R.L. Watts. 1992. The investment opportunity set and corporate financing, dividend and compensation policies. *Journal of Financial Economics* 5: 263–92.

Spero, L.L. 1979. The extent and cases of voluntary disclosure of financial information in three European capital markets: An exploratory study. Unpublished Doctoral Dissertation, Harvard University.

Welker, M. 1995. Disclosure policy, information asymmetry and liquidity in equity markets. *Contemporary Accounting Research* 11 (Spring): 801–27.

White, H. 1980. A heteroscedasticity-consistent covariance matrix estimator and a direct test for heteroscedasticity. *Econometrica* 48: 817–38.

Yermack, D. 1995. Do corporations award CEO stock options effectively? *Journal of Financial Economics* 39: 237–69.

CHAPTER 7

The Effects of Multinationality on Earnings Response Coefficients

INTRODUCTION

The relation between unexpected returns and unexpected earnings has been found to be affected by firm-specific characteristics. Multinationality may proxy for all these firm characteristics as it involves large firms, with quality preannouncement information, traded on the major stock exchange and with a certain level of earnings unpredictability. Accordingly, this chapter examines the effect of multinationality on the relation between unexpected returns and unexpected earnings.

We investigate the effect of multinationality by using the familiar linear relation between unexpected stock returns (UE), with five hundred firm-year observations collected over a five-year period, 1995–99. Multinationality is measured by foreign profits/total profits. Our results indicate a systematic relation between multinationality and the information content of earnings. Firms with relatively more (less) multinationality appeared to have smaller (larger), less significant (more significant) earnings response coefficients.

RELATED RESEARCH AND HYPOTHESIS

The relation between unexpected returns and unexpected earnings has been found to be affected by firm-specific characteristics such as the differential quality of preannouncement information, firm size (Atiase, 1985; Freeman, 1987), the exchange on which a firm's stock is traded (Grant, 1980; Atiase, 1987), the effect of earnings predictability (Lipe, 1990), and the effects of ex-ante earnings uncertainty (Imhoff and Lobo, 1992). Multinational firms are mostly of large size, have good-quality preannouncement information, are generally traded in the major stock exchanges such as the NYSE and NASDAQ, and have a relatively high ex-ante earnings uncertainty (Ball, 1995; Morck and Yeung, 1991; Riahi-Belkaoui, 1994). One may easily argue that multinationality can proxy for all the firm characteristics found to affect the relation between unexpected returns and unexpected earnings. Based on this notion, the amount of "unexpected" information conveyed to the market by actual earnings reports is inversely related to the firm's level of multinationality, other things being equal. Greater multinationality is expected to result in small earnings response coefficients. The findings reported in this study strongly support the hypothesis that the degree of unexpected security price changes is inversely related to the level of multinationality of the firm.

METHODOLOGY AND SAMPLE

Models

The relation between unexpected return and unexpected earnings used in previous words is expressed as follows:

$$UR_{it} = \alpha + \beta UE_{it} + E_{it} \tag{1}$$

where

UR_{it} = Cumulative unexpected security returns during the earnings announcement period.
UE_{it} = Cumulative earnings for firm i in period t.

The next step is to test the impact of multinationality on the relation expressed in equation (1). Firms are classified into three groups depending on their level of multinationality: high, medium, and low. The potential impact of multinationality on the earnings coefficient for a two-day period $(-1, 0)$ surrounding the annual earnings announcement is tested by the following model:

$$UR_{it} = \alpha_1 + \alpha_2 M_M + \alpha_3 M_H + \beta_1 UE_{it} + \beta_2 M_M UE_{it} + \beta_3 M_H UE_{it} \tag{2}$$

where the new variables are:

M_M = a dummy variable equal to 1 when a firm-year level of multinationality is in the MIDDLE multinationality group for that year, and 0 otherwise.
M_H = a dummy variable equal to 1 when a firm-year observation is in the HIGH multinationality group for that year, and 0 otherwise.

This model, also used by Imhoff and Lobo (1992), allows the intercept and response coefficients to vary across multinationality groups. The intercept and response coefficients are respectively:

1. α_1 and β_1 for the low multinationality group.
2. $\alpha_1 + \alpha_2$ and $\beta_1 + \beta_2$ for the middle multinationality group.
3. $\alpha_1 + \alpha_3$ and $\beta_1 + \beta_3$ for the high multinationality group.

Therefore, the differences in the intercepts and response coefficients respectively between the middle (high) and low multinationality groups are $\alpha_2 + \beta_2$ ($\alpha_3 + \beta_3$). The hypotheses to be tested are as follows:

$Ho_1: \beta_2 = \beta_3 = 0 \quad H_{A1}: \beta_2 < 0; \beta_3 < 0$, and
$Ho_2: \beta_2 - \beta_3 = 0 \quad H_{A2}: \beta_3 < \beta_2$

The expectations in this study are that (a) differences in response coefficients between the middle (high) and low multinationality group will be negative, and (b) the response coefficient for the high multinationality group will be less (more negative) than the response coefficient for the middle group. Lower response coefficients are expected as the level of multinationality increases.

Sample

Both the annual *Forbes* survey of the largest U.S. multinational firms and the International Brokers Estimate System (I/B/E/S) database for the 1995–99 period were used to identify the firms to be included in the sample based on the availability of data in both survey and database. The final sample consisted of five hundred observations.

MEASUREMENTS

The empirical testing of the hypothesis relies on three variables: unexpected stock returns (UR), unexpected annual earnings (UE), and level of multinationality.

Measuring Unexpected Returns

The market model was used to eliminate marketwide sources of price changes:

$$R_{it} = a_i + b_t R_{Mt} + E_{it} \tag{3}$$

where

R_{it} = Return on firm i on day t.

R_{Mt} = Return on CRSP value-weighted market index on day t.

E_{it} = A stochastic disturbance term, and a_i and b_i = intercept and slope coefficient, respectively for firm i.

Ordinary least squares (OLS) regression was performed on R_{it} and R_{Mt} for twenty weeks preceding day three. The estimated coefficients a_i and b_i were used to compute UR_{it}, the cumulative unexpected security returns during the earnings announcement periods, as follows:

$$UR_{it} = \sum_{t=-1}^{0} [R_{it} - (\hat{a}_i + b_i R_{Mt})]$$

(4)

The results from equation (2) represent the cumulative two-day returns on the day of and the day preceding the earnings announcement in the *Wall Street Journal*.

Measuring Unexpected Earnings

The choice of a measure of unexpected earnings may have an effect on the results obtained on the information content of earnings announcement. Following prior work and suggestions made by Imhoff and Lobo (1992), the following measure of unexpected earnings was used:

$$UE_{it} = \frac{A_{it} - F_{it}}{P_{it}}$$

where

A_{it} = Actual earnings for firm i in period t.

F_{it} = Expected annual earnings for firm i in period t, measured as the mean security analyst's annual earnings forecast on the I/B/E/S tape in the month immediately preceding that of earnings announcement.

P_{it} = Stock price for firm i two trading days before the annual earnings announcement date.

Measuring Multinationality

Previous research has attempted to measure three attributes of the degree of multinationality:

1. Performance in terms of what goes on overseas (Tsetsekos, 1991).

2. Structure in terms of how resources are used overseas (Shopford and Wells, 1972).

3. Attitude or conduct in terms of what is top management orientation (Dunning, 1995).

Table 7.1

Descriptive Statistics and Correlation of Three Measures of Multinationality for *Forbes*'s **"The Most International 100 U.S. Firms" for the 1995–99 Period**

Panel A: Descriptive Statistics

	FP/TP[a]	FP/TP[b]	FP/TP[c]
Maximum	816.2	91	92
Third Quartile	63.2	48.2	41.5
Median	41.3	32.6	38.5
First Quartile	2.8	24.8	21.2
Minimum	0.3	5.9	2.8
Mean	58.26	38.26	39.72

Panel B: Correlations

	FP/TP	FS/TS	FA/TA
FP/TP	1.000		
FS/TS	0.281	1.000	
FA/TA	0.041	0.193*	1.000

*Denotes p-Value<0.05.
[a]FP/TP=Foreign profits/total profits.
[b]FS/TS=Foreign sales/total sales.
[c]FA/TA=Foreign assets/total assets.

Nine measures were identified to include: (1) foreign sales as a percentage of total sales (FS/TS), (2) research and development intensity (RDI), (3) advertising intensity (AI), (4) export sales as a percentage of total sales (ES/TS), (5) foreign profits as a percentage of total profits (FP/TP), (6) foreign assets over total assets (FA/TA), (7) overseas subsidiaries as a percentage of total subsidiaries (OS/TS), (8) top management's international experience (TMIE), and (9) psychic dispersion of international operations (PDIO) (Perlmutter, 1969).

Of these nine measures, an item-total analysis showed the five variables of FS/TS, FA/TA, OS/TS, PDIO, and TMIE to have a high reliability in the construction of a homogeneous measure of multinationality (Sullivan, 1994). We follow a similar approach in this study, using an ensemble of variables to measure multinationality. Three measures of multinationality generally available are used in this study: foreign sales/total sales (FS/TS), foreign profits (FP/TP), and foreign assets/total assets (FA/TA). Descriptive statistics and correlations among the three measures of multinationality are shown in table 7.1. Correlations among the variables are positive, and with one exception, all are significant. The nonsignificant correlation is between FP/TP and FA/TA. The low correlations between FP/TP, FS/TS, and FA/TA indicate that each variable can make a unique contribution as a measure of multinationality. To obtain a unique contribution, a factor analysis is used to isolate the factor common to the three measures of multinationality. All the observations were subjected to factor anal-

Table 7.2
Selected Statistics Related to a Common Factor Analysis of Three Measures of Multinationality for *Forbes*'s "The Most International 100 U.S. Firms" for the 1995–99 Period

1. Eigenvalues of the Correlation Matrix:

Eigenvalues	1	23	
	1.3826	0.9676	0.6703

2. Factor Pattern

FACTOR1

FS/TS	0.8231
FP/TP	0.5232
FA/TA	0.6821

3. Final Communality Estimates: Total = 1.361489

FS/TS	FP/TP	FA/TA
0.6528	0.2513	0.4725

4. Standardized Scoring Coefficients

FACTOR1

FS/TS	0.5213
FP/TP	0.3116
FA/TA	0.4928

5. Descriptive Statistics of the Common Factor Extracted from the Three Measures of Multinationality

Maximum	2031.24
Third Quartile	78.2
Median	56.7
First Quartile	40.21
Minimum	5.22
Mean	68.56

Table 7.3
Relation between Unexpected Earnings (UE) and Unexpected Returns (UR) for the Period 1995–99

Period	Number of Observations	$UR_{it}=\alpha+\beta UE_{it}+E_{it}$ [a]		
		α	β	Adjusted R^2
1990-1999	987	-0.00072	0.006235	0.0213
		(-1.025)	(4.256)*	

a. UR_{it}=Unexpected two-day return of firm i for the day before and the day of the annual earnings announcement (1,0).
   UE_{it}=Unexpected earnings for firm i, measured as the difference between actual earnings and the mean I/B/E/S deflated by stock price two trading days before the earnings announcement.
   α,β=Intercept and slope (response coefficient).
   E_{it}=Residual for firm i in period t.
b. *Significant at α=0.01.

ysis, and one common factor was found to explain the intercorrelations among the three individual measures. Table 7.2 reports the results of the common factor analysis. One common factor appears to explain the intercorrelations among the three variables, as the first eigenvalue alone exceeds the sum of the commonalities. The common factor is significantly and positively correlated with the three measures. Based on these factor scores, high multinationality firms were chosen from the top 1/3% of the distribution factor scores, while low multinationality firms were chosen from the bottom 1/3%. Middle multinationality firms were chosen from the remaining 1/3% of the distribution factor scores.

RESULTS

Equations (1) and (2) are estimated using ordinary least squares (OLS) regressions. Table 7.3 reports a summary of the OLS regression results for equation (1) for the two-day period surrounding the earnings announcement date. As expected and similarly to previous research, the earnings coefficient β is positive and significant with a t-statistic of 4.256.

Table 7.4 reports the results of the OLS regression for equation (2). Using the pooled results, the response coefficients are equal to $\beta_1 = 0.82$ for the low multinationality group, $\beta_1 + \beta_2 = 0.3936$ for the middle multinationality group, and $\beta_1 + \beta_3 = 0.007$ for the high multinationality group.

Table 7.4
Effects of Multinationality on the Unexpected Earnings—Unexpected Returns Relation

$$UR_{it} = \alpha + \alpha_2 M_t + \beta UE_{it} + \beta_2 M_t UE_{it} + \beta_3 M_t UE_{it}$$

Pooled Results	α_1	α_2	α_3	β_1	β_2	β_3	Actg R_2	$Ho: \beta_2 = \beta_3$ t (sign)	$Ho: \beta_2 = \beta_3 = 0$ t (sign)
1990-1991	-0.0018* (-3.012)	0.00231 (1.231)	0.00321 (1.351)	0.8251* (3.821)	-0.4315* (-2.017)	-0.8321* (-3.521)	0.091	17.2312* (0.0001)	5.3112 (0.0001)
Year-by-Year									
1990	-0.00231* (-1.2321)	0.00312 (1.023)	0.00931 (1.032)	1.1231* (1.812)	-0.6321 (0.8121)	-0.9101 (0.9121)	0.113	1.2312 (0.1521)	1.521 (0.0512)
1991	-0.00321* (-3.127)	0.00321* (3.105)	0.00915 (1.256)	1.0312 (1.0521)	-0.5312 (-1.031)	-0.8128 (0.5123)	0.121	5.235* (0.0131)	2.6931 (0.0058)
1992	-0.0003* (-1.021)	0.00123 (1.156)	0.00315 (1.281)	1.125 (1.121)	-0.2631* (-2.151)	-0.5127* (2.310)	0.118	6.212* (0.0111)	1.2371 (0.1361)
1993	-0.00137* (-3.218)	0.00231 (0.951)	0.00321 (1.151)	0.9212* (1.713)	-0.3120 (-0.9512)	-0.5171 (0.815)	0.091	0.937 (0.0521)	2.5891 (0.073)
1994	-0.00216* (-3.358)	0.00251 (0.987)	0.00328 (1.251)	1.7832* (2.351)	-0.0521 (-1.021)	-0.2316 (1.130)	0.871	6.213* (0.014)	-2.873 (0.7120)
1995	-0.00211* (-3.278)	0.00312* (2.205)	0.00518* (2.231)	1.8131* (2.452)	-0.2631* (-2.511)	-0.5120* (3.012)	0.109	4.312* (0.013)	1.532 (0.0921)
1996	-0.00191* (-3.251)	0.00123 (0.915)	0.00418 (1.238)	0.9316 (1.012)	-1.2513* (-2.521)	-1.6231* (2.312)	0.101	5.112* (0.0112)	2.7191 (0.0059)
1997	-0.00121* (-3.521)	0.00315* (2.521)	0.00512 (1.051)	1.6132* (2.871)	-1.3111 (0.9912)	-1.5212* (0.8121)	0.103	1.352 (0.1521)	1.2571 (0.01469)
1998	-0.00312* (-3.621)	0.00412* (3.918)	0.00527* (1.251)	1.8131* (2.710)	-1.2101 (-1.021)	-1.7121 (-1.011)	0.115	2.352* (0.0189)	2.6799 (0.081)
1999	-0.00412* (-3.725)	0.00139 (1.0521)	0.00218 (1.251)	0.8131* (1.876)	-0.5816* (2.521)	-0.9152* (-3.012)	0.091	5.321* (0.0131)	2.8231 (0.0059)

a. UR_{it} =Unexpected two-day return for portfolio i in period $(-1,0)$.
   UE_{it} =Unexpected earnings for firm i in period t, measured as the difference between actual earnings and the means I/B/E/S forecast deflated by stock price two trading days before the earnings announcement.
   $M_M = 1$ for firms ranked in the middle multinationality group, 0 otherwise.
   $M_H = 1$ for firms ranked in the high multinationality group, 0 otherwise.
b. White's (1980) adjusted t statistics:

Both alternate hypotheses are accepted in favor of the rejection of hypothesis H_{01} and H_{02}. Basically, the results in Table 7.3 indicate that greater multinationality leads to lower response coefficients. The effect of the null hypothesis that $\beta_2 = \beta_3$ is rejected at $\alpha = 0.0001$. Similarly, H_{02} is rejected given that β_3 is significantly more negative than β_2. In other words, greater levels of multinationality yields lower levels of response coefficients. These results hold also on an annual basis. $\beta_2 < 0$, $\beta_3 < 0$ and $\beta_2 < \beta_3$ hold in ten of ten cases.

To check if multinationality was acting like a proxy for other variables that have been found to affect the UR-UE relationship, equation (2) was estimated after the addition of market value of equity as a measure of size, and the number of analyst's forecasts in the month preceding the earnings announcement as a measure of the quantity of information available about the firm, a procedure also used by Imhoff and Lobo (1992). Both variables were insignificant, indicating that the results were strictly driven by the multinationality variable.

CONCLUSIONS

The role of multinationality in managerial decisions and outcomes is expanded in this study to an investigation of its role and effect on the earnings coefficient of U.S. multinational firms. The results of this study indicate a systematic effect of multinationality in the relation between unexpected returns and unexpected earnings. Firms with relatively more (less) multinationality appeared to have smaller (larger), less significant (more significant) earnings response coefficients. Multinationality appears to be a good proxy for variables that have been found to affect the UR-UE relationship; namely, the size of the firm, the quality of preannouncement information, the exchange trade in which a firm's stock is traded, the earnings predictability, and the ex-ante earnings uncertainty.

REFERENCES

Atiase, R. 1985. Predisclosure information, firm capitalization and security price behavior around earnings announcements. *Journal of Accounting Research* 23 (Spring): 21–35.

———. 1987. Market implications of predisclosure information: Size and exchange effects. *Journal of Accounting Research* 25 (Spring): 168–76.

Ball, R. 1995. Making accounting more international: Why, how, and how far will it go? *Journal of Applied Corporate Finance* 8: 19–29.

Dunning, J. 1995. Reappraising the eclectic paradigm in an age of alliance capitalism. *Journal of International Business Studies* 26: 461–92.

Freeman, R.N. 1987. The association between accounting earnings and security returns for large and small firms. *Journal of Accounting & Economics* 9 (July): 195–228.

Grant, E. 1980. Market implications of differential amounts of interim information. *Journal of Accounting Research* 18 (Spring): 255–68.

Imhoff, E.A., Jr., and G.J. Lobo. 1992. The effects of ex-ante earnings uncertainty on earnings response coefficients. *The Accounting Review* 67: 427–39.

Lipe, R. 1990. The relation between stock returns and accounting earnings given alternative information. *The Accounting Review* 65 (January): 49–71.

Morck, R., and B. Yeung. 1991. Why investors value multinationality. *Journal of Business* 64: 165–87.

Perlmutter, H.U. 1969. The tortuous evaluation of multinational corporations. *Columbia Journal of World Business* 4: 9–18.

Riahi-Belkaoui, A. 1994. *International and Multinational Accounting*. London: International Thompson.

Shopford, J.M., and L.T. Wells. 1972. *Managing the Multinational Enterprise*. New York: Basic Books.

Sullivan, D. 1994. Measuring the degree of internationalization of a firm. *Journal of International Business Studies* 5: 325–34.

Tsetsekos, G.P. 1991. Multinationality and common stock offering. *Journal of International Financial Management and Accounting* 3: 1–16.

White, H. 1980. A heteroscedasticity-consistent covariance matrix estimator and a direct test for heteroscedasticity. *Econometrica* 48: 817–38.

CHAPTER 8

The Effects of Multinationality on Earnings Persistence

INTRODUCTION

Accounting researchers have relied on time-series models to obtain measures of earnings persistence and to form earnings expectations (e.g., Lev, 1983; Collins and Kothari, 1989). While it is still an open question of whether analysts, managers, and investors rely on time-series models to form earnings expectations, it is appropriate to investigate what economic characteristics cause earnings to behave in a persistent fashion and which persistence measure derived from alternative time-series models provides the best association.

With regards to the choice of potential economic characteristics, a more robust and clear test is to identify a measure of firm complexity that can proxy for most of the variables found to be potential determinants of earnings persistence. One measure to be examined in this study is the multinationality variable; that is, the degree of international involvement of the firm in terms of revenues, profits, and assets.

With regards to the alternative time-series model that can provide the best association between persistence and multinationality, a higher-order Autoregressive, Integrated, Moving-Average (ARIMA) model is expected to provide a far higher association.

This inquiry is related to prior work investigating the economic criterion for the choice of a specific time-series model (Lev, 1983; Baginski et al., 1999). Lev (1983) investigated the question whether interfirm differences in first and second order autocorrelation coefficients of earnings changes, return on equity changes, and sales can be explained by the firm's economic environment. His findings indicate that autocorrelation and variability of annual earnings and earnings over equity changes are systematically associated with the following factors: the type of product, the height of industry barriers-to-entity (a surrogate for degree of competition), the degree of capital intensity (operating leverage), and the firm size. Relying on the same economic characteristics, Baginski et al. (1999) investigated whether persistence estimated from the earnings time-series captures the joint effect of these economic variables, and whether differenced, higher-order ARIMA model measures of persistence do so to a great extent. Their findings replicated the significant impact of the economic characteristics on persistence, but also showed that differenced, higher-order ARIMA models used to measure earnings persistence yield higher adjusted R^2 in the 10–12% range than lower-order ARIMA models. Results based on earnings persistence measures derived from higher-order ARIMA models: (2, 1, 0) and (4, 1, 0) yield respectively adjusted R^2 of 10.3% and 12.5%. Persistence measures from a higher-order ARIMA reflect the economic characteristics that give rise to earnings persistence. They will be used in this study to investigate the association between multinationality and earnings persistence.

MULTINATIONALITY AS A DETERMINANT OF EARNINGS PERSISTENCE

Previous research relied on the economic and strategic literatures to identify four observable economic characteristics that are expected to yield profits that persist, namely: firm size, product type, barriers to entity, and capital intensity (Lev, 1983; Baginski et al., 1999). This study relies instead on the international business and accounting literature to present multinationality as the determinant of earnings persistence of U.S. multinational firms. The choice of multinationality as the essential economic characteristic to yield profits that persists is supported by the following arguments:

1. Theories of foreign direct investment promise numerous benefits of geographical dispersion (Ostry, 1998; Buckley and Casson, 1998; Dunning, 1998), and empirical evidence shows a degree of a relationship between multinationality and performance (Gomes and Ramaswanny, 1999; Tallman and Li, 1996).

2. Given the rarity of observing perfectly positive correlations between fluctuations in the economies of two or more countries, risk can be reduced through diversification across national boundaries which, as a result, increases the stabilization of profits (Hughes et al., 1975; Rugman, 1977, 1979; Miller and Pras, 1980; Fatemi, 1984; Shaked, 1986; Grant, 1987; Amit and Livnat, 1988; Kim et al., 1989; Amit and Wernerfeld, 1990; Morck and Yeung, 1991, Qian, 1997a, 1997b).

3. The political risk literature provides an additional explanation between earnings stability and a firm's level of multinationality. High multinationality firms are more susceptible to political pressure, government intervention, and even expropriation (Brewer, 1981, 1983; Farge and Wells, 1982; Jodia 1989). High multinationality firms

can, therefore, be expected to engage in less risky production and investment activities in order not to draw foreign governments to large variation in earnings (Monti-Belkaoui and Riahi-Belkaoui, 1998; Farge and Wells, 1982).

SAMPLE AND VARIABLE MEASUREMENT

Sample and Models

The sample for this study consists of the one hundred largest U.S. multinational firms from *Forbes*'s annual survey for 1990 to 1999. The only requirement for inclusion is the availability of consecutive data on earnings and multinationality. The final sample consisted of 878 firm-year observations.

The firms in the sample are assumed and expected to have unstable characteristics which cause noise in the ARIMA parameter estimation, expected not to be severe. The model building rests on an assumption of stability.

Annual Persistence Measures

Earnings persistence is generally measured by estimating an ARIMA true series earnings process (e.g., Kormendi and Lipe, 1987). It measures the impact of a current shock on the whole stream of future realizations of the earnings series. A formula adapted from Flavin (1981) and Kormendi and Lipe 1987), and used by both Collins and Kothari (1989, 198) and Baginski et al. (1999, 110) indicates that for a given ARIMA (p, d, q) model specification, persistence is a function of the autoregressive and moving-average parameters as follows:

$$
PER = \frac{1 - \sum_{i=1}^{q} B^i \theta_i}{(1 - B)^d \left(1 - \sum_{j=1}^{p} B^j \varphi_j \right)} - 1
\tag{1}
$$

where:

$B = 1/(1+r)$ where r is the appropriate rate for discounting expected future earnings, and r is set at .10, providing similar results with $r = .04$ and .20.[1]

θ_i = Moving-average parameter of order i.

d = Level of consecutive differencing.

φ_j = Autoregressive parameter of order j.

Following the results of the superiority of higher-order models by Baginski et al. (1999), this study uses the (2, 1, 0) and (4, 1, 0) autoregressive processes to generate the earnings persistence measures.

Measuring Multinationality

Previous research has attempted to measure the following attributes of multinationality:

1. *Performance*—in terms of what goes on overseas (Dunning, 1995),
2. *Structure*—in terms of resources used overseas (Stopford and Wells, 1972), and,
3. *Attitude or Conduct*—in terms of what is top management's orientation (Perlmutter, 1969).

Sullivan (1994) developed nine measures, of which five were shown to have a high reliability in the construction of a homogeneous measure of multinationality: (1) foreign sales as a percentage of total sales (FS/TS), (2) foreign assets over total assets (FA/TA), (3) overseas subsidiaries as a percentage of total subsidiaries (OS/TS), (4) top management's international experience (TMIE), and (5) psychic dispersion of international operation (PDIO). In this study, we follow a similar approach by measuring multinationality through, three measures: (1) foreign sates/total sales (FS/TS), (2) foreign profits/total profits (FP/TP), and (3) foreign assets/total assets (FA/TA). Descriptive statistics and correlations among the three multinationality measures are shown in table 8.1. Correlations among the variables are positive, and with one exception, all significant. The nonsignificant correlation is between FP/TP and FA/TA. The low correlations between FP/TP, FS/TS, and FA/TA indicate that each variable can make a unique contribution as a multinationality measure. Thus, a factor analysis of all observations is used to isolate the factor common to the three measures. All the observations were subjected to factor analysis. Table 8.2 reports the results. One common factor appears to explain the intercorrelations among the three variables, as the first eigenvalue alone exceeds the sum of the commonalities. The common factor is significantly positively correlated with the three measures. The factor score for each firm will be used as the index of multinationality for that firm.

DESCRIPTIVE STATISTICS

The descriptive statistics for the variable used in the study are shown in table 8.3. As expected, the earnings persistence measure for the (2, 1, 0) ARIMA model is higher than the persistence measure in the (4, 1, 0).

Table 8.4 presents univariate Spearman rank order correlations for all the variables used in the study. As expected, the persistence measures were highly correlated (.86) at a high significance level ($p < .01$). Multinationality and size are also highly correlated (.78) at a 0.01 significance level.

Table 8.1
Descriptive Statistics and Correlation of Three Measures of Multinationality for
Forbes's "The Most International 100 U.S. Firms" for the 1990–99 Period

Panel A: Descriptive Statistics

	FP/TP[a]	FP/TP[b]	FP/TP[c]
Maximum	813.5	92	93
Third Quartile	69.2	47.3	42.5
Median	40.2	33.8	38.7
First Quartile	2.7	33.8	29.3
Minimum	0.4	6.9	3.8
Mean	57.36	66.36	39.81

Panel B: Correlations

	FP/TP	FS/TS	FA/TA
FP/TP	1.000		
FS/TS	0.282	1.000	
FA/TA	0.031	0.182*	1.000

*Denotes p-Value <0.05.
[a]FP/TP=Foreign profits/total profits.
[b]FS/TS=Foreign sales/total sales.
[c]FA/TA=Foreign assets/total assets.

REGRESSION RESULTS

The model used in this study calls for the estimation of the cross-sectional
relation between a multinationality index and size as independent variables and
alternative earnings persistence measures as follows:

$$PER = B_0 + B_1 SIZE_i + B_2 MULTY_i + e_i \qquad (2)$$

where

PER = Persistence of annual earnings derived from equation (1) using the following
ARIMA models: (1) (2, 1, 0) and (2) (4, 1, 0).

$SIZE_i$ = The average of the log of market value over the entire sample period.

$MULTY_i$ = The multinationality score for firm i.

B_i = Coefficients estimated using ordinary least squares regression in the cross-section.

Table 8.2

Selected Statistics Related to a Common Factor Analysis of Three Measures of Multinationality for *Forbes*'s "The Most International 100 U.S. Firms" for the 1990–99 Period

1. Eigenvalues of the Correlation Matrix:

Eigenvalues	1	23	
	1.2838	0.9856	0.67630

2. Factor Pattern

   FACTOR1

FS/TS	0.8321
FP/TP	0.5312
FA/TA	0.6741

3. Final Communality Estimates: Total = 1.361489

FS/TS	FP/TP	FA/TA
0.6638	0.2623	0.4835

4. Standardized Scoring Coefficients

   FACTOR1

FS/TS	0.5328
FP/TP	0.3217
FA/TA	0.4521

5. Descriptive Statistics of the Common Factor Extracted from the Three Measures of Multinationality

Maximum	2052.34
Third Quartile	76.3
Median	58.2
First Quartile	41.32
Minimum	5.23
Mean	67.26

Table 8.3
Descriptive Statistics for Dependent and Independent Variables

Variables	Mean	Standard Deviation	Tenth Percentile	Median	Nineteenth Percentile
ARIMA (2, 1, 0) Persistence (PER)[a]	8.62	11.38	5.62	7.31	14.81
ARIMA 4, 1, 0) Persistence (PER)[a]	11.32	14.62	3.62	7.02	19.73
Firm Size (SIZE)[b]	7.20	1.31	5.21	6.32	9.31
MULTY[c]					

[a]PER=Persistence in annual earnings using firm-specific parameter estimates of (2, 1, 0) and (4, 1, 0) ARIMA models. The formula for PER is:

$$PER = \frac{1 - \sum_{i=1}^{q} B^i \theta_i}{(1 - B)^d \left(1 - \sum_{j=1}^{p} B^j \varphi^j\right)} - 1$$

where:

$B = 1/(1+r)$ where r is the appropriate rate for discounting expected future earnings ($r=.10$ for this table).
θ_i = Moving-average parameter of order i.
d = Level of consecutive differencing.
φ_j = Autoregressive parameter of order j.
[b]SIZE=Average of the logs of the market value of equity over the 1990–99 period.
[c]MULTY=Multinationality index.

Size is used as a control variable following its importance in prior work. The estimates of equation (2) for the earnings persistence measures derived from equation (1) are shown in table 8.5. The results are obtained after the dependent variable was unwinsorized at two standard deviations from the mean.

R^2 from their higher-order ARIMA derived persistence measures are high: 0.112 and 0.132, results similar to those obtained by Baginski et al. (1999). The model with the greatest explanatory power is, as expected, the (4, 1, 0) ARIMA structure, where the derived earnings persistence seems to better capture mean reversion of earnings through time.[2]

As hypothesized, the results show a positive relationship with size and a negative relationship in the multinationality. Both size and multinationality appear as strong determinants of the earnings persistence measures derived from higher-order ARIMA models, a result consistent with previous work on the use of higher-order ARIMA models (Baginski et al., 1999). A rerun of the regressions using (a) unwinsorized data, (b) size measured as the average of

Table 8.4
Spearman Rank Order Correlation

(p-values in parentheses)

	PER (2, 1, 0)	PER (4, 1, 0)	SIZE	MULTY
PER (2, 1, 0)		0.86	-0.060	-.18
		(0.001)	(0.867)	(.456)
PER (4, 1, 0)			-0.070	-.13
			(0.628)	(.862)
SIZE				.78
				(.001)
MULTY				

All variables are defined in table 8.3.

the logarithm of sales, and (c) the dependent variable redefined as the value minus its sample mean and divided by its sample standard deviation, yielded similar results on the significance of size and multinationality as determinants of earnings.

To test whether accounting rule changes and earnings management may have interfered with the relation between persistence and multinationality, the earnings persistence measure was replaced by the sales persistence measure as a dependent variable. The results yielded a higher level of R^2s (0.121 and 0.146) and significant positive relationship with multinationality. The negative relationship of multinationality with persistence was not affected by any of the noise introduced by accounting rule changes and earnings management.

Additional tests for ascertaining the sensitivity of the results to alternative specifications of the dependent and independent variables included: (a) replacing the index of multinationality (MULTY) by foreign revenues/total revenues, foreign profits/total profits, or foreign assets/total assets; and (b) measuring earnings persistence as the fourth-order scaled variance. They define the estimated Kth ordinate of the scaled variogram as:

$$R(k) = \frac{\sigma^2(k)}{K\sigma^2(1)} \frac{n-1}{n-k} \tag{3}$$

where n = sample size, K = lag, and σ^2 = variance of the differenced annual earnings at the K lag. The measurement of the fourth-order scaled variance is accomplished by setting k equal to 4. These supplemental tests were supportive of the main findings.

To check if multinationality was acting like a proxy for other variables found to be associated with earnings persistence, equation (2) was estimated after the addition of a one (zero) indicator variable for durable (nondurable) goods; cap-

Table 8.5
Association of Earnings Persistence Measures (PER) and Multinationality (1990–99; n=878)

model: $PER = B_0 + B_1 SIZE_i + B_2 MULTY_i + e_i$

Variables	Expected Sign	Coefficient Estimates (White [1980] Adjusted Statistics in Parentheses) PER Computed Using ARIMA Models	
		(2, 1, 0)	(4, 1, 0)
Intercept	?	11.32	19.82
		(5.62)	(4.89)*
SIZE	+	0.61	0.32
		(0.38)	(0.51)
MULTY	-	-5.863	-8.632
		(4.32)*	(4.86)*
Adjusted R²		0.112	0.132
F Statistic		6.32	7.31*

*Significant at .01 level in one-tail test (two-tailed for intercept).
All variables are defined in table 8.3.

ital intensity variable measured as the average values of depreciation, depletion, and amortization expense over the 1993–99 period, deflated by average sales over the same period; and a barrier-to-entry variable measured as the average values of research and development expense and advertising expense over the 1990–99 period, deflated by average sales over the same period. These new variables were all insignificant, indicating that the results were strictly driven by the multinationality variable.

CONCLUSIONS

This study shows a negative relationship between the level of multinationality of a firm and earnings persistence measures derived from higher-order ARIMA models. The results verify the generally accepted thesis of (a) a negative relationship between multinationality and performance, and (b) a reduced risk through diversification across national boundaries and greater stabilization of profits. The multinationality level of multinational firms may be used to assess earnings persistence as computed from higher-order ARIMA models.

NOTES

1. R is set at .10, providing similar results when set at .04 and .20.
2. As explained in both Lipe and Kormendi (1994) and Baginski et al. (1999), the reduction in median persistence may be attributed to the third- and fourth-order autoregressive parameters in the (4, 1, 0) ARIMA model, capturing the negative autocorrelations of earnings at higher lags relative to the (2, 1, 0) ARIMA model.

REFERENCES

Amit, R., and J. Livnat. 1988. Diversification strategies, business cycles and economic performance. *Strategic Management Journal*: 99–110.
Amit, R., and B. Wernerfeld. 1990. Why do firms reduce business risk? *Academy of Management Journal*: 520–33.
Baginski, S.P., K.S. Lorek, G.L. Willinger, and B.C. Branson. 1999. The relationship between economic characteristics and alternative annual earnings persistence measures. *The Accounting Review* 74: 105–20.
Brewer, T.J. 1981. Political risk assessment for foreign direct investment decisions: Better methods for better results. *Columbia Journal of World Business* 16: 5–13.
———. 1983. Political sources of risk in the international money markets: Conceptual, methodological, and interpretive refinements. *Journal of International Business Studies* 19: 161–64.
Buckley, P.J., and M.C. Casson. 1998. Models of the multinational enterprise. *Journal of International Business Studies* 29: 21–44.
Collins, D., and S. Kothari. 1989. An analysis of intertemporal and cross-sectional determinants of earnings response coefficients. *Journal of Accounting and Economics* 11 (July): 143–82.
Dunning, J.H. 1995. Reappraising the electric paradigm in an age of alliance capitalism. *Journal of International Business Studies* 26: 461–92.
———. 1998. Location and the multinational enterprise. *Journal of International Business Studies* 29: 45–66.
Farge, N., and L.T. Wells, Jr. 1982. Bargaining power of multinational and host governments. *Journal of International Business Studies* 13: 9–23.
Fatemi, A.M. 1984. Shareholder benefits from corporate international diversification. *Journal of Finance*: 1325–44.
Flavin, M. 1981. The adjustment of consumption to changing expectations about future income. *Journal of Political Economy* 89: 974–1009.
Gomes, L., and K. Ramaswanny. 1999. An empirical examination of the form of the relationship between multinationality and performance. *Journal of International Business Studies* 30: 173–88.
Grant, R.M. 1987. Multinationality and performance among british manufacturing companies. *Journal of International Business Studies*: 79–89.
Hughes, J.S., D.E. Logue, and R. Sweeney. 1975. Corporate international diversification and market assigned measures of risk and diversification. *Journal of Financial & Quantitative Analysis*: 627–37.
Jodia, D.A. 1989. French in political risk assessment: Prospects for the future. In *International Political Risk Management: New Dimensions*, eds. F. Ghadar and T.H. Moran. New York: Ghadar and Associates, 81–95.
Kim, W.C., P. Hwang, and W.P. Burgers. 1989. Global diversification, strategy and corporate profit. *Strategic Management Journal*: 45–57.
Kormendi, R., and R. Lipe. 1987. Earnings innovations, earnings persistence, and stock returns. *Journal of Business* 60: 323–45.

Lev, B. 1983. Some economic determinants of time-series properties of earnings. *Journal of Accounting and Economics* 5: 31–48.

Miller, J.C., and B. Pras. 1980. The effects of multinational and export diversification on the profit stability of U.S. corporations. *Southern Economic Journal*: 792–805.

Monti-Belkaoui, J., and A. Riahi-Belkaoui. 1998. *The Nature, Estimation and Management of Political Risk*. Westport, CT: Quorum Books.

Morck, R., and B. Yeung. 1991. Why investors value multinationality. *Journal of Business*: 165–87.

Ostry, Sylvia. 1998. Technology, productivity and the multinational enterprise. *Journal of International Business Studies* 29: 85–100.

Perlmutter, Howard V. 1969. The tortuous evaluation of the multinational corporation. *Columbia Journal of World Business* 4: 9–18.

Qian, Gongming. 1997a. An analysis of the risk performance of the largest U.S. firms 1981–92. *Journal of Global Business* 8: 45–56.

———. 1997b. Assessing product-market diversification of U.S. firms. *Management International Review*: 127–49.

Rugman, A.M. 1977. International diversification by financial and direct investment. *Journal of Economics & Business*: 31–37.

———. 1979. *International Diversification & the Multinational Enterprise*. Lexington, MA: Health.

Shaked, I. 1986. Are multinational corporations safer? *Journal of International Business Studies*: 83–106.

Stopford, J.M., and L.T. Wells. 1972. *Managing the Multinational Enterprise*. New York: Basic Books.

Sullivan, D. 1994. Measuring the degree of the internationalization of a firm. *Journal of International Business Studies* 25: 235–342.

Tallman, S., and J. Li. 1996. Effects of international diversity and product diversity in the performance of multinational firms. *Academy of Management Journal* 39: 179–96.

CHAPTER 9

The Association between Performance Plan Adoption and Organizational Slack

Recent accounting research has argued that managerial compensation contracts influence managerial decision making (Watts and Zimmerman, 1978; Hagerman and Zmijewski, 1979; Dukes et al., 1981; Horwitz and Kolodny, 1981) and motivate executives to improve firm performance by working harder, lengthening their decision horizons, and becoming less risk-averse in their investment decisions (Baril, 1988; Larcker, 1983; Smith and Watts, 1982). The evidence shows that performance plan adoption was associated with an increase in capital expenditures (Larcker, 1983; Gaver, Gaver, and Furze, 1989).[1] The resources used for the increased capital expenditures are derived from organizational slack.

Organizational slack is a cushion of actual resources used by organizations to adapt successfully either to internal pressures for adjustments, or to external pressures for change in policy (Bourgeois, 1981; March, 1978).[2] A review of the concept of organizational slack and its use in theory indicates that there are two measures (Bourgeois, 1981; Singh, 1983, 37–49). Organizational slack is conceptualized as *unabsorbed slack*, which corresponds to the excess, uncommitted resources in organizations. It is also conceptualized as *absorbed slack*, which corresponds to excess costs in organizations (Williamson, 1964). This distinction raises the following question: How does performance plan adoption affect changes in absorbed and unabsorbed slack? The question is investigated here. The empirical results indicate that multinational U.S. firms adopting performance plans (relative to similar nonadopting firms) decrease the amount of unabsorbed slack they were holding.

These results make a significant contribution to research for two reasons. First, they demonstrate a relationship between performance plan adoption and unabsorbed slack. It suggests that some of the resources needed for investment following the adoption of performance plans, as shown by Larcker (1983), come from the organization's unabsorbed slack. Second, they show that the adoption of a performance plan is not sufficient to reduce absorbed slack. This means that managers have incentives to invest unused resources, but that the plan is insufficient to get them to give up perks.

The remainder of the chapter consists of four sections: The first section introduces the concept of organizational slack, the second discusses the theoretical linkages between performance plan adoption and organizational slack, the third describes the methodology used, and the fourth presents the empirical results. Finally, the research findings are discussed and summarized.

ORGANIZATIONAL SLACK

Slack arises from the tendency of organizations and individuals to refrain from using all the resources available to them. It describes a tendency not to operate at peak efficiency. In general, two types of slack have been identified in the literature: organizational and budgetary. Organizational slack refers to an unused capacity, in the sense that the demands put on the resources of the organization are less than the supply of these resources. Budgetary slack refers to the intentional distortion of information that results from an understatement of budgeted sales and overstatement of budgeted costs. The interest in this study is with organizational slack. It is a buffer created by management in its use of available resources to deal with internal as well as external events that may arise and threaten an established coalition. Organizational slack, therefore, is used by management as an agent of change in response to changes in both the internal and external environments.

Cyert and March (1963) explain organizational slack in terms of cognitive and structural factors. They provide a rationale for the unintended creation of organizational slack. Individuals are assumed to "satisfice," in the sense that they set aspiration levels for performance rather than a maximization goal. The aspirations adjust upward or downward, depending on actual performance, and in a slower fashion than actual changes in performance. It is this lag in adjustment that allows excess resources from superior performance to accumulate in the form of organizational slack. This form is then used as a stabilization force to absorb excess resources in good times without requiring a revision of aspiration and intentions regarding the use of these excess resources.

O.E. Williamson (1964) proposed a model of slack based on managerial incentives. This model provides the rationale for managers' motivation and desire for slack resources. Under conditions where managers are able to pursue their own objectives, the model predicts that excess resources available after target levels of profit have been reached are not allocated according to profit maximization rules. Organizational slack becomes the means by which a manager achieves his or her personal goals, as characterized by four motives: income, job security, status, and discretionary control over resources. Williamson makes the assumption that the manager is motivated to maximize his or her personal goals subject to satisfying organizational objectives and that the manager achieves this by maximizing slack resources under his or her control.

The slack, as identified by Cyert and March (1963) and/or Williamson (1964), can be conceptualized as unabsorbed, corresponding to the excess uncommitted resources, or absorbed, corresponding to the excess costs in organization (Bourgeois, 1981). They are assumed in this study to be affected by the adoption of performance plans. A rationale for this thesis follows.

PERFORMANCE PLANS AND ORGANIZATIONAL SLACK

In essence, organizational slack is the difference between resources available to management and the resources used by management. Management uses it as a buffer to deal with internal as well as external events that may arise and/or threaten an established coalition (Cyert and March, 1963, 36). The performance plan adoptions motivate management to improve firm performance as evidenced by the increase in capital expenditures reported by Larcker (1983). The resources needed by management for such endeavors can be easily provided by the excess resources of organizational slack, the use of which may, however, depend on whether the slack is absorbed or unabsorbed.

First, performance plans are based on accounting measures of corporate performance. The adoption of performance plans will encourage managers to allocate their efforts to the improvement of the short-term accounting performance measure through reduction of costs. Accordingly, absorbed slack, also labeled administrative slack, is expected to decrease following the adoption of a performance plan.

Second, the adoption of a performance plan will encourage the managers to allocate their efforts to the improvement of long-term accounting performance measures by searching, and spending for, new investment opportunities. Some of the resources needed for the new investment may come from unabsorbed slack. Accordingly, unabsorbed slack is expected to decrease following the adoption of a performance plan.

The following research hypotheses are examined in the subsequent empirical study.

H1: The adoption of a performance plan is associated with a decrease in absorbed slack.

H2: The adoption of a performance plan is associated with a decrease in unabsorbed slack.

METHODS

This study uses a longitudinal design because the relationship between performance plan adoption and organizational slack occurs over time.

Sample and Data Collection

A list of corporate incentive plans was obtained from previous research (Larcker, 1983) and through independent historical research. Each experimental firm was required to satisfy two criteria. First, the performance plan adoption must have occurred during the 1971–82 period. Second, a firm passing the criterion must have a matching control firm.

A total of seventy multinational U.S. experimental firms were identified. The control firms were required to satisfy the following criteria:

1. same industry as the experimental firms.[3]
2. similar size as the experimental firm measured by corporate sales in the year prior to performance plan adoption by the experimental firm.
3. similar fiscal year as the experimental firm.

The plans were all long-term, consisting of forty-four performance unit plans and twenty-six performance share plans. To measure the effect of the performance plan, organizational slack is analyzed before and after the change, while controlling for one categorical variable and two covariates.

Dependent Variables

Financial statement data for years -5 to $+5$ (relative to the year of adoption of the performance plan by the experimental company) for each firm were collected from *Compustat*. Year 0, the year of adoption of the performance plan, was excluded from the analysis to avoid confounding the slack measures with outcomes during the transition. The data collected were on absorbed slack and unabsorbed slack. Various measures of slack have been used. Rosner (1968) used profit and excess capacity as slack measures. Lewin and Wolf (1976) suggested selling, general, and administrative expenses as surrogates for slack.

A case for financially derived measures of slack was made by Bourgeois (1981), and Bourgeois and Singh (1983). A two-component concept of slack was proposed that made the distinction between absorbed slack, referring to slack absorbed as costs in organizations, and unabsorbed slack, referring to uncommitted resources. Analogously, absorbed slack was measured by (a) the ratio of selling, general, and administrative expenses to cost of goods sold in order to capture slack absorbed in salaries, overhead expenses, and various administrative costs, and (b) the ratio of working capital to sales in order to capture the absorption of slack related to capital utilization. Unabsorbed slack was computed as cash plus marketable securities minus current liabilities divided by sales, in order to capture the amount of liquid resources uncommitted to liabilities in the near future (Singh, 1986).

Table 9.1
Results of Overall Analysis of Covariance for Absorbed Slack Computed as Selling, General, and Administrative Expenses/Cost of Goods Sold*

Sources	F	P
A: Firm Effect (Experimental Control)	0.92	0.217
B: Performance Plan Adoption (before/after)	0.89	0.3382
A X B Interaction	21.79	0.3462
Control Variables: Early/ Late adoption	28.27	0.0001
Covariates: Size	71.87	0.0001
Rate of return on assets	61.80	0.0001

*$R^2=0.1607$
Overall F=20.88 (p=0.0001)

Control Variable and Covariates

One control variable and two covariates were used to control for possible intervening effects.

First, to control for size and profitability, total assets and rate of return on assets were used as covariates.

Second, an influence on the use of slack may have advantages or disadvantages resulting from early or late adoption of performance plans within a set of competitors. Another argument is that imitators may learn from first adopters' mistakes and can benefit from the adoption of performance plans. To control for innovation effects, the experimental firms were coded into two groups, with the first thirty early adopters of performance plans classified as early adopters and the rest as late adopters.

Data Analysis

Analysis of covariance was used to test the overall relationship between (1) slack and firm effect, (2) slack and performance plan adoption, and (3) the interaction of firm effect and performance plan adoption on slack. The model's control variable was early/late adoption and covariates included assets and rate of return on assets.

Table 9.2
Results of Overall Analysis of Covariance for Absorbed Slack Computed as Working Capital/Sales*

Sources	F	P
A: Firm Effect (Experimental Control)	0.13	
B: Performance Plan Adoption (before/ after)	3.19	0.0748
A X B Interaction	0.06	0.8093
Control Variables: Early/ Late adoption	1.58	0.2094
Covariates: Size	35.52	0.0001
Rate of return on assets	136.79	0.0001

*R^2=0.2084
Overall F=29.54 (p=0.0001)

Table 9.3
Results of Overall Analysis of Covariance for Unabsorbed Slack Computed as (Cash + Marketable Securities-Current Liabilities)/Sales*

Sources	F	P
A: Firm Effect (Experimental Control)	5.09	0.0245
B: Performance Plan Adoption (before/ after)	14.13	0.0002
A X B Interaction Control Variables:	4.38	0.0368
Early / Late adoption	0.01	0.9217
Covariates: Size	7.11	0.0079
Rate of return on assets	165.10	0.0001

*R^2=0.2255
Overall F=32.67 (p=0.0001)

Table 9.4
T Tests and Slack Means by Firm Group before and after Performance Plan
Adoption

	Before Adoption	After Adoption	*T*
Slack 1			
Experimental Group			
_____Mean	0.2571	0.30571	1.4962
Control Group			
_____Mean	0.3216	0.3215	0.0021
Slack 2			
Experimental Group			
_____Mean	0.1928	0.21166	1.3015
Control Group			
_____Mean	0.1992	0.2135	0.9486
Slack 3			
Experimental Group			
_____Mean	- 0.1881	- 0.1236	- 2.1209
Control Group			
_____Mean	- 0.0713	- 0.1252	- 2.9442

RESULTS

Tables 9.1, 9.2, and 9.3 present the overall results for the two measures of
absorbed slack and the measure of unabsorbed slack. Table 9.4 presents the
means and standard deviations of each of the slack measures before and after
the adoption of the performance plan for both the experimental and control
groups of firms.

The first measure of absorbed slack is the ratio of selling, general, and administrative expenses as a percentage of cost of goods sold. It captures slack
absorbed in salaries, overhead expenses, and various administrative costs. The

results for this measure of absorbed slack are reported in table 9.2 and show that the main firm effects and performance plan adoption, as well as the interactive effects on slack are both insignificant. The same result is found in Table 9.4 for this measure.

The second measure of absorbed slack is the ratio of working capital of sales, which is used to capture the absorption of slack related to capital utilization. These results are summarized in table 9.2 and show that the main firm effects and performance plan adoption, as well as the interaction effects on slack are all insignificant. The same result is found in table 9.4 for this measure.

The measure of unabsorbed slack is the ratio of cash plus marketable securities minus current liabilities to sales. This measure is used to capture the amount of liquid resources uncommitted to liabilities in the near future. These results are summarized in Table 9.3 and show that the following relationships are all significant at $\square = 0.05$: (a) between slack and firm effect, (b) between slack and performance plan adoption, and (c) between firm effect-performance plan adoption interactions and slack. An examination of the mean results on absorbed slack in table 9.4 shows a significant reduction in unabsorbed slack taking a place subsequent to the adoption of the performance plan. This result is consistent with Hypothesis 2. That is, unabsorbed slack declines following the adoption of the performance plan. It suggests that following the implementation of compensation plans, managers do seek new investment opportunities as shown in Larcker (1983). It also suggests that some of the resources needed for the new investment come from the unabsorbed slack existing in the firms. The amount of liquid resources uncommitted to liabilities in the near future appears as the first resources to be invested by managers following the adopting of performance plans.

DISCUSSION AND SUMMARY

The hypothesis that changes in executive compensation contracts and is associated with changes in managerial decision is important to the incentive research taking place in management, accounting, and economics. One incentive question investigated in this study concerns the association between performance plan adoption and organizational slack. A differentiation was made between absorbed slack and unabsorbed slack. The results on absorbed slack were insignificant. However, the empirical results indicate that, when compared to similar nonadopting firms, those firms that adopt performance plans exhibit a significant reduction in unabsorbed slack following plan adoption. A logical interpretation is that the performance plan encourages managers to allocate their efforts towards improving accounting-based, long-term performance measures by increasing capital investment. That investment leads to a reduction of the unabsorbed slack, which is used to fund some of the increase in capital investment. Before these results can be generalized, future research should investigate the impact of the use of different measures of organizational slack, different firms, and different periods.

NOTES

1. Other related evidence indicates that the adoption of a performance plan was associated with (a) a decrease in corporate risk (Gaver, Gaver, and Furze, 1989), and (b) mixed evidence on the stock market reaction to the announcement of performance plan adoption (Larcker, 1983; Brickley, Bhagat, and Lease, 1985; Gaver, Gaver, and Battistel, 1992; Kumar and Sopariwala, 1991).

2. There is a clear differentiation between organizational slack, which refers to the difference between the available and used resources, and budgetary slack, which refers to the use of the budget process for the creation of attainable budgets.

3. For the seventy matched pairs, forty-six had the same two-digit SIC code, five had the same five-digit SIC code, and nineteen had the same four-digit SIC code.

REFERENCES

Baril, C.P. 1988. Long term incentive compensation, ownership, and the decision horizon problem. Working paper, McIntyre School of Commerce, University of Virginia, Charlottesville.

Bourgeois, L.J. 1981. On the measurement of organizational slack. *Academy of Management Review* 6 (October): 29–39.

Bourgeois, L.J., and J.V. Singh. 1983. Organizational slack and political behavior within top management teams. *Academy of Management Proceedings* : 43–47.

Brickley, J.A., S. Bhagat, and R.C. Lease. 1985. The impact of long-range managerial compensation plans on shareholder wealth. *Journal of Accounting and Economics* 7 (April): 115–29.

Cyert, R.M., and J.G. March. 1963. *A Behavioral Theory of the Firm.* Englewood Cliffs, NJ: Prentice Hall.

Dukes, R., T.R. Dyckman, and J. Elliot. 1981. Accounting for research and development costs: The impact on research and development expenditures. *Journal of Accounting Research* (Supplement) 18: 1–26.

Gaver, J.J., K.M. Gaver, and G.P. Battistel. 1992. The stock market reaction to performance plan adoptions. *The Accounting Review* 1 (January): 172–82.

Gaver J.J., K.M. Gaver, and S. Furze. 1989. The association between performance plan adoption and corporate investment decisions. Working paper, University of Oregon.

Hagerman, R.L., and M.E. Zmijewski. 1979. Some economic determinants of accounting policy choice. *Journal of Accounting and Economics* 1: 141–61.

Horwitz, B., and R. Kolodny. 1981. The economic effects of involuntary uniformity in the financial reporting of R&D expenditures. *Journal of Accounting Research* (Supplement) 18: 38–74.

Kumar, R., and P.R. Sopariwala. 1991. The effect of adoption of long-term performance plans on stock prices and accounting numbers. Working paper, Virginia Polytechnic Institute and State University.

Larcker, D.F. 1983. The association between performance plan adoption and corporate capital investment. *Journal of Accounting and Economics* 5 (April): 9–30.

Lewin, A.Y., and C. Wolf. 1976. The theory of organizational slack: A critical review. *Proceedings: Twentieth International Meeting of ITMS*: 648–54.

March, J.G. 1978. Bounded rationality, ambiguity, and the engineering of choice. *Bell Journal of Economics* 9: 587–608.

Rosner, M.M. 1968. Economic determination of organizational innovation. *Administrative Science Quarterly* 12: 614–25.

Singh, J.V. 1983. Performance, slack, and risk taking in strategic decisions: Test of a structural equation model. Unpublished Doctoral Dissertation, Graduate School of Business, Stanford University, Palo Alto, CA.

——. 1986. Performance, slack, and risk taking in organizational decision making. *Academy of Management Journal* 3 (September): 562–85.

Smith, C.W., and R.L. Watts. 1982. Incentive and tax effects of U.S. executive compensation plans. *Australian Journal of Management* 7 (December): 39–157.

Tehranian, H., and J.F. Waegelein. 1985. Market reaction to short-term executive compensation plan adoption. *Journal of Accounting and Economics* 7 (April): 131–44.

Watts, R.L., and J.L. Zimmerman. 1978. Towards a positive theory of the determination of accounting standards. *The Accounting Review* (January): 112–34.

Williamson, O.E. 1964. *The Economics of Discretionary Behavior: Managerial Objectives in a Theory of the Firm.* Englewood Cliffs, NJ: Prentice Hall.

CHAPTER 10

Corporate Disclosure Quality and Corporate Reputation of U.S. Multinational Firms

INTRODUCTION

This chapter investigates the link between a firm's overall disclosure quality and its corporate reputation. This study adds to the growing literature on the determinants of corporate reputation by suggesting that corporate audiences construct the reputation of firms by interpreting information signals about the firms' corporate disclosure quality. What results is that firms that constantly make timely and informative disclosures are more likely to avoid withholding value-relevant unfavorable information. Consequently, these firms are given a high reputational ranking.

The results of this study conform to the above argument. A firm's corporate reputation is measured by executives' evaluation of corporate practices, available annually from *Fortune Magazine*. A firm's disclosure policy is measured by financial analysts' evaluation and corporate disclosures policy available from the annual volume of the *Report of the Financial Analysts Federation Corporate Information Committee*. Results show that the measure of corporate reputation is positively related to the disclosure measure, after controlling for market and accounting signals indicating the size of the assets, market assessment of the value of assets in place, and rate of return on assets.

The study extends the investigation of both the determination of corporate reputation and the consequences of disclosure quality by showing evidence of a link between disclosure quality and corporate reputation of large U.S. multinational firms. Although the signals used in previous studies show attendance by corporate audiences to market and accounting cues, the results here suggest that disclosure quality also influences reputation building for large U.S. multinational firms.

This chapter is organized as follows: hypothesis development, research methodology, sample description report of the results, and the conclusions and inferences.

HYPOTHESIS DEVELOPMENT

The reputation of a firm is an initial signal of the firm's organizational effectiveness. Favorable reputations can lead to favorable situations for firms that includes (1) the generation of excess returns by inhibiting the mobility of rivals in an industry (Caves and Porter, 1977; Wilson, 1985); (2) the capability of charging premium prices to customers (Klein and Leffler, 1981; Milgrom and Roberts, 1986a); and (3) the creation of a better image in the capital markets and to investors (Beatty and Ritter, 1986; Milgrom and Roberts, 1986b).

Various studies examined the determinants of reputational building (Belkaoui, 1992; Fombrun and Shanley, 1990; and Riahi-Belkaoui and Pavlik, 1991). The reputational rankings were found to be related to various accounting and market signals of financial performance. This study extends these analyses by relating assessments of reputations to various information signals about a firm's corporate disclosure quality. Basically, corporate audiences try to assess the reputation of a firm based on all available information. One of the factors likely to affect their assessments is the probability that the firm is withholding value-relevant unfavorable information, as they perceive this information to decrease their reputation ranking of the firm. The larger this probability as assessed by corporate audiences, the smaller the corporate reputation ranking they would assign to the firm.

One way to assess whether the firm is withholding adverse information is to examine the past performance on corporate disclosure quality. Corporate audiences may be inclined to examine the adequacy of disclosure in annual and quarterly reports, the frequency of press releases, and the availability of timely information to financial analysts. If a firm scores high on these activities, it will be perceived as having achieved quality in its corporate disclosures. As a result, corporate audiences will attach a lower probability that the firm has withheld adverse private information and assign to it a high reputation ranking. This leads to the main hypothesis of the study:

H1: A firm's corporate reputation score is positively related to the quality of its disclosures.

METHODOLOGY

The impact of corporate disclosures on a firm's corporate reputation is examined using the following model:

$$CR_{t+1} = f(DISC_t, \text{Control Variables}) \tag{1}$$

where CR_{t+1} is the corporate reputation ranking issued in year $t + 1$ and $DISC_t$ is a means of disclosure quality over a period of years ending in year t. These variables and the control variables are discussed below.

Measure of Corporate Reputation (CR)

The main dependent variable of reputation is the combined score obtained in an annual *Fortune* magazine. The *Fortune* survey covers every industry group comprising four or more companies. The industry groups are based on categories established by the U.S. Office of Management and Budget (OMB). The survey asked executives, directors, and analysts in particular industries to rate a company on the following eight key attributes of reputation:

1. Quality of management
2. Quality of products/service offered
3. Innovativeness
4. Value as a long-term investment
5. Soundness of financial position
6. Ability to attract/develop/keep talented people
7. Responsibility to the community/environment
8. Wise use of corporate assets

Ratings were on a scale of 0 (poor) to 10 (excellent). The score met the multiple-consistency ecological model view of organization effectiveness. For the purpose of our study, the 1986 to 1990 *Fortune* magazine surveys were used. They contain the overall scores for the firms' ratings in 1986 to 1990. The use of the overall score rather than a factor analysis of the eight scores is based on the facts that: (a) it is the overall score which is published in *Fortune* magazine rather than the eight scores on the attributes, and (b) it is then the overall score that is perceived by the readers as well as the respondents of the survey as the reputation index. From previous experience, the respondents know that the means of their scores on the eight attributes will be published as the overall score of reputation.

Besides the overall score, the eight individual scores on the eight key attributes of reputation were also used as dependent variables to evaluate their differential relations with corporate disclosure.

The Disclosure Quality Management (DISC)

To measure disclosure quality, this study uses data from the annual volumes of the *Report of the Financial Analysts Federation Corporate Information Com-*

mittee (FAF, 1986–90). It is generally considered as a comprehensive measure of the informativeness of a firm's disclosure policy (Lang and Lundholm, 1993, 1996; Farragher et al., 1984; Welker, 1995; Sengupta, 1998; Botosan, 1997). The data measure the firm's effectiveness in communicating with investors and the extent to which the firm provides information so that investors have the information necessary to make informed judgement across all types of disclosures. The disclosures provided through annual reports, quarterly reports, proxy statements, published information in the form of press releases and fact books, and direct disclosures to and communications with analysts are used for the evaluation of the firm's disclosure practices. In the FAF report, analysts evaluate the complete range of a firm's disclosures, summarizing their evaluations by a score (out of one hundred possible points) on the firm's total disclosure efforts, and separate scores for the different disclosure categories. Although these scores are based on analysts' perceptions of corporate disclosure practices, any potential biases or errors are minimized by a procedure that (a) requires the reporting of average scores (across industry analysts), and (b) rests on the use of detailed guidelines and a comprehensive checklist of criteria that allow a standardization of the rating process both within and across industries.

Because corporate audiences may be expected to consider both past and present disclosures in their reputation assessments, the disclosure metric, DISC, to be used in this study is the average of the total disclosure score of a firm over three consecutive years (years t, t − 1, and t − 2).

The Control Variables

The control variables were selected with the basis of a survey of prior research on the determinants of corporate reputation (Belkaoui, 1992; Formbum and Shanley, 1990; and Riahi-Belkaoui and Pavlik, 1991). Those studies typically explain reputation building for large U.S. firms in terms of market and accounting signals of performance. Based on these studies, the following control variables were included:

ROA: rate of return on assets. A firm's efficient use of its assets is best reflected by its rate of return on assets. Corporate audiences will assign a better reputation the greater a firm's rate of return on assets.

LR: logarithm of total revenues as a measure of size. Corporate audiences appreciate better the information quality of larger firms and assign them a better reputation.

QV: the market value relative to the accounting value, denoted q-Value, is computed as the ratio of the market value of the firm to the better value of its assets. As both a measure of managerial performance and a measure of agency costs, QV can also be interpreted as a signal of asset management performance. Corporate audiences will assign a better reputation the greater a firm's QV.

The Model

The main hypothesis may be expressed by the following model:

$$CR_{it+1} = a_{0t} + a_{1t} \, DISC_{it} + LR_{it} + ROA_{it} + QV_{it} + e_{it} \tag{2}$$

where

CR_{it} = Overall score of reputation
CR_{2t} = Score in quality of management
CR_{3t} = Score in quality of products/services offered
CR_{4t} = Score in innovativeness
CR_{5t} = Score in value as a long-term investment
CR_{6t} = Score in soundness of financial position
CR_{7t} = Score in ability to attract/develop/keep talented people
CR_{8t} = Score in responsibility to the community/environment
CR_{9t} = Score in wise use of corporate assets
$DISC_t$ = Average of total FAF disclosure score over the years t, t − 1 and t − 2
LR_t = logarithm of total revenues at the end of year t
ROA_t = Net income of year t divided by total assets of year t
QV = q-Value computed as total market value in year t over total assets of year t

The model was run for the 1986–90 period.

SAMPLE

To ensure the greatest sample of firms for which data would be available for all variables, the initial sample chosen was for all multinational firms included in *Fortune*'s 1986 to 1990 studies of corporate reputation and in the annual volumes of the *Report of the Financial Analysts Federation Corporate Information Committee* (FAF, 1986–90). The disclosure scores of each firm were averaged over three consecutive years (years t, t − 1, and t − 2) to obtain the disclosure metric (DISC) capturing a firm's current and past corporate disclosure performance. Accounting data for these firms' control variables was obtained from Standard & Poor's *Compustat* industrial and business segment tapes. The final sample amounted to 347 firm-year observations.

RESULTS

Descriptive Statistics and Corporate Analysis

Table 10.1 presents the descriptive statistics for all the variables used for the study. The median disclosure score is 56.3. A wide dispersion of the scores is

Table 10.1
Summary Statistics and Variable Definitions

Panel A: Summary Statistics

Variables	Number of Observation	Mean	Standard Deviation	Median	Minimum	Maximum
CR	374	6.604	0.95	6.601	3.30	8.97
DISC	374	57.86	6.89	56.31	47.31	76.73
ROA	374	0.057	0.05	0.057	0.08	0.2
LR	374	9.195	0.896	9.027	7.74	11.75
QV	374	0.8949	0.79	0.665	0.01	5.00

Variable Definitions:
CR: Corporate reputation score
DISC: FAF disclosure score
ROA: Rate of return on assets
LR: Logarithm of total revenues
QV: q-Value computed

present with a minimum of 47.31, a maximum of 76.73, and a standard deviation of 6.89. The median logarithm of revenues of 9.027 indicates a sample of large U.S. firms, with a wide variation as indicated by the minimum and maximum values. The corporate reputation score also varies across firms, with a minimum of 3.30 and a maximum of 8.97. Table 10.2 presents the intercorrelations among variables in the study. The low intercorrelation among the predictor variables used in the model indicates no reason to suspect multicollinearity, and various diagnostic tests run on the derived regression models confirmed that it was not a problem.

Effect of Disclosure Quality on Corporate Reputation

The tests of H_1 is performed by running regression (2). Table 10.3 presents the results of the regression coefficients for all the independent variables, using all the measures of corporate reputation as dependent variables. The Breusch and Pagan (1979) test for heteroscedasticity yielded an X^2 of a minimum of 143.73 and a maximum of 172.325 for all the regressions, indicating that heteroscedasticity could be a problem in these regressions. Accordingly, the reported t-statistics are based on White's (1980) heteroscedasticity corrected covariance matrix. Hypothesis 1 predicts that corporate disclosure quality will positively affect reputation. The results, in all cases, corroborate the hypothesis that corporate audiences tend to assign higher (better) reputations to firms with

Table 10.2
Correlations among Selected Variables*

	CR	DISC	ROA	LR	QV
CR	1.000 0.00	-0.0005 (0.999)	0.536 (0.0001)	0.114 (0.026)	0.515 (0.0001)
DISC		1.000 0.00	-0.285 (0.0001)	0.499 (0.0001)	-0.457 (0.0001)
ROA			1.000 0.00	-0.136 (0.0004)	0.459 (0.0001)
LR				1.000 0.00	-0.320 (0.0001)
QV					1.000 0.001

*p-Values for two-tailed tests are provided in parentheses.
Variables are defined in table 10.1.

better corporate disclosure. The magnitude of the coefficients for DISC indicates that a 1% increase in the disclosure measure results in approximately 0.02% increase in corporate reputation in most cases.

The control variables were all significant and have expected signs supporting the results of previous research on the determinants of corporate reputations.

CONCLUSION

This chapter has hypothesized that corporate audiences will construct reputational ranking on the basis of a firm's overall disclosure quality. More significantly, the results of an empirical study of large U.S. firms supported the general hypothesis that corporate audiences construct reputations on the basis of information about a firm's overall disclosure policy in addition to market and accounting signals indicating the size of the firm, the market assessment of the value of assets, and the rate of return on assets. Given the potential that reputation ranking may crystallize the status of firms within an industrial social system (Shrum and Wuthnow, 1988), firms, through a thorough understanding of the informational medium from which corporate audiences construct reputations, signal these audiences about their overall disclosure quality through annual reports, quarterly reports, proxy statements, other published information such as press releases and fact books, and direct disclosures to the analysts in the form of meetings and responses to analyst inquiries.

Table 10.3
Explaining Corporate Reputation

Independent/ Dependent Variables	Intercept	DISC	LR	ROA	QV	F	Adjusted R^2 (%)
Overall Corporate Reputation	2.733 (5.629)*	0.019 (1.877)**	0.214 (2.646)*	5.462 (4.829)*	0.486 (5.955)*	59.375*	38.44
Quality of Management	3.351 (5.498)*	0.019 (1.811)**	0.189 (1.668)**	6.548 (4.613)*	0.375 (3.664)*	34.536	96.40
Quality of Products/ Services Offered	5.032 (10.475)*	0.005 (1.82)**	0.139 (1.741)**	3.020 (2.702)*	0.439 (5.439)*	34.77*	26.53
Innovativeness	4.184 (7.449)*	0.032 (2.766)	0.040 (1.728)**	4.191 (3.203)*	0.363 (3.847)*	23.173	19.17
Value as a Long-Term Investment	1.479 (2.757)*	0.030 (2.727)*	0.249 (2.797)*	6.181 (4.946)*	0.576 (6.390)*	66.161*	41.07
Soundness of Financial Position	0.1244 (0.206)	0.030 (2.727)*	0.500 (4.976)*	8.087 (5.757)*	0.705 (6.965)*	89.485*	48.62
Ability to Attract/ Develop/ Keep Talented People	2.167 (4.075)*	0.023 (2.069)	0.238 (2.685)*	5.410 (4.366)*	0.484 (5.420)*	49.863*	34.33
Responsibility to Community/ Environment	3.412 (8.105)*	0.006 (1.769)**	0.315 (4.494)*	2.042 (2.083)*	0.472 (6.629)*	46.323*	32.65
Wise Use of Resources	3.857 (6.151)*	0.018 (1.894)**	0.127 (1.846)**	6.634 (5.379)*	0.449 (5.057)*	53.946*	36.15

Variables are defined in table 10.1.
*Absolute value of t-statistics in parentheses, significant at $\alpha=0.01$.
**Significant at $\alpha=0.05$.
***Significant at $\alpha=0.00$.

REFERENCES

Beatty, R.P., and J.R. Ritter. 1986. Investment banking, reputation, and underpricing of initial public offerings. *Journal of Financial Economics* 15: 213–32.

Belkaoui, A. 1992. Organizational effectiveness, social performance and economic performance. *Research in Corporate Social Performance and Policy* 12: (Forthcoming).

Botosan, C. 1997. Disclosure level of the cost of equity capital. *The Accounting Review* 72 (July): 323–49.

Breusch, T., and A. Pagan. 1979. A simple test for the heteroscedasticity and random coefficient variation. *Econometrica* 47: 1287–94.

Caves, R.E., and M.E. Porter. 1977. From entry barriers to mobility barriers. *Quarterly Journal of Economics* 91: 421–34.

Farragher, E., R. Kleiman, and M. Baza. 1994. Do investor relations make a difference? *Quarterly Review of Economics and Finance* 34 (Winter): 403–12.

Financial Analysts Federation (FAF). 1986–90. *Report of the Financial Analysts Federation Corporate Information Committee*. New York: FAF.

Klein, B., and K. Leffler. 1981. The role of market forces in assuring contractual performance. *Journal of Political Economy* 89: 615–41.

Lang, M., and R. Lundholm. 1993. Cross-sectional determinants of analyst ratings of corporate disclosure. *Journal of Accounting Research* 31 (Autumn): 246–71.

———. 1996. Corporate disclosure policy and analyst behavior. *The Accounting Review* 71 (October): 467–92.

Milgrom, P., and J. Roberts. 1986a. Price and advertising and signals of products quality. *Journal of Political Economy* 94: 796–821.

———. 1986b. Relying on the information of interested parties. *Rand Journal of Economics* 17: 18–32.

Riahi-Belkaoui, A., and E. Pavlik. 1991. Asset management performance and reputation building for large U.S. firms. *British Journal of Management* 2: 231–38.

Sengupta, P. 1998. Corporate disclosure quality and the cost of debt. *The Accounting Review* 4 (October): 459–74.

Shrum, W., and R. Wuthnow. 1988. Reputational status of organizations in technical systems. *American Journal of Sociology* 93: 882–912.

Smith, C.W., and R. Watts. 1992. The investment opportunity set and corporate financing, dividend, and compensation policies. *Journal of Financial Economics*: 263–92.

Welker, M. 1995. Disclosure policy, information asymmetry and liquidity in equity markets. *Contemporary Accounting Research* 11 (Spring): 801–27.

White, H. 1980. A heteroscedasticity-consistent covariance matrix estimator and a direct test for heteroscedasticity. *Econometrica* 48: 817–38.

Wilson, R. 1985. Reputations in games and markets. In A.E. Roth, ed., *Game-theoric Models of Bargaining*. New York: Cambridge University Press, 65–84.

CHAPTER 11

Growth Opportunities, Multinationality, and Reputation Building

INTRODUCTION

The reputation of a firm is important for various decisions including resource allocations, career decisions, and product choices, among others (Dowling, 1986; Riahi-Belkaoui and Pavlik, 1992). Reputation is an important signal of the firm's organizational effectiveness. Favorable reputations can create favorable situations for firms, including: (1) the generation of excess returns by inhibiting the mobility of rivals in an industry (Caves and Porter, 1977; Wilson, 1985); (2) the capability of charging premium prices to consumers (Beatty and Ritter, 1986; Milgrom and Roberts, 1986b); and (3) the creation of a better image in the capital markets and investors (Klein and Leffler, 1981; Milgrom and Roberts, 1986a).

With few exceptions, most previous empirical studies on reputation have examined the relationship of earnings performance and social performance (Karpik and Belkaoui, 1989; Ullman, 1985). However, four studies investigated the relationship between reputation and various economic and noneconomic criteria that may be used by corporate audiences to construct reputations.

Although the signals used in these four studies show attendance by corporate audiences to different information cues, this chapter postulates that the most important is placed on signals about asset management performance. Therefore, this study proposes specific hypotheses relating assessments of reputation to various information signals about the firm's asset management performance, specifically using signals that indicate size of the firm, the level of the firm's investment opportunity set, and multinationality.

RELATED RESEARCH

Four studies have investigated the determinants of reputation building. Based on the thesis that an organization's social performance is an indistinguishable component of its effectiveness, Belkaoui (1991) and Riahi-Belkaoui and Pavlik (1992) expanded the definition of social performance to include organizational effectiveness, and investigated the relationship between organizational effectiveness and economic performance. Following the ecological model, organizational effectiveness by constructs' reputational ranking of firms was used (Connolly, Conlon, and Deutsh, 1980; Scott, 1981). Reputational rankings were found to be positively related to profitability, size, and price/earnings ratio, and negatively related to systematic risk. Using a similar approach, Fombrun and Shanley (1990) found the same reputational rankings, for a different period and a different sample, to be related to the firm's risk-return profiles, resource allocations, social responsiveness, institutional ownership, media exposure, and corporate diversification. These are all signals about a firm's projects and generate reputations.

Riahi-Belkaoui and Pavlik (1991) presented empirical evidence that supported the general hypotheses that corporate audiences construct reputations on the basis of information about firms' asset management performance, specifically using market and accounting symbols indicating the size of the assets, market assessment of the value of the assets in place, turnover, and profit margin.

Finally, Riahi-Belkaoui (1999) hypothesized that corporate audiences will construct reputation rankings on the basis of the extent of earnings management. The empirical study of the one hundred most international U.S. firms supported the hypothesis that corporate audiences construct reputations on the basis of information about the firm's extent of earnings management by assigning higher reputation for firms with a higher cash flow from operations and lower reputations for firms with higher total accruals.

REPUTATION BUILDING

Objective Function and Stewardship

This chapter hypothesizes that corporate audiences use different features of firms' asset management performance in constructing reputational rankings. In particular, the focus on asset management performance rather than other attributes of firm performance results from specific expectations of corporate audiences about the objectives of management and the nature of asset stewardship.

Organizations are social units deliberately constructed and reconstructed to seek specific goals (Etzioni, 1964). J.D. Thompson (1967) differentiated between goals held for an organization and goals of an organization. The former goals are held by outside members of the organization who have a given interest in the activities of the firm, while the latter are the goals held by persons and/or managers who are part of the "dominant coalition" in terms of holding enough control to commit the organization to a given direction. The same distinction is made by Perrow (1961) as official goals versus operative goals. The main difference between the goals arises when the official goals held by corporate audiences conform to a management-welfare-maximization model (Belkaoui, 1980). The shareholder-wealth-maximization model holds that the operative goals are to maximize the wealth of stockholders. The firm accepts all projects yielding more than the cost of capital, and therefore is only interested in an efficient use of the assets of the firm. The management-welfare-maximization model holds that managers operate firms for their own benefit (Branch, 1973). It follows that corporate audiences committed to a shareholder-wealth-maximization view of operative goals will construct reputations on the basis of information about the firm's asset management performance.

The stewardship concept is basically a feature of the principle-agent relationship, whereby the agent is assumed to safeguard the resources of the principal. The stewardship concept has evolved over time. Birnberg (1980) distinguished four periods: (1) the pure custodial period; (2) the traditional custodial period; (3) the asset utilization period; and (4) the open-ended period. The first two periods refer to the need for the agent to return the resources intact to the principal by performing minimal tasks to fulfill the custodial function. The third period refers to the need for the agent to provide initiative and insight in using the assets to conform to agreed-upon plans. Finally, the open-ended period differs from the asset utilization period by providing more flexibility in the use of assets and enabling the agent to chart the course of asset utilization. The third and fourth periods are more reflective of the contemporary concept of stewardship. It follows that corporate audiences holding these views of stewardship will construct reputations on the basis of information about firms' asset management performance.

Interpreting Ambiguous Signals about Asset Management

Based on the shareholder-wealth-maximization model for operative goals of firms, and the asset utilization and open-ended use of assets for views of stewardship, corporate audiences are assumed to construct reputations on the basis of informational signals about firms' asset management performance. Asset management performance is perceived to be a combination of firm size, level of the investment opportunity set, and level of multinationality.

Size

Large firms are more politically sensitive than small firms (Watts and Zimmerman, 1986). If their profits are also large, they fear government actions (Alchian and Kessel, 1962; Jensen and Meckling, 1978). The amount and quality of information of large firms will be larger in response to the increased scrutiny (Arbel and Sltreber, 1984; Freeman, 1987). As a result, it can be postulated that corporate audiences will better appreciate the information quality of large firms and assign them a better reputation. The following hypothesis will be tested:

Hypothesis 1: The larger the firm, the better its reputation.

Level of the Investment Opportunity Set

The level of the investment opportunity set is a measure of the growth opportunities or the firm's future investment opportunities. It can be perceived as a measure of future and present managerial performance. As such, the level of the investment opportunity set can also be interpreted as a signal of asset management performance. The following hypothesis will be tested:

Hypothesis 2: The greater the level of the investment opportunity set of a firm, the better its reputation.

Level of Multinationality

A firm's efficient use of its assets can be measured by the degree to which it takes advantage of both local and foreign opportunities, which can be expressed by the level of multinationality. Given the profit-related results of multinationality, the level of multinationality can be perceived as a good signal of asset management performance. The following hypothesis will be tested:

Hypothesis 3: The greater a firm's level of multinationality, the better its reputation.

THE MODEL

The three hypotheses may be expressed by the following model:

$$REP_{it} = a_{0t} + a_{1t} \, SIZE + a_{2t} \, IOS + a_{3t} \, MULTY + M_{it}$$

where

REP_{1t} = Overall score of reputation
REP_{2t} = Score on quality of management
REP_{3t} = Score on quality of products/service offered
REP_{4t} = Score on innovativeness
REP_{5t} = Score of value as a long-term investment
REP_{6t} = Score on soundness of financial position
REP_{7t} = Score on ability to attract/develop/keep talented people
REP_{8t} = Score on responsibility to the community/environment
REP_{9t} = Score on use of corporate assets
$SIZE$ = Firm size

Table 11.1
Descriptive Statistics

Variables	Mean	Standard Deviation	Minimum	Maximum
MULTY	35.073	14.962	6.600	76.100
IOS	0.5611	0.824	-8.787	7.383
SIZE	15,013	18,953	9,318	126,932

Variable Definitions:
MULTY=Multinationality measured as foreign revenues/total revenues.
IOS=Level of investment opportunity set.
SIZE=Total revenues in thousands.

IOS = Investment opportunity set level

MULTY = Multinationality level

The model was run for the period 1986–90.

THE DATA

Dependent Variable

The main dependant variable of reputation is the combined score obtained in an annual *Fortune* magazine survey, which covers every industry group comprising four or more companies. The industry groups are based on categories established by the U.S. Office of Management and Budget (OMB). The survey asked executives, directors, and analysts in particular industries to rate a company on the following eight key attributes of reputation:

1. Quality of management
2. Quality of products/service offered
3. Innovativeness
4. Value as a long-term investment
5. Soundness of financial position
6. Ability to attract/develop/keep talented people

Table 11.2
Correlations

Variables	MULTY	IOS	SIZE
MULTY	1.000 (0.000)	0.0404 (0.4571)	-0.0167 (0.7243)
IOS		1.000 (0.000)	0.0181 (0.7385)
SIZE			1.000 (0.000)

7. Responsibility to the community/environment

8. Wise use of corporate assets

Ratings were on a scale of 0 (poor) to 10 (excellent). The score met the multiple-consisting ecological view of organization effectiveness. For the purpose of this study, the 1986–90 *Fortune* magazine surveys were used. The use of the overall score is based on the facts that: (a) it is the overall score which is published in *Fortune* magazine rather than the eight scores on the attributes, (b) the overall score is perceived by the readers as the reputation index, and (c) from previous experience, the respondents know that the means of their scores on the eight attributes will be published as the overall score of reputation. Besides the overall score, the individual scores on the eight key attributes of reputation were also used as dependent variables to evaluate their differential relations with asset management performance.

Independent Variables

The independent variables include firm size, level of the investment opportunity set, and level of multinationality. Firm size was measured by the logarithm of total revenues. The level of the investment opportunity set was measured by the earnings/price ratio. The level of multinationality was measured by the foreign revenues/total revenues ratio.

Sample

To ensure the greatest sample of firms for which data would be available for all variables, the initial sample chosen was all the firms included in *Fortune*'s 1986–90 studies of corporate reputation and the *Forbes* list of the one hundred most international U.S. firms for the same period. Table 11.1 presents the basic descriptive statistics for all the variables in the model. Table 11.2 presents the

Table 11.3
Explaining Corporate Reputation

Independent Variables/Dependent Variables	Intercept	SIZE	IOS	MULTY	R^2	F
Overall Corporate Reputation	5.079 (7.616)*	0.115 (1.734)***	0.1340 (1.715)***	0.0132 (3.450)*	0.062	6.375*
Quality of Management	5.486 (7.081)*	0.0931 (1.788)***	0.1543 (1.679)***	0.0100 (2.226)*	0.034	3.407*
Quality of Products/ Services Offered	6.4614 (10.645)*	0.0158 (1.825)***	0.0991 (1.689)***	0.0156 (4.437)*	0.078	8.187*
Innovativeness	5.901 (8.455)*	0.0010 (1.782)**	0.1310 (1.683)***	0.0099 (2.438)*	0.034	3.399*
Value as a Long- Term Investment	4.256 (5.602)*	0.1821 (2.370)*	0.1499 (1.663)***	0.0134 (3.047)*	0.097	10.354*
Soundness of Financial Position	2.838 (3.227)*	0.3526 (3.964)*	0.1775 (1.702)***	0.0184 (3.599)*	0.097	10.354*
Ability to Attract / Develop / Keep Talented People	4.2646 (6.095)*	0.1744 (2.464)*	0.1355 (1.634)***	0.0156 (3.847)*	0.077	8.065*
Responsibility to Community/ Environment	5.1881 (9.252)*	0.0882 (1.756)***	0.0987 (1.884)***	0.0128 (3.884)*	0.068	7.000*
Wise Use of Resources	5.7553 (7.890)*	0.0191 (1.759)***	0.1264 (1.864)***	0.0100 (2.357)*	0.030	3.053*

1. Absolute value of t-statistics in parentheses.
2. * Significant at 0.01.
   ** Significant at 0.05.
   *** Significant at 0.10.

intercorrelations among the variables. The low intercorrelations among the predictor variables used in the model gave no reason to suspect multicollinearity; various diagnostic tests run on derived regression models confirmed that it was not a problem.

RESULTS

Table 11.3 presents the results of the regression coefficients for all independent variables, using all the measures of reputation as dependent variables for the 1986–90 period.

Hypothesis 1 predicts that the firm size, as measured by the logarithm of total revenues, will positively affect reputation. With no exception, the results corroborate the hypothesis that corporate audiences tend to assign higher (better) reputations to firms with higher size as measured by the logarithm of total revenues.

Hypothesis 2 predicts that the level of the investment opportunity set, as a measure of the firm's future investment opportunities, will positively affect reputation. With no exceptions, the results for the 1986–90 period corroborate the hypothesis that corporate audiences tend to assign higher reputations to firms with a higher level of investment opportunity set.

Hypothesis 3 predicts that the level of multinationality significantly influences reputational judgements. With no exceptions, the results for the periods examined indicate that corporate audiences tend to assign higher reputations to firms with a higher level of multinationality.

In short, the overall reputation of firms, as well as the eight component scores of reputation, is positively related to the firm's size, level of investment opportunity set, and level of multinationality. An interesting result is provided by the results on reputation as measured by soundness of financial position. It offers the highest R^2. As expected, the results regarding reputation as measured by soundness of financial position is related to the three dependent variables.

DISCUSSION AND CONCLUSIONS

Both the shareholder-wealth-maximization model and the open-ended stewardship concept maintain that corporate audiences are concerned by managers' use of the assets of the firm. This chapter has hypothesized that, consequently, corporate audiences will construct reputational rankings on the basis of the asset management performance. The results of an empirical study of large U.S. firms supported the general hypothesis that corporate audiences construct reputations based on information regarding a firm's asset management performance, specifically using market and accounting signals that indicate the size of the firm, the level of the investment opportunity set, and the level of multinationality. Given the potential that reputation rankings may crystallize the status of firms within an industrial social system, firms, through a thorough understanding of the informational medium from which corporate audiences construct reputations, signal these audiences about their asset management performance through both accounting and market signals. An interesting signal identified in this study is the level of the investment opportunity set. In other words, corporate audiences construct reputations on the basis of their perceptions of the level of growth opportunities experienced by the firms being evaluated.

REFERENCES

Alchian, A.A., and R. Kessel. 1962. Competition, monopoly and the pursuit of money. In *Aspects of Labor Economics*, ed. H.G. Lewis. New Jersey: Princeton University Press, 157–75.

Arbel, A., and P. Sltreber. 1984. The neglected and small firm effects. *Journal of Financial Economics* (July): 283–94.

Beatty, R.P., and J.R. Ritter. 1986. Investment banking, reputation, and underpricing of initial public offerings. *Journal of Financial Economics* 15: 213–32.

Belkaoui, A. 1980. *Conceptual Foundations of Management Accounting* (Reading, MA: Addison Wesley.

———. 1991. Organizational effectiveness, social performance and economic performance. *Research in Corporate Social Performance and Policy* 12: 143–53.

Birnberg, J.C. 1980. The role of accounting in financial disclosure. *Accounting, Organizations and Society* (June): 71–80.

Branch, B. 1973. Corporate objectives and market performance. *Financial Management* (Summer): 24–29.

Caves, R.E., and M.E. Porter. 1977. From entry barriers to mobility barriers. *Quarterly Journal of Economics* 91: 421–34.

Connolly, T., E. Conlon, and S.J. Deutsh. 1980. Organizational effectiveness: A multi-constituency approach. *Academy of Management Review* 5: 211–17.

Dowling, G.R. 1986. Managing your corporate images. *Industrial Market Management* 15: 109–15.

Etzioni, A. 1964. *Modern Organization*. Englewood Cliffs, NJ: Prentice Hall.

Fombrun, C.J., and M. Shanley. 1990. What's in a name? Reputation building and corporate strategy. *Academy of Management Journal* 33: 233–58.

Freeman, R.N. 1987. The association between accounting earnings and security returns for large and small firms. *Journal of Accounting and Economics* (July): 195–228.

Jensen, N.C., and W.H. Meckling. 1978. Can the corporation survive? *Financial Analysts Journal* (January–February): 31–37.

Karpik, P.G., and A. Belkaoui. 1989. Determinants of the corporate decisions to disclose social information. *Accounting, Auditing and Accountability Journal* 2: 36–51.

Klein, B., and K. Leffler. 1981. The role of market forces in assuring contractual performance. *Journal of Political Economy* 89: 615–41.

Milgrom, P., and J. Roberts. 1986a. Price and advertising signals of product quality. *Journal of Political Economy* 94: 796–821.

———. 1986b. Relying on the information of interested parties. *Rand Journal of Economics* 17: 18–32.

Perrow, C. 1961. The analysis of goals in complex organizations. *American Sociological Review* 6: 854–66.

Riahi-Belkaoui, A. 1999. Earnings management and reputation building for large U.S. firms. *Accounting and Business Review* 6, 2: 159–70.

Riahi-Belkaoui, A. and E. Pavlik. 1991. Asset management performance and reputation building for large U.S. firms. *British Journal of Management* 2: 231–38.

———. 1992. *Accounting for Corporate Reputation*. Westport, CT: Greenwood Publishing.

Scott, W.R. 1981. *Organizations: Rational, Natural Operational Systems*. Englewood Cliffs, NJ: Prentice Hall.

Thompson, J.D. 1967. *Organizations in Action*. New York: McGraw Hill.

Ullman, A.A. 1985. Data in search of a theory: A critical examination of the relationship among social performance, social disclosure and economic performance of U.S. firms. *Academy of Management Review* 10: 540–52.

Watts, R.L., and J.L. Zimmerman. 1986. *Positive Accounting Theory*. Englewood Cliffs, NJ: Prentice Hall.

Wilson, R. 1985. Reputation in games and markets. In *Game-Theoretical Models of Bargaining*, ed. A.E. Roth. New York: Cambridge University Press, 65–84.

CHAPTER 12

Net Value Added and Earnings Determination for U.S. Multinational Firms

INTRODUCTION

The research on earnings management is primarily concerned with the influence and importance of accounting accruals in arriving at a summary value of earnings (Schipper 1989; Dechow et al. 1995). This chapter does not refute the existence and potential of earnings management as a deliberate process of managing the components of earnings or of supplementary disclosures. Instead, it presents earnings management as a second-stage operation preceded by a process of earnings determination. Basically, a value of earnings is first determined as the appropriate signal the firm should be sending to the market. Second, a variety of accrual options available under generally accepted accounting principles, and susceptible to manipulation, are used for managing earnings to arrive at the same value obtained in the process of earnings determination.

Earnings determination is modeled as a response to the net wealth generated by the firm or net value added, and as an adjustment to the previous level of earnings. The main purpose of this chapter is to empirically test this net value added earnings policy model. The model is estimated annually for nonfinancial U.S. multinational firms over the period 1976 through 1995. The evidence is consistent with the role of net value added and the previous level of earnings in the determination of earnings.

The chapter contributes to the emerging literature on earnings determination and earnings management. By relying on a broad section of firms, the study documents the overall descriptive behavior of the net value added earnings policy model and lays the foundation for more contextually specific approaches.

Thus, the evidence in support of this model should be of great interest to accounting researchers and those who require estimation of net earnings of a firm.

The chapter proceeds as follows: The next section presents the policy model and its testable implications. The following sections describe the sample selection and present descriptive statistics and the empirical results. The final section presents a conclusion.

A SAMPLE VALUE ADDED EARNINGS POLICY MODEL AND TESTABLE IMPLICATIONS

The Value Added Concept in Accounting

Value added is a measure of wealth that can be easily derived from published accounting numbers (AAA, 1991; ASSC, 1975; Askren et al., 1994; Bannister et al., 1991; Bao and Bao, 1996; Burchell et al., 1985; Deegan and Hallman, 1991). It represents the total return of the firm earned by all providers of capital, plus employees and the government. It can be expressed as follows:

$$S - B = W + I + DP + DD + T + R \tag{1}$$

or

$$S - B - DP = W + I + DD + T + R \tag{2}$$

where:

R = Retained earnings

S = Sales revenue

B = Purchases of material and services

W = Wages

I = Interest

DD = Dividends

T = Taxes

DP = Depreciation

Equation (1) expresses the gross value added; equation (2) expresses the net value added. In both equations, the left side (the subtractive side) shows the value added (gross or net) and the right side (the additive side) shows the distribution of wealth among the stakeholders (Gray and Maunders, 1979; Karpik and Riahi-Belkaoui, 1994).

Value Added Earnings Policy Model

The fundamental assumption underlying the value added earnings policy model, derived from equations (1) and (2), is that earnings are related to per-moment net value added in a period. A simple linear specification of this is:

$$E_t = \alpha_0 + \alpha_1 NAV_t^* + \mu_t \tag{3}$$

where E_t and NAV_t^* denote earnings and permanent net value added in period t, respectively. Permanent net value added refers to the observed wealth that the firm can produce in perpetuity (Maunders, 1985; McLeay, 1983; Meek and Gray, 1988; Morley, 1979; Sinha, 1983). The factor of proportionality in (3), α_1, is referred to as the net value added response coefficient. μ_t is a mean zero random distribution term that includes all the potential variables other than per-manent net value added that affect earnings. The intercept α_0, represents the mean of the missing variables. If the observed net value added, NVA_t is used as a proxy for the unobservable permanent net value added in perpetuity, NVA_t^*, then the net value added and earnings relations in equation (3) may be estimated again in level forms as follows:

$$E_t = \alpha_0 + \alpha_1 NAV_t + \mu_t \tag{4a}$$

The disturbance term in equation (4a) includes all the variables that affect earn-ings other than net value added. The results of income-smoothing hypothesis suggest that managers adjust earnings to a new desired level derived from a new level of permanent wealth or net value added. This adjustment process can be obtained by a lagged level as an additional variable in equation (4a):

$$E_t = \alpha_0 + \alpha_1 NAV_t + \alpha_2 E_{t-1} + \mu_t \tag{4b}$$

We refer to α_1 as the net value added response coefficient and α_2 as the earnings adjustment coefficient. Equation (4b) generates the testable cross-sectional im-plications of the permanent net value added earnings model. It implies that earnings may be determined as a response to a level of observed net value added and as an adjustment to the previous earnings level.

SAMPLE SELECTION AND DESCRIPTIVE STATISTICS

Sample Selection

The availability of data for each of the variables included in equation (4b) defined the sample used. The firms examined in this study represented all the NYSE and AMEX multinational firms that have available data over the period 1976–95 in *Compustat*. The data extract resulted in a sample of 4,018 firm-year

Table 12.1
Summary Statistics for Variables of Earnings Policy Model

	Mean	Standard Deviation	Minimum	1st Quartile	Median	2nd Quartile	Maximum
Net Value Added (NVA_t)	1514.098	3400.364	1862.480	125.809	490.9606	1429.925	48,471.17
Earnings (E_t)	229.2392	607.599	4408.540	11.927	56.620	196.531	7275.884

Table 12.2
Correlation Matrix

	Net Value Added (NVA_t)	Earnings (E_t)	Previous Year Earnings (E_{t-1})
Net Value Added (NVA_t)	1.000		
Earnings (E_t)	0.23914	1.000	
Previous Year Earnings (E_{t-1})	0.63774	0.32969	1.000

observations. To limit the impact of extreme observations, values NVA_t, E_t, and E_{t-1} within the top and bottom 1% of their respective annual distribution were excluded. This left 3,998 observations (95.5% of the initial sample). All the variables are scaled by total assets.

Descriptive Statistics and Correlation Analysis

Table 12.1 presents the descriptive statistics of the three variables employed in the empirical analyses. Table 12.2 includes the correlation matrix. The only significant correlation exists between net value added (NVA_t) and previous-year level of earnings.

RESULTS

The value added earnings policy model, as summarized by equation (4b), is examined empirically via cross-sectional regressions. The results are reported in Table 12.3. The regression using the pooled (all years) sample yields estimated coefficients α_1, of 0.0075 (t-statistic = 2.513) and α_2 of 0.6928 (t-statistic = 48.623). Further both α_1 and α_2 are significant at the 0.05 level or better in all eighteen years. The R^2 are important enough, deviating from a low of 18.65% to a high of 74.66%. To investigate the potentials bias in the coefficients due to cross-sectional correlation in the error terms of the regression, we assumed that each annual regression is independent. Therefore, the mean and standard error of the coefficients obtained from the annual regressions are used to test whether this mean is statistically different from zero. The computation is shown in the last line of table 12.3. Both coefficients α_1 and α_2, are statistically different

Table 12.3

Earnings and Net Value Added [White (1980) t-Statistic in Parentheses] Model

$$E_{it} = \alpha_{0t} + \alpha_{1t} NVA_{it} + \alpha_2 E_{it-1} + \beta_{it}$$

Year	Number of Forms	α_0	α_1	α_2	Adjusted R^2
1976	207	0.0275 [1] (5.420)*	0.0080 (2.134)**	0.5682 (13.834)*	53.26%
1978	206	-0.041 (-0.802)	0.0086 (2.173)**	0.8657 (17.329)*	62.28%
1979	218	0.0211 (5.201)*	0.0059 (2.861)*	0.7938 (18.921)*	65.66%
1980	228	0.0056 (1.418)	0.0038 (2.560)*	0.9014 (22.064)*	72.09%
1981	230	0.0096 (2.936)*	0.0132 (2.869)*	0.8044 (23.366)*	74.66%
1982	236	0.0167 (3.963)*	0.0131 (2.796)*	0.9220 (20.309)*	65.45%
1983	237	0.0082 (1.455)	0.0262 (3.235)*	0.9102 (10.616)*	57.49%
1984	224	0.0144 (1.374)*	0.0214 (2.186)**	0.6060 (14.785)*	51.05%
1985	211	0.0026 (0.280)	0.0112 (2.778)*	0.8091 (10.616)*	34.42%
1986	208	0.0060 (0.815)	0.0384 (2.791)*	0.5291 (8.813)*	32.83%
1987	202	0.0080 (1.657)**	0.0065 (2.616)*	0.9208 (19.109)*	67.84%
1989	203	-0.0035 -(0.4150)	0.0370 (2.477)*	0.5251 (8.012)*	30.98%
1990	205	0.0289 (3.825)*	0.0060 (2.429)*	0.3689 (6.241)*	18.65%
1991	194	0.0408 (6.995)*	0.0009 (2.088)**	0.4392 (8.715)*	30.24%
1992	203	0.0347 (50530)*	0.0168 (2.488)*	0.6813 (11.371)*	39.90%
1993	257	-0.0049 -(0.884)	0.0012 (2.103)**	0.8357 (15.022)*	50.45%
1994	256	0.0314 (1.862)**	0.0033 (2.035)**	0.6900 (11.261)*	33.52%
1995	256	-0.0151 -(1.609)**	0.0294 (2.449)*	0.8628 (10.947)*	33.25%
All years	3998	0.0124 (7.555)*	0.0075 (2.513)*	0.6928 (48.623)*	40.74%
Mean^2			0.0145*	0.8074	

1. t-statistics are provided in parentheses.

*Significant at $\alpha \leqslant 0.01$.

*Significant at $\alpha \leqslant 0.05$.

2. This is the mean of the yearly coefficients estimated to control for the effect of cross-sectional correlation in the error terms.

Data for 1978 and 1988 purposely excluded.

from zero at the 0.05 level for α_1 and 0.01 level for α_2. We concluded that the significance of the two coefficients is unlikely to be the result of potential cross-sectional correlations.

To investigate potential collinearity among the variables in equation (4b), we computed the condition indexes advocated by Belsley, Kuh, and Welsh (1980) for detecting multicollinearity. The highest condition index obtained was 3.5, and in most yearly regressions the maximum condition index was 3.5. Thus, collinearity does not seem to influence our results, following Belsley, Kuh, and Welsh's suggestion of a mild collinearity for a maximum index between 5 and 10.

The final specification tests we performed were several analyses on the residuals from each multivariate regression that included checks for normality and use of various scatter plots. A null hypothesis of normality could not be rejected at the 0.01 level in all cases. Finally, the t-statistics were computed after correcting for the heteroscedasticity as described by White (1980).

Overall, the evidence suggests that the net value added level (NAV$_t$ and the previous-year level of earnings ($E_t - 1$) are relevant to explaining current earnings. In a sense, earnings determination may be a process of a response to a level of net value added and an adjustment to the previous earnings level.

SUMMARY AND CONCLUSION

This study shows that earnings is determined as a process of response to the wealth generated by the firm, measured by net value added, and a process of adjustment to the previous earnings level.

The first result implies the existence of a positive net value added response coefficient, in the sense that the management of the firm determines the level of earnings proportionally to the level of wealth generated as measured by the net value added. The net value added response coefficient represents how much the firm changes its earnings in response to the new level of net value added.

Basically, wealth generation precedes earnings determination. A knowledge of the wealth created in a given year as measured by the net value added and the existence of a net earnings response model are used by management to determine the level of earnings compatible with the wealth generated.

The second result implies the existence of earnings adjustment coefficient, in the sense that management determines the level of earnings in a given year proportionally to the previous-year level of earnings. The earnings adjustment coefficient represents how much the firm changes its earnings. The previous-year level of earnings acts as an anchor before adjustments are made to send a signal to the market of an ascending trend in earnings.

REFERENCES

Accounting Standards Steering Committee (ASSC). 1975. *The Corporate Report*. London: Accounting Standards Steering Committee.

American Accounting Association (AAA). 1991. Committee on accounting and audition measurement, 1989–1990. *Accounting Horizons* (September): 81–105.

Askren, B.J., J.W. Bannister, and E. Pavlik. 1994. The impact of performance plan adoption on value added and earnings. *Managerial Finance* 20, no. 9: 27–43.

Bannister, J.W., and A. Riahi-Belkaoui. 1991. Value added and corporate control in the U.S. *Journal of International Financial Management and Accounting* (Autumn): 241–57.

Bao, B., and D. Bao. 1996. The time series behavior and predictive ability results of value added data. *Journal of Business Finance and Accounting* (April): 449–60.

Belsley, D.A., E. Kuh, and R.E. Welsh. 1980. *Regression Diagnostics: Identifying Influential Data and Sources of Collinearity*. New York: Wiley.

Burchell, S., C. Clubb, and A. Hopwood. 1985. Accounting and its social context: Towards a history of value added in the United Kingdom. *Accounting Organizations and Society* 10: 381–413.

Dechow, P.M., R.G. Sloan, and A.P. Sweeney. 1995. Detecting earnings management. *The Accounting Review* 2: 193–225.

Deegan, C., and A. Hallman. 1991. The voluntary presentation of value added statements in Australia: A political cost perspective. *Accounting and Finance* (May): 1–29.

Gray, S. 1980. *Value Added Reporting: Uses and Measurement*. London: Association of Certified Accountants.

Gray, S., and K.T. Maunders. 1979. Recent developments in value added disclosures. *Certified Accountant* (August): 255–56.

Karpik, P., and A. Riahi-Belkaoui. 1994. The effects of the implementation of the multidivisional structure on shareholders' wealth: The contingency of diversification strategy. *Journal of Business Finance and Accounting* (April): 349–66.

Maunders, K.T. 1985. The decision relevance of value added reports. In *Frontiers of International Accounting: An Anthology*, eds. F.D. Choi and G.G. Mueller. Ann Arbor, MI: UMI Research Press, 225–45.

McLeay, S. 1983. Value added: A comparative study. *Accounting Organizations and Society* 8, no. 1: 31–56.

Meek, G.K., and S.J. Gray. 1988. The value added statement: An innovation for the U.S. companies. *Accounting Horizons* (June): 73–81.

Morley, M.F. 1979. The value added statement in Britain. *The Accounting Review* (May): 618–89.

Rahman, M.Z. 1990. The local value added statement: A reporting requirement for multinationals in developing host countries. *International Journal of Accounting* (February): 87–98.

Schipper, K. 1989. Commentary on earnings management. *Accounting Horizons* 3: 91–102.

Sinha, G. 1983. *Value Added Income*. Calcutta: Book World.

Suojanen, W.W. 1954. Accounting today and the large corporation. *The Accounting Review* (July): 391–98.

White, H. 1980. A heteroscedasticity-consistent covariance matrix estimator and a direct test for heteroscedasticity. *Econometrica* 48 (May): 817–38.

CHAPTER 13

The Substitution of Net Value Added for Earnings in Equity Valuation

INTRODUCTION

In this chapter, we investigate the usefulness of the substitution of net value added for earnings in equity valuation for multinational firms. The primary models motivating this research, as developed by Ohlson (1995) and Feltham and Ohlson (1999), map book value and abnormal earnings into equity value, with a residual factor representing the predictable effects of value-relevant information other than abnormal earnings. Net value added represents the total wealth generated by the firm before distribution to shareholders, bondholders, labor, and government (Bao and Bao, 1996; Askren et al., 1994). Substituting net value added for earnings in the equity valuation models of Ohlson and Feltham and Ohlson provides two benefits: (a) a better measure of wealth than earnings, and (b) the inclusion of value-relevant information other than earnings in the equity valuation models. The substitution is expected to result in a better explanatory equity valuation model that will explicitly differentiate between the effects of abnormal earnings and nonearnings, not value-added components.

The results provide evidence that the substitution of net value added for earnings in the equity valuation models of Ohlson and Feltham and Ohlson results in a better association with equity value of multinational firms.

The relevance of net value added variable suggests new opportunities in the search of equity valuation models. It adds to the evidence on the predictive power of net value added, and to the need for a better disclosure of its components.

The models including earnings and net value added in the equity valuation

models are presented in the next section. The data and sample selection procedure are described in the following section, and empirical analyses of the equity
valuation models including either earnings or net value added are presented after
that, followed by the summary and conclusions.

EQUITY VALUATION MODELS AND MEASURES
OF WEALTH

Equity Valuation Model Based on Earnings

The accounting-based equity valuation models developed by Ohlson (1995)
and Feltham and Ohlson (1999) are the theoretically consistent attempts to map
accounting variables into stock price.

The Feltham and Ohlson (1999) model relates a firm's market value to accounting data on its operating and financial activities. The model relies on the
following:

P_t = Market value of the firm's equity at date t

Fa_t = Financial assets, net of financial obligations, at date r

oa_t = Operating assets, net of operating liabilities, at date t

x_t = Earnings for the period t − 1 through t

ox_t = Operating earnings for the period t − 1 to t

d_t = Dividends, net of capital contributions, at date t

Based on a *present value relation* (PVR) assumption, the model presents the
market value, P_t, as the present value of expected dividends discounted at the
riskless rate, r_L:

$$P_t = \sum_{t=1}^{\infty} R_L^{-\gamma} E_t [d_{t+\sim}], \text{ where } R_t = 1 + r_f$$

(1)

The model relies also on a *clean surplus relation* (CSR), requiring all changes
in book value (bv) to result in either income or dividends, and a *net interest
relation* (NIR), requiring net financial assets to earn interest at the risk-free rate.
They may be expressed as follows:

$$bv_t = bv_{t-1} + x_t - d_t$$

(2)

and

$$i_t = (R_f - 1)bv_{t-1}$$

(3)

In addition, the model defines abnormal earnings x_t^a, as earnings minus a capital charge on beginning of period book value:

$$x_t^a = x_t - (R_f - 1)bv_{t-1} \tag{4}$$

As a result, abnormal operating earnings ox_t^a is defined as follows:

$$ox_t^a = ox_t - (R_f - 1)oa_t \tag{5}$$

Given that NIR do not generate abnormal earnings, it follows that abnormal earnings x_t^a is equal to abnormal operating earnings ox_t^a.

Feltham and Ohlson (1999) assume that all information evolves according to the following *linear information model* (LIM).

$$ox_{t+1}{}^a + \omega_{11}ox_t^a + \omega_{12}oa_t^a + v_{rt} + \varepsilon_{1t+1} \tag{6}$$

$$ox_{t+1} + \omega_{22}\,oa_t + v_{2t} + \varepsilon_{2t+1} \tag{7}$$

$$v_{1t+1} = \gamma_1\,v_{1t} + \varepsilon_{3t+1} \tag{8}$$

$$v_{2t+1} = \gamma_2\,v_{2t} + \varepsilon_{4t+1} \tag{9}$$

The parameters in the LIM represent persistence in abnormal operating earnings, operating, ω_{11} growth in operating assets, ω_{12} and either unbiased to ($\omega_{12} = 0$) or conservative ($\omega_{12} > 0$) accounting.

The LIM leads to a closed form, linear valuation function:

$$P_t = Bv_t + \alpha_1\,ox_t^a + \alpha_2\,oa_t + \beta v_t e^{i\theta} \tag{10}$$

Equation (10) holds that equity value equals (1) the book value, Bv_t, (2) a multiple of abnormal operating earnings, $\alpha_1 ox_t^a$, (3) an adjustment for conservative accounting, $\alpha_2 oa_t$, and (4) the effects of other value-relevant information, $B_t v$.

If we treat all assets as operating assets and liabilities, or equivalently net operating assets as book value of owners' equity, then the following model is obtained:

$$P_t = Bv_t + \alpha_1\,ox_t^a + \beta v_t \tag{11}$$

In equation (11), equity value equals the book value of owners' equity plus a multiple of abnormal operating earnings $\alpha_1 ox_t^a$, and the effects of other value-relevant information, $B_t v$. This study examines the model based on equation (11).

Equity Valuation Model Based on Net Value Added

The measure of wealth used for the derivation for equation (11) is based on the conventional measure of earnings. Another measure considered by multinational firms is value-added data. Inclusion of such data in the financial reports of U.S. corporations has been suggested by the American Accounting Committee on Accounting and Auditing (1991), and by the international accounting and research literature. Value added represents the total wealth of the firm that could be distributed to all capital providers, employees, and the government. Earnings represent the return to shareholders, while other value-added components reflect the return to the other shareholders—i.e., the bondholders, the government, and the employees.

The value-added statement is a supplement to the income statement, which reports upon the income earned by a large group of "stakeholders," all capital providers, employees, and government. It can be easily computed by the following rearrangement of the income statement:

$$S - B = W + I + DP + D + T + R \tag{12}$$

or

$$S - B - DP = W + I + D + T + R \tag{13}$$

where:

R = Retained earnings

S = Sales revenue

B = Bought-in material and services

DP = Depreciation

W = Wages

I = Interest

D = Dividends

T = Taxes

Equation (12) expresses the gross value added, while equation (13) expresses the net value added. In both equations, the left side (the "subtractive" side) shows the value added (gross or net), and the right side (the "additive" side) shows how value added is divided among the stakeholders. In equation (13), the right side includes $D + R$, the earnings components of net value added, and $W + I + T$, the nonearnings components of net value added.

Returning to equation (11) and expressing wealth as net value added (NVA) rather than earnings, the following models are derived:

$$P_t = Bv_t + \alpha_1 ONVA_t^a \tag{14}$$

or

$$P_t = Bv_t + \alpha_1 ox_t^a + \infty_2 NVATX_t^a \tag{15}$$

where:

$ONVA_t^a$ = Abnormal net value added, or net value added minus a capital charge on beginning-of-the-year total assets rather than book value because all assets generate NVA

$NVATX_t^a$ = Abnormal nonearnings net value-added components

= $ONVA_t^a - ox_t^a$

The difference between equation (11) and equation (15) is the substitution of the effects of value-relevant information $B_t v$, by the effects of abnormal non-earnings net value-added components. In a sense, equation (15) relates equity value of a firm to the components of the abnormal net value added, namely $\alpha_1 ox_t^a$, the abnormal earnings, and $\alpha_2 NVATX_t^a$, the abnormal nonearnings net value-added components. Equation (15) generalizes the Feltham and Ohlson (1999) model to accommodate a more exhaustive function of wealth that captures the predictable effects of value-relevant information other than abnormal earnings.

In the empirical analyses, we examine the equity value models implied by equation (11) and equation (15), with equation (11) relying on an earnings-based measure of wealth and equation (15) as a net value-added measure of wealth.

DATA AND SAMPLE SELECTION

The availability of data for each of the variables included in equations (11) and (15) defined the sample used. The accounting variables in both equations were calculated as follows (*Compustat* data item numbers in parentheses):

1. Net Value Added (NVA_t = the sum of labor expenses, corporate taxes, dividends, interest expense, minority shareholders in subsidiaries, and retained earnings ($42 + 6 + 19 + 21 + 49 + 36 + 36_{t-1}$)

2. Common equity = $bv_t(60_t)$

3. x_t = income before extraordinary items (18_t) - preferred dividends (19).

4. x_t^a = abnormal earnings
   = income available to common, - "normal" earnings
   = $x_t - r.bv_{t+1}$

Table 13.1
Descriptive Statistics

	#obs.	Mean	Sd.	25%	Median	75%
P	3999	21.1371	57.7802	6.8138	14.060	25.622
X^n	3999	-1.8015	13.7311	-2.0523	-0.8606	-0.1860
BV	3999	15.8652	47.1189	4.1938	9.3652	18.7914
NVAX	3999	16.7565	60.1661	4.4032	9.7892	20.0388

Table 13.2
Correlation Matrix

	P	X^n	BV	$NVAX^n$
P	1.000			
X^n	-0.3447	1.000		
BV	0.8270	-0.4040	1.000	
$NVAX^n$	0.8588	-0.5680	0.0718	1.000

a. Lower triangle contains Spearman correlation coefficients.
b. All correlations are significant at the 0.001 level.
c. Variable definitions (all per-share): P=price; X^n=abnormal earnings; BV=book value; $NVAX^n$=abnormal nonearnings component of net value added.

where r = cost of equity capital.

The firms examined in this study represented all the NYSE and AMEX multinational firms that have available data over the period 1978–95 in *Compustat*. The data extract resulted in a sample of 4,018 firm-year observations. To limit the impact of extreme observations, values of NAV_t and within x_t the top and bottom 1% of their respective annual distribution were excluded. This left 3,999 observations (95.5% of the sample). Tables 13.1 and 13.2 present, respectively, the descriptive statistics and the correlation table.

EMPIRICAL ANALYSES

All the variables are expressed in per-share form. Converting equations (11) and (15) to a cross-sectional model required adding a firm subscript, I, to the accounting variables leading to empirical models, labeled models 1 and 2, respectively:

$$\text{Model 1: } P_{it} = \alpha_{01} + \alpha_{1t}x_{it}^a + \alpha_{2t}bv_{it} + e_{it} \tag{16}$$

$$\text{Model 2: } P_{it} = \alpha_{01}^1 + \alpha_{1t}^1 x_{it}^a + \alpha_{2t}^1 bv_{it} + \alpha_3^1 NVATX_{it}^a + e_{it}^1 \tag{17}$$

Table 13.3
Estimate of Equation [White (1980) t-Statistics in Parentheses]

$$P_{it} = \alpha_{1t} + \alpha_{1t}X_t^a + \alpha_{2t}BV_{it} + e_{it}$$

Year	Number of Forms	α_0	α_1	α_2	Adjusted R^2
1978	207	-0.4198 (-0.198)	19.3305 (3.602)**	3.0422 (4.615)*	0.5791
1979	206	-0.007 (-0.008)	1.9779 (2.576)*	1.0509 (6.715)*	0.7518
1980	218	-6.9819 (-2.998)*	17.565 (3.127)*	3.3529 (4.905)*	0.7149
1981	228	-14.774 (-5.077)*	13.999 (3.111)*	3.636 (6.685)*	0.8049
1982	230	-47.224 (-11.923*)	92.832 (9.228)*	13.297 (11.115)*	0.9414
1983	236	-23.438 (-9.897)*	48.6229 (8.457)*	7.1616 (10.410)*	0.9740
1984	237	-6.650 (-5.299)*	19.536 (7.513)*	3.2198 (10.315)*	0.9840
1985	224	-1.155 (-0.889)	17.805 (6.986)*	2.927 (9.532)*	0.9782
1986	211	-2.262 (-2.033)	6.1555 (3.933)*	1.6926 (7.607)*	0.9266
1987	208	2.471 (3.069)*	4.472 (3.810)*	1.4104 (9.838)*	0.9499
1988	202	7.194 (6.087)*	6.034 (7.886)*	1.513 (5.603)*	0.5440
1989	203	3.4756 (3.166)*	12.555 (5.617)*	7.304 (8.353)*	0.6335
1990	205	28.3255 (15.503)	-15.504 (-6.405)*	-1.880 (-8.779)*	0.4934
1991	194	16.493 (9.388)*	-0.0205 (2.077)*	0.6903 (7.734)*	0.2511
1992	203	19.775 (9.964)*	-4.247 (-6.028)*	0.062 (2.512)**	0.2598
1993	257	16.539 (10.919)*	-0.015 (-2.669)*	0.6113 (9.200)*	0.2442
1994	256	20.497 (11.879)*	0.5404 (2.925)*	0.637 (6.393)*	0.2039
1995	256	15.686 (11.145)*	8.016 (4.172)*	1.478 (6.161)*	0.3002
All years	3998	5.0509 (9.319)*	-0.053 (-2.229)**	1.007 (84.5590)*	0.6839
Mean		1.570*	13.869**	2.844*	

Variable definitions: P=price; X^n=abnormal earnings; BV=book value.
*Significant at α=0.01.
**Significant at α=0.05.

Table 13.4

Estimate of Equation [White (1980) t-Statistics in Parentheses]

$$P_t = \alpha_{0t}{}^1 + \alpha_{1e}{}^1 X_{it}{}^a + \alpha_{2t}{}^1 NVATX_{it}{}^a + X_{3t}{}^1 Bv_{it} + e_{it}{}^1$$

Year	Number of Forms	α_0	α_1	α_2	α_3	Adjusted R^2
1978	207	-2.5509 (-1.202)	24.343 (4.586)*	-0.6330 (-4.131)	4.316 (6.116)	0.6097
1979	206	1.667 (.987)**	1.6479 (2.476)**	0.5051 (7.159)*	0.3158 (1.944)*	0.8008
1980	218	-5.5909 (-2.469)*	15.454 (2.847)*	0.9141 (4.273)*	2.136 (2.982)*	0.7359
1981	228	-7.1766 (-2.469)*	7.6602 (2.012)**	2.0380 (9.988)*	0.2876 (2.732)*	0.8643
1982	230	-25.244 (-5.824)*	48.822 (4.769)*	1.687 (8.436)*	5.651 (4.087)*	0.9552
1983	236	-23.870 (-9.504)*	49.490 (8.258)*	-0.076 (-2.533)*	7.360 (9.351)*	0.9739
1984	237	-7.263 (-5.856)*	20.492 (8.010)*	-0.2762 (-3.423)*	3.672 (11.040)*	0.9847
1985	224	-0.7958 (-0.663)	17.562 (6.879)*	0.0812 (8.383)**	2.786 (8.559)*	0.9782
1986	211	-1.9291 (-1.703)***	6.175 (3.432)*	-0.1435 (-2.107)*	1.947 (7.847)*	0.9278
1987	208	2.6381 (3.355)*	3.598 (3.070)*	0.2300 (3.442)*	1.047 (6.340)*	0.9574
1988	202	7.3109 (6.304)*	4.766 (8.251)*	0.172 (8.999)*	1.192 (4.177)*	0.5615
1989	203	4.143 (3.925)*	10.187 (4.652)*	0.214 (4.637)*	1.779 (6.219)*	0.6674
1990	205	13.323 (9.598)*	-2.573 (-2.564)*	1.861 (-8.837)*	-0.7071 (-4.837)*	0.8090
1991	194	12.211 (7.929)*	-0.7064 (2.998)*	0.6692 (9.173)*	0.3119 (3.611)*	0.4774
1992	203	14.459 (7.739)*	-2.165 (-3.218)*	0.580 (7.831)*	-0.088 (2.820)**	0.4307
1993	257	12.860 (9.347)*	0.3666 (7.918)*	0.3826 (9.161)*	0.3915 (6.246)*	0.4297
1994	256	15.621 (9.534)*	1.249 (2.340)*	0.4428 (8.488)*	0.4427 (4.855)*	0.3779
1995	256	12.3530 (8.372)*	8.315 (4.554)*	0.2434 (5.336)*	1.407 (6.160)*	0.3689
All years	3998	4.856 (10.481)*	0.8143 (19.558)*	0.8403 (38.378)*	0.1251 (4.973)*	0.7690
Mean		1.231*	12.005*	0.4495*	1.902*	

Variable definitions: P=price; X^n=abnormal earnings; BV=book value; $NVATX_a$=abnormal nonearnings component of net value added.

*Significant at $\alpha=0.01$.

**Significant at $\alpha=0.05$.

Model 1 represents the Feltham-Ohlson model based on earnings as the measure of wealth. Model 2 represents the Feltham-Ohlson model based on net value added as a measure of wealth. These regression models are estimated for the pooled cross-section and time-series samples as well as for each year (t) of available data. The results from regression of model 1 and model 2 are reported in tables 13.3 and 13.4. In both tables, in the regression using the pooled sample of all 3,998 firm-year observations as well as in the annual cross-sectional regressions, the coefficients are significant at the 0.01 or 0.05 levels. The RZ from the pooled regressions based on model 2 is 76.90%, compared to the RZ of 68.39 year regressions, the RZ from the net percent from model i. For the year-by-value, model 2 is higher than the RZ from the earnings model 1 in the eighteen years used in the study. These results indicate that in the Feltham-Ohlson equity valuation, price is better correlated with accounting variables, when wealth is measured by net value added.

To investigate potential collinearity among the variables in both models, we computed the condition indexes advocated by Belsley, Kuh, and Welsch (1980) for detecting multicollinearity. The highest condition index obtained was 3.6. Thus, collinearity does not seem to influence our results, suggestion of a mild collinearity for maximum index between 5 and 10.

As final specification tests, we performed several analyses on the residuals from each multivariate regression that included checks for normality and uses of various scatter plots. A UII hypothesis of normality could not be rejected at the 0.01 level in all cases. Finally, the t-statistics were computed after correcting for the heteroscedasticity as described by White (1980).

Overall, the evidence suggests that net value added-based equity valuation model is better at explaining price than the earnings-based equity valuation model. Stated differently, the equity valuation model based on earnings needs to include as additional value-relevant information the effects of the nonearnings components of net value added.

SUMMARY AND CONCLUSIONS

This study provides first a test of the descriptive validity of the Feltham and Ohlson (1999) model. In addition, it shows that when net value added is substituted as a measure of wealth for earnings, the resulting accounting valuation model is better descriptive than the conventional Feltham-Ohlson (1999) model. This is consistent with net value added as a better measure of wealth than earnings. The results suggest that the net value added model plays a significant role in equity valuation and needs to be considered in capital market research as an alternative to conventional earnings.

REFERENCES

Accounting Standards Steering Committee (ASSC). 1975. *The Corporate Report.* London: Accounting Standards Steering Committee.

American Accounting Association (AAA). 1991. Committee on accounting and auditing measurement, 1989–1990. *Accounting Horizons* (September): 81–105.

Askren, B.J., J.W. Bannister, and E.L. Pavlik. 1994. The impact of performance plan adoption on value added and earnings. *Managerial Finance* 20: 27–43.

Bao, B. and D. Bao. 1996. The time series behavior and predictive ability results of value added data. *Journal of Business Finance and Accounting* (April): 449–60.

Belsley, D.A., E. Kuh, and R.E. Welsch. 1980. *Regression Diagnostics.* New York: John Wiley & Sons.

Feltham, G.A., and J.A. Ohlson. 1995. Valuation and clean surplus accounting for operating financial activities. *Contemporary Accounting Research* 11 (Spring).

Ibbotson, R.G., and R.A. Sinquefield. 1989. *Stocks, Bonds, Bills, and Inflation: Historical Returns (1926–1987).* Charlottesville, VA: The Research Foundation of the Institute of Chartered Financial Analysts.

Meek, G.K., and S.J. Gray. 1988. The value added statement: An innovation for the U.S.? *Accounting Horizons* (June): 73–81.

Ohlson, J.A. 1995. Earnings, book values, and dividends in equity valuation. *Contemporary Accounting Research* 11 (Spring): 661–87.

Riahi-Belkaoui, A. 1996. *Performance Results of Value Reporting.* Westport, CT: Greenwood Publishing.

Stober, T.L. 1997. Do prices behave as if accounting is conservative? Cross-sectional evidence from the Feltham-Ohlson valuation model. Working paper, University of Notre Dame (October).

Suojanen, W.W. 1954. Accounting today and the large corporation. *The Accounting Review* (July): 391–98.

White, H. 1980. A heteroscedasticity-consistent covariance matrix estimator and a direct test for heteroscedasticity. *Econometrica* 48 (May): 817–838.

CHAPTER 14

Implementation of the M-Form Organizational Structure and Shareholders' Wealth of Multinational Firms

INTRODUCTION

The question of whether there is a preferred, possibly optimal, structure for managing large, diverse (multiproduct) multinational firms has been a recurrent topic in the economic literature. It is generally agreed that the multidivisional (M-form) structure has various advantages over a unitary centralized functional (U-form) structure for control of large, and generally growing, multiproduct firms.

These studies emphasize the profit-increasing and risk-reducing aspects of implementing the M-form, but with the exception of the evidence on German firms provided by R. Buhner and P. Moiler (1985), the literature does not provide direct evidence regarding the effect of M-form on shareholders' wealth and systematic risk of multinational firms.

The first objective of this study is to formally investigate whether the firm's organizational structure change affects its market value and systematic risk. It is an attempt to provide evidence on whether divisionalization is a wealth-increasing corporate decision. Specifically, to the extent that reorganizing the firm's operations promotes internal efficiency and profitability, announcing the implementation of the M-form structure should result in abnormal returns on the affected firm's stock and/or reduction in its systematic risk.

The second objective of this study is to examine whether the market reaction (risk changes and/or abnormal returns) to the announced implementation of the M-form structure is contingent on the firm's existing diversification (related, unrelated, or vertical). In agreement with the theory and empirical evidence on the M-form hypothesis, regardless of a firm's existing diversification strategy, adopting the M-form structure is generally expected to reduce the firm's systematic risk.

According to Chandler (1962), since the early 1920s corporations have adopted the M-form in response to the complex administrative problems created by increased firm size and diversity under the U-form. Williamson (1970, 1975) identifies two problems encountered by U-form structured firms: cumulative control loss, and the compounding of the strategic and operating decision-making process increases the risk of failing to achieve least-cost, profit-maximizing behavior. He maintains that as firm size increases, people reach their limits of control because of bounded rationality and start resorting to opportunism, thereby threatening efficiency and profitability. The M-form is proposed as a unique structural framework that overcomes these difficulties by favoring goal pursuits and least-cost behavior, which are more consistent with neoclassical wealth maximization.

In his using "transaction cost analysis," Williamson (1975) contends that firms tend to choose the M-form because the continued expansion of the U-form creates (cumulative control loss) effects that have adverse internal efficiency consequences. These analyses motivated investigations of the links between the M-form structure and better performance (Teece, 1981). Recent anecdotal evidence suggests that inappropriate use of the M-form, with its autonomous subunit management structure, can lead to problems: costly management duplication; marketing difficulties due to inefficient sales strategies; units competing against each other, making similar but incompatible products; and subunits acting in their short-term self-interest at expense of long-run overall company goals.

The empirical results to date provide evidence supporting various interpretations: (1) M-form implementation affects (improves) performance in large corporations regardless of other contingencies, (2) mixed results, or (3) M-form adoption effects are contingent on a firm's diversification strategy (vertical, related, or unrelated, or vertical). However, most of the studies use accounting return and annual stock return variability as risk surrogates. It is unclear how the relative magnitude of systematic risk (betas) measured using monthly and/or daily returns differs among firms with different diversification strategies.

The theory and evidence of the wealth impact of the M-form adoption on unrelated diversifying firms is inconsistent. Unrelated diversification is generally not associated with increased shareholder wealth. The evidence shows that unrelated diversification is associated with both lower economic returns and lower risk, and stockholders can diversify their own portfolios more efficiently than a firm can. However, adopting the M-form management structure in a firm with an existing unrelated diversification strategy is a different question. It was argued that the M-form structure is a good match for firms with unrelated diversification strategies, resulting in more efficient capital allocation compared to external capital markets. Most unrelated diversifying firms are expected to operate under an M-form structure.

Firms employ vertical integration of stages of production to increase economies of scale and other efficiencies, such as reduced duplication of services.
Positive results—increased profitability and stock returns—are generally associated with these benefits from vertical integration. The vertically integrated
firm's various stages of production become divisions under an M-form implementation. Providing operational autonomy to each division and applying decentralized performance evaluation are at odds with the required coordination
along the stages of production and actual performance criteria. However, if top
management can free up more time for strategic planning by allocating some
operational decision making to vertically integrated divisions, this should reduce
risk and may increase returns. The empirical evidence on the relationship between stock or accounting returns and M-form adoption in vertically integrated
firms is inconsistent. Armour and Teece (1978) find that M-form adopters out-
performed (return on equity) U-form firms in one period (1955–68), but not in
another period (1969–73) for a sample of petroleum firms. R.A. Bettis and A.
Chen's (1986) replication using stock returns indicated reduced systematic risk,
but no increase in returns due to M-form adoption. The empirical results generally indicate reduced risk.

The effect of M-form adoption on related diversified firms is the intermediate
case between the unrelated diversification and vertical integration cases. However, related diversified firms may be able to uniquely combine divisional synergistic economies such as: sharing distribution channels, advertising, technical
information (termed "economies of scope") (Teece, 1982), and reduced risks
from combining different business divisions. The empirical results have been
inconclusive. R.P. Rumelt (1974) found no profitability differences between M-
form and U-form related diversified firms. Buhner and Moiler (1985) show positive risk adjusted returns and reduced systematic risk for M-form adopting
German firms.

The study in this chapter differs from previous studies in terms of the data,
variables, and test methods in several significant ways: (1) the sample includes
U.S. firms rather than German firms; (2) stock returns are daily rather than
weekly; (3) the event date is the specific announcement date of M-form implementation rather than the annual statement revelation period, which in Germany
can extend up to seven weeks; and (4) M-form adoption is classified by diversification strategy (unrelated, related, or vertical) rather than typically related
strategies.

DATA AND METHODOLOGY

The sample included sixty-two U.S. multinational firms that adopted the M-
form according to previous research, and uses Rumelt's methodology to classify
the firms in three strategic groups: twenty-four vertically integrated, twenty-two
related diversified, and sixteen unrelated diversified firms. The methodology uses
a criterion based on three ratios to classify firms according to their diversification

strategy. The same sample of firms is used in this study to provide complimentary evidence on the stock price and systematic risk reactions to multidivisional announcements, and to test whether the reactions are contingent on the existing diversification strategy. Because of data availability (Center for Research on Security Prices daily returns data), forty-four of these firms are used in this study. Table 14.1 lists the firms, the date of the multidivisionalization announcement, and the existing diversification strategy.

The M-form event date is that of the specific announcement as reported by the *Wall Street Journal*, usually announced during the annual meeting (twenty-one of forty-four) or, lacking that, the annual meeting date in the year of implementation. There are ten of forty-four specific announcements at other than annual meeting dates of M-form adoption reported in the *Wall Street Journal*.

This study investigates the stock price reaction to an event using an event study methodology. The event date is defined as the first announcement of implementing the M-form. The methodology focuses on the pattern of daily return residuals, prediction errors, or abnormal returns surrounding the event, controlling for overall market movements and the systematic risk of each individual firm.

An abnormal return for the common stock of firm i and period (day) t is defined as:

$$AR_{it} = R_{it} - (a_i + b_i R_{mt}) \tag{1}$$

where a_i and b_i are ordinary least squares estimates of the market-model parameters; R_{it} is the return on security i for day t; and R_{mt} is the rate of return in the CRSP value weighted index on event day t. The estimation period (200 days) is from $t = -230$ to $r = -31$ relative to the announcement date, day $t = 0$. A T test (distributed with $n - 2$ degrees of freedom where n equals the number of days in the estimation period) is used to examine whether the firms' average daily abnormal return is statistically different from zero. The test statistic is calculated as:

$$T_{it} = AR_{it} IS_{it} \tag{2}$$

where s is the standard error of firm i's returns (R_{it}) in the estimation period. For the total sample and subsamples of firms, and over the interval $i = -30$ to $+30$, the average daily abnormal returns are calculated. The average abnormal return for N firms for each day (AR_{Nt}) is obtained by summing AR_{it} across N firms and dividing by N as follows:

$$AR_{Nt} = \sum_{i=1}^{N} AR_{it}/N \tag{3}$$

Table 14.1
Sample Description

No. Firm Name	CUSIP Number	Event Date
Related Diversified Firms		
1 Allied Chemical	01908710	720424
2 Aluminum Co. of America	02224910	680418
3 Ashland Oil	04454010	700826
4 Bendix Corp.	08168910	650224
5 Borden, Inc.	09959910	680417
6 CPC International Inc.	12614910	670426
7 Celanese Company	15084310	630410
8 Coca-Cola Co.	19121610	680506
9 Dow Chemical Co.	26054310	630508
10 H.J. Heinz Co.	42307410	670908
11 Ingersoll-Rand Co.	45686610	640428
12 IBM	45920010	650427
13 Monsanto Co.	61166210	710423
14 Philip Morris	71815410	670425
15 Proctor & Gamble	74271810	661011
16 Quaker Oats Co.	74740210	711117
17 RJR Nabisco Inc.	74960110	700408
18 Ralston Purina Co.	75127710	681212
19 J.P. Stevens & Co.	86016310	710302
20 Unisys (Burroughs) Co.	90921410	660322
21 White Motor Corp.	96406610	690423
Unrelated Diversified Firms		
22 Borg Warner Corp.	09972510	700417
23 Brunswick Corp.	11704310	690425
24 Colt Industries Inc.	19686470	680503
25 DAYCO	23953010	660228
26 Esmark Inc.	29647010	700429
27 Gulf + Western Inc.	40206410	670920
28 ITT Corp.	45067910	680508
29 Lear Siegler Inc.	52189410	621107
30 Ogden Corp.	67634610	690525
31 SCM	78401510	621013
32 U.S. Industries	91207810	690417

Table 14.1 cont'd

No. Firm Name   CUSIP Number   Event Date

Vertically Integrated Firms

No. Firm Name	CUSIP Number	Event Date
33 City Service	17303610	670425
34 Crown Zellerbach	22866910	680425
35 Goodyear Tire & Rubber	38255010	760404
36 George A. Hormel & Corp.	44045210	661220
37 International Paper	46014610	730410
38 Kennecott Corp.	48931410	660503
39 Marathon Oil Co.	56584510	630502
40 Occidental Petroleum	67459910	720516
41 Phillips Petroleum	71850710	750429
42 St. Regis Paper	79345310	690423
43 Sun Co. Inc.	86676210	710420
44 Unocal Corp.	91528910	640414

A T test is used to examine whether the average daily abnormal returns across N firms is statistically different from zero. In addition, a binomial test examines whether the proportion of positive to negative residual returns is statistically significant compared to the null hypothesis.

EMPIRICAL RESULTS

Overall Sample

The daily average raw returns (R), daily abnormal returns (AR), AR t-values, and the percentage of positive over negative abnormal returns for the sample, for the period -15 to $+15$ days relative to the announcement date ($t = 0$), are shown in table 14.2. Notable from table 14.2 total sample results is that the announcements of the implementation of the M-form are, on average, associated with no abnormal returns on the announcement day ($t = 0$); and the average abnormal return is -0.00012 (with a t-value $= -0.05$), statistically insignificant, at any conventional level. However, the abnormal returns on the preannouncement date ($t = -1$) is statistically different from zero (AR $= -0.0048$, t-value $= -2.62$, which is significant at a .01 level). These results suggest that the reorganization announcement is anticipated or known a day before the announcement date, resulting in small but significant negative changes in stockholders' wealth. This falls within the typical research event window of the day before and the day of the event announcement (from $t = -1$ to 0). These results imply that multidivisional restructuring is perceived by investors as bad news (the benefits in terms of profitability relative to risk are perceived as less than the costs associated with the changes in organizational structure).

DIVERSIFICATION STRATEGY AND EXCESS RETURNS

The second objective of this study was to investigate if the price effect of the M-form implementation is contingent on the firm's existing diversification strategy. Accordingly, the total sample is divided into three groups of firms according to the diversification strategies: unrelated, related, or vertical.

Table 14.2 presents the average raw returns (R) and average daily abnormal returns (AR) over the period encompassing the fifteen days before and following the event date (t = -15 to $+15$), their AR t-values, and the percentage of positive versus negative abnormal returns for each firm diversification strategy group (Panel A: Unrelated Diversification, Panel B: Related Diversification, and Vertical Integration). As suspected, three different results emerge from table 14.2.

The first type of results concerns firms adopting an unrelated diversification strategy (see Panel A). In this case, the M-form announcement date as well as the trading days preceding and following the announcement were not associated with significant abnormal returns. Two types of explanations may be offered. The first explanation relies on the evidence that unrelated diversification is associated with lower economic return and lower risk. Stockholders can diversify their own portfolios more quickly and at a lower cost than a firm can, and thus have little to gain from the risk-reducing aspects of unrelated diversification. Thus, the benefits equate costs for changing the managerial structure relationships between basically independent businesses. A second explanation is that because the M-form structure is a good match for firms with unrelated diversification strategies, and such firms are expected to operate under an M-form structure, there is no news. This market nonresponse to expected events is consistent with the findings for abnormal returns associated with dividend announcements.

The second type of results concerns the firms adopting a related diversification strategy (see Panel B). The announcement of the diversification is associated with abnormal returns anticipated a day before the announcement date (at day f = $+1$, AR = -0.00782, t-value = -3.04, which is statistically significant at .01). Although related diversification may be in the stockholders' best interests, it requires the adoption of the appropriate structure and control systems, skill transfers, and resource sharing in order to enable a more efficient utilization of resources, thereby increasing firm productivity. These significant negative abnormal performance findings indicate that stockholders doubt that these mechanisms will be efficiently adopted, so that they will not result in net cost savings

Table 14.2
Daily Average Abnormal Returns (AR), Raw Returns (R), AR t-Values

Number of Positive: Negative ARs

Abnormal Returns of OLS Market Model Using 200 Prior Days [-230 to –31] Only Results for

Days –15 to +15 Shown

Total Sample: All Firms Adopting a Multi-Divisional Structure (N=44)

Event Day	AR	Average (Raw) R	AR t-Value	%AR>0
-15.	-0.00204	-0.00050	-1.13	45.5
-14.	0.00190	0.00447	0.67	47.7
-13.	-0.00028	0.00124	-0.13	50.0
-12.	0.00034	0.00067	0.15	50.0
-11.	0.00106	0.00280	0.31	47.7
-10.	-0.00100	0.00127	-0.33	50.0
-9.	0.00592	0.00765	2.32*	59.1
-8.	0.00020	0.00271	0.09	47.7
-7.	-0.00447	-0.00464	-2.04*	38.6
-6.	-0.00010	0.00174	-0.04	61.4
-5.	0.00199	0.00351	0.81	52.3
-4.	0.00343	0.00293	1.22	56.8
-3.	-0.00140	-0.00084	-0.58	40.9
-2.	0.00352	0.00494	1.43	56.8
-1.	-0.00488	-0.00412	-2.62**	27.3
0.	-0.00012	0.00150	-0.05	43.2
1.	-0.00207	-0.00135	-0.69	47.7
2.	0.00500	0.00544	1.59	54.5
3.	0.00291	0.00315	1.35	63.6
4.	0.00112	-0.00045	0.41	43.2
5.	-0.00086	-0.00099	-0.47	45.5
6.	-0.00020	0.00084	-0.11	56.8
7.	0.00225	0.00272	1.16	59.1
8.	-0.00003	0.00054	-0.01	38.6
9.	-0.00046	-0.00024	-0.24	40.9
10.	-0.00399	-0.00650	-1.60	38.6
11.	-0.00084	-0.00199	-0.34	43.2
12.	0.00576	0.00554	1.62	50.0
13.	-0.00214	-0.00174	-0.86	54.5
14.	0.00090	-0.00062	0.31	43.2
15.	0.00014	0.00006	-0.06	50.0

Table 14.2 cont'd

Daily Average Abnormal Returns (AR), Raw Returns (R), AR t-Values, Number of Positive:

Negative ARs, and Significance of Binomial Tests Abnormal of OLS Market Model Using 200

Prior Days [-230 to –31] Only Results for Days –15 to +15 Shown

Panel A: Subsample with a Strategy of Unrelated Diversification (N=11)

Event Day	AR	Average (Raw) R	AR t-Value	%AR>0	Positive: Negative	Binomial Significance
-15.	-0.00480	-0.00103	-1.34	27.3	3:8	.1133
-14.	0.00814	0.01201	1.07	63.6	7:4	.2744
-13.	0.00057	0.00391	0.13	54.5	6:5	.5000
-12.	0.00381	0.00799	0.55	54.5	6:5	.5000
-11.	-0.00517	-0.00265	-0.87	45.5	5:6	.5000
-10.	-0.01363	-0.01406	-2.10	36.4	4:7	.2744
-9.	0.00434	0.00449	0.57	54.5	6:5	.5000
-8.	-0.00487	-0.00322	-0.72	36.4	4:7	.2744
-7.	-0.00501	-0.00533	-1.17	36.4	4:7	.2744
-6.	0.00247	0.00657	0.44	54.5	6:5	.5000
-5.	0.00213	0.00433	0.32	45.5	5:6	.5000
-4.	0.00308	-0.00113	0.49	63.6	7:4	.27444
-3.	-0.00649	-0.00854	-1.68	27.3	3:8	.1133
-2.	0.00104	0.00194	0.19	63.6	7:4	.2744
-1.	0.00015	-0.00139	0.04	45.5	5:6	.5000
0.	0.00042	0.00324	0.07	27.3	3:8	.1133
1.	-0.00357	-0.00500	-0.52	36.4	4:7	.2744
2.	0.00507	0.00586	0.52	54.5	6:5	.5000
3.	-0.00031	-0.00056	-0.06	54.5	6:5	.5000
4.	-0.00170	-0.00822	-0.27	27.3	3:8	.1133
5.	-0.00465	-0.00487	-1.53	27.3	3:8	.1133
6.	-0.00625	-0.00468	-1.72	45.5	5:6	.5000
7.	0.00205	0.00323	0.47	63.6	7:4	.2744
8.	0.00223	0.00129	0.46	54.5	6:5	.5000
9.	0.00054	0.00148	0.10	54.5	6:5	.5000
10.	-0.00771	-0.01372	-1.22	36.4	4:7	.2744
11.	0.00054	-0.00754	0.12	63.6	7:4	.2744
12.	0.00515	0.00811	0.60	54.5	6:5	.5000
13.	-0.00726	-0.00258	-1.06	54.5	6:5	.5000
14.	0.00951	0.00394	1.11	63.6	7:4	.2744
15.	0.00631	0.00144	0.92	72.7	8:3	.1133

Table 14.2 cont'd

Daily Average Abnormal Returns (AR), Raw Returns (R), AR t-Values, Number of Positive:

Negative ARs, and Significance of Binomial Tests Abnormal of OLS Market Model Using 200

Prior Days [-230 to −31] Only Results for Days −15 to +15 Shown

Panel B: Subsample with a Strategy of Unrelated Diversification (N=21)

Event Day	AR	Average (Raw) R	AR t-Value	%AR>0	Positive: Negative	Binomial Significance
-15.	-0.00104	0.00110	-0.45	52.4	11:10	.5000
-14.	-0.00422	-0.00239	-1.89	38.1	8:13	.1917
-13.	-0.00177	-0.00028	-0.72	42.9	9:12	.3318
-12.	0.00128	-0.00013	0.43	57.1	12:9	.3318
-11.	0.00868	0.01039	1.51	57.1	12:9	.3318
-10.	0.00295	0.00604	0.64	52.4	11:10	.5000
-9.	0.00688	0.00902	2.29*	66.7	14:7	.0946
-8.	0.00172	0.00368	0.67	52.4	11:10	.5000
-7.	-0.00237	-0.00184	-0.67	42.9	9:12	.3318
-6.	-0.00215	-0.00079	-0.47	61.9	13:8	.1917
-5.	0.00279	0.00578	0.77	47.6	10:11	.5000
-4.	0.00634	0.00871	1.56	52.4	11:10	.5000
-3.	0.00240	0.00479	0.63	47.6	10:11	.5000
-2.	0.00029	0.00149	0.09	42.6	9:12	.3318
-1.	-0.00782	-0.00644	-3.04**	19.0	4:17	.0036
0.	0.00157	0.00289	0.65	47.6	10:11	.5000
1.	-0.00067	0.00050	-0.14	61.9	13:8	.1917
2.	0.00376	0.00429	1.12	57.1	12:9	.3318
3.	0.00237	0.00267	0.77	61.9	13:8	.1917
4.	0.00358	0.00461	0.94	47.6	10:11	.5000
5.	0.00283	0.00333	0.99	57.1	12:9	.3318
6.	0.00206	0.00214	0.83	57.1	12:9	.3318
7.	0.00109	0.00146	0.37	47.6	10:11	.5000
8.	-0.00348	-0.00212	-1.32	28.6	6:15	.0392
9.	0.00157	0.00276	0.69	42.9	9:12	.3318
10.	-0.00478	-0.00597	-1.70	33.3	7:14	.0946
11.	-0.00542	-0.00553	-2.13*	28.6	6:15	.0392
12.	0.00748	0.00674	1.29	47.6	10:11	.5000
13.	0.00076	0.00050	0.26	61.9	13:8	.1917
14.	-0.00183	-0.00201	-0.51	38.1	8:13	.1917
15.	-0.00514	-0.00292	-2.03	28.6	6:15	.0392

Table 14.2 cont'd

Daily Average Abnormal Returns (AR), Raw Returns (R), AR t-Values, Number of Positive:

Negative ARs, and Significance of Binomial Tests Abnormal of OLS Market Model Using 200

Prior Days [-230 to −31] Only Results for Days −15 to +15 Shown

Panel C: Subsample with a Strategy of Vertical Integration (N=12)

Event Day	AR	Average (Raw) R	AR t-Value	%AR>0	Positive: Negative	Binomial Significance
-15.	-0.00126	-0.00280	-0.29	50.0	6:6	.6128
-14.	0.00687	0.00955	1.07	50.0	6:6	.6128
-13.	0.00157	0.00144	0.27	58.3	7:5	.3872
-12.	-0.00449	-0.00464	-2.46*	33.3	4:8	.1938
-11.	-0.00656	-0.00547	-1.47	33.3	4:8	.1938
-10.	0.00365	0.00698	0.96	58.3	7:5	.3872
-9.	0.00568	0.00815	1.42	50.0	6:6	.6128
-8.	0.00218	0.00643	0.71	50.0	6:6	.6128
-7.	-0.00764	-0.00888	-2.24*	33.3	4:8	.1938
-6.	0.00111	0.00173	0.34	66.7	8:4	.1938
-5.	0.00047	-0.00118	0.15	66.7	8:4	.1938
-4.	-0.00136	-0.00347	-0.27	58.3	7:5	.3872
-3.	-0.00336	-0.00362	-0.75	41.7	5:7	.3872
-2.	0.01146	0.01372	2.45*	75.0	9:3	.0730
-1.	-0.00433	-0.00256	-1.32	25.0	3:9	.0730
0.	-0.00357	-0.00253	-0.92	50.0	6:6	.6128
1.	-0.00314	-0.00124	-0.78	33.3	4:8	.1938
2.	0.00710	0.00706	1.38	50.0	6:6	.6128
3.	0.00682	0.00739	2.25*	75.0	9:3	.0730
4.	-0.00059	-0.00216	-0.11	50.0	6:6	.6128
5.	-0.00385	-0.00501	-1.21	41.7	5:7	.3872
6.	0.00140	0.00363	0.36	66.7	8:4	.1938
7.	0.00445	0.00444	1.44	75.0	9:3	.0730
8.	0.00395	0.00448	0.82	41.7	5:7	.3872
9.	-0.00492	-0.00705	-1.56	25.0	3:9	.0730
10.	0.00080	-0.00082	0.15	50.0	6:6	.6128
11.	0.00589	0.00928	0.91	50.0	6:6	.6128
12.	0.00330	0.00108	0.92	50.0	6:6	.6128
13.	-0.00251	-0.00488	-0.57	41.7	5:7	.3872
14.	-0.00222	-0.00239	-0.60	33.3	4:8	.1938
15.	0.00271	0.00402	0.68	66.7	8:4	.1938

*Significant at $\alpha=.05$ level.
**Significant at $\alpha=.01$ level.

Table 14.3
Risk Measure (Beta) Paired T Test Results

Panel A: Monthly Beta Analysis

(OLS Betas for 60 months prior versus following the event period [12 months before and after

the announcement month], i.e., Betas for months -72 to -13 versus Betas for months +13 to +72).

Class/Subclass by Diversification (Sample N=)	Mean Diff.	Monthly Betas [Change after event]	Std. Dev.	t-value (Prob.)	Sign Rank (Prob.)
Total sample		-0.25907	0.34551	-4.9168	-345.5
(N = 42)*				(0.0001)	(0.0001)
Unrelated		-0.44818	0.38806	-3.8304	-33.0
(N = 11)				(0.0033)	(0.0039)
Related		-0.23381	0.31872	-3.3617	-83.5
(N = 21)				(0.0031)	(0.0039)
Vertical		-0.11818	0.29175	-1.3435	-13.5
(N = 10)				(0.2088)	(0.1851)

or may even cause wasteful duplication of managerial functions at both the central and divisional levels.

The third type of result concerns the firms adopting a vertical diversification strategy (see Panel C). Here again, the M-form announcement date (t = 0) is associated with normal returns (AR = -0.00357, t-value = -0.92, which is not significant). However, the anticipation of the announcement of a vertical diversification strategy two days before the announcement (t = -2) and the full adoption of the information two days after the announcement date (r = $+2$) are associated with positive abnormal returns. This is consistent with previous results on the M-form hypothesis showing improved profitability and risk reduction for firms adopting a vertical strategy. The positive abnormal returns two days prior and two days following the announcement date suggest that the advantages associated with a vertical strategy were perceived to outweigh the costs associated with implementing the M-form structure.

DIVERSIFICATION STRATEGY AND RISK CHANGES

Table 14.3 shows the changes in systematic risk (Panel A: monthly betas; Panel B: daily betas) after the event date for the total sample and by diversification subgroups (unrelated, related, or vertical). The significant post divisionalization decline in monthly betas for the total sample is consistent with the findings of using six-year annual betas for German firms. For each diversification subgroup, the average beta declined after the M-form adoption. The mag-

Table 14.3 cont'd

Panel A: Monthly Beta Analysis

(OLS Betas for 200 days prior versus following the event period [30 days before and after the announcement month], i.e., Betas for months -230 to -31 versus Betas for months +31 to +230).

Class	Daily Betas [Change after event]		t-value	Sign Rank
(Sample N=)	Mean Diff.	Std. Dev.	(Prob.)	(Prob.)
Total sample	-0.080704	0.480177	1.20246	-75.0
(N = 44)			(0.2357)	(0.3846)
Unrelated	-0.16545	0.46166	-1.18865	-18.0
(N = 11)			(0.2620)	(0.1197)
Related	0.14000	0.39851	1.6099	43.5
(N = 21)			(0.1231)	(0.1350)
Vertical	0.22583	0.57332	1.36452	11.0
(N = 10)			(0.1997)	(0.4101)

*Note: Insufficient monthly returns creates smaller sample than for daily return analysis.

nitude of the changes and their statistical significance (both T test and the nonparametric sign rank test) are clearly associated with the type of diversification strategy. As expected, combining unrelated lines of business results in the greatest decrease in beta and greatest statistical significance, the vertical case (encompassing a similar line of business) results in the least decrease in beta (not statistically significant), and the related case results in intermediate declines and significance. The results for daily betas (Panel B) indicate no statistically significant changes. In fact, the related and vertical strategy firms slightly increase their daily betas, while the unrelated strategy group shows a small decline. The daily beta findings are consistent with firms having stable systematic risk in the short run.

CROSS-SECTIONAL REGRESSION ANALYSIS

To obtain additional insights into the price effects of the M-form implementation, the following regression is estimated:

$$CAR_{(t=-1.0)} = a_0 + b_1DS + b_2ROCE + b_3SIZE \tag{4}$$

where for firm i:

$CAR_{(t=-1.0)i}$ = two-day $(r = -1$ to $0)$ cumulative abnormal return
DS_i = diversification strategy: 0 if unrelated, and 1 if related or vertical

$ROCE_i$ = return on common equity in previous year

$SIZE_i$ = firm size measured as the log of revenue in previous year

The DS_i variable is included to test whether the price reaction is contingent on the firm's diversification strategy. The return on common equity is a profitability measure that serves as a surrogate for management's ability to successfully implement the M-form management structure. The return on common equity has also been used in prior research. Finally, the size variable is included because there may be a minimum size required to gain economic advantages from adopting the M-form.

Table 14.4 reports the results of the regression analysis. The model has statistically significant explanatory power (the F value of 6.602 is significant at a less than .001 level). The model appears to be well specified, with the sequential parameter estimates indicating stable coefficients as variables added to the model. The ROCE coefficient is positive and is highly significant (at a less than .01 level). The size and diversification strategy variable coefficients are both negative, but are not significant at a .10 level. These size results for abnormal price reactions imply that M-form implementation may be less beneficial for the larger size firms in the sample. The weaker diversification strategy results indicate that the M-form announcement CARs are less if firms are classified as related diversified or vertically integrated, versus unrelated diversified. Recall that vertically integrated firms on average show highly significant positive abnormal returns at day $t = -2$ and $r = +3$, just outside the event window of days $t = -1$ to 0. Thus, the results for the vertically integrated group appear to be sensitive to the typically used two-day window definition compared to using a wider event window.

SUMMARY AND CONCLUSIONS

This chapter has investigated firms' abnormal share price changes and risk changes associated with the announcement of a multidivisional corporate structure (M-form). The evidence suggests that both price effects and risk changes are contingent on the sample firm's existing type of diversification strategy (unrelated, related, or vertical). The abnormal return results point to significant market anticipation or a response to prereleased information just prior to the reported announcement dates (at day $t = -1$ or -2) for the vertically integrated and related diversified firms, respectively. Significantly negative average abnormal returns occur in the case of the related strategy, versus abnormal positive returns for the vertical strategy. No significant abnormal returns are found for the unrelated diversification case. The cross-sectional regression results help clarify previous findings on the benefit associated with each type of diversification strategy. Armour and Teece's (1978) finding that M-form adopters had greater returns on equity than U-form firms in one period (1955–68) but not in another (1969–73) can be reconciled with Bettis and Chen's (1986) replication

Table 14.4
OLS Regression Estimates of Equation (4)

MODEL: $CAR_{(t=1.0)} = b_0 + b_1DS + b_2ROCE + b_3SIZE$

Dependent Variable: $CAR_{(t=1.0)}$ = Cumulative Abnormal Returns

SOURCE	DF	SUM OF SQUARES	MEAN SQUARE	F VALUE	PROB>F
MODEL	3	0.00459	0.00153	6.602	0.0010
ERROR	39	0.00904	0.00023		
C TOTAL	42	0.001362			

$R^2 = 0.3368$

$ADJ\ R^2 = 0.2858$

Root MSE = 0.01522

PARAMETER ESTIMATES:

Independent Variable	Coefficient Estimate	Standard Error	t-Value HO: b = 0	PROB>T	Standard Estimate
INTERCEPT	0.0108	0.0205	0.528	0.6008	0
DS	-0.0053	0.0056	-0.938	0.3542	-0.12546
ROCE	0.1697	0.0442	3.836	0.0004	0.50126
SIZE	-0.0044	0.0029	-1.520	0.1365	-0.20376

Variable		Definition
DS	=	Diversification Strategy: Unrelated = 0, and Related or Vertical =1;
ROCE	=	Lagged Return on Common Equity;
SIZE	=	Lagged Log of Total Revenue

SEQUENTIAL PARAMETER ESTIMATES

Coefficients in Model	Added Variable	INTERCEPT	DS	ROCE	SIZE
b0	INTERCEPT	-0.0050			
b0 b1	DS	.0001	-.0078		
b0 b1 b2	ROCE	-.0185	-.0072	0.1737	
b0 b1 b2 b3	SIZE	.0108	-.0053	0.1697	-.0044

using stock returns indication of reduced *systematic* risk but no increase in returns due to M-form adoption. The market reacts favorably to M-form adoption only if there is a recent record of profitability. Firms with a record of greater *returns* on common equity exhibit a highly significant positive association with abnormal returns associated with the M-form announcement. Thus, firms with lower profitability may be inappropriately adopting the M-form as a desperate attempt to increase profits, or such firms may be facing intense competition or other difficulties, and may not have the resources needed to effectively install this type of management structure. The coefficients on firm size and diversification strategy (DS) are both negative, but are not statistically significant at even the 0.10 level. This can be viewed as mild evidence of more favorable market response to M-form announcements by smaller firms and unrelated diversifiers versus firms with related diversification or vertical integration strategies. Further research on a larger sample with a greater range of firm sizes would help clarify these relationships.

The findings relative to risk (beta) changes show unrelated diversification results in the greatest decrease in beta and greatest statistical significance, the vertical case results in the least decrease in beta (not statistically significant), and the related diversification results in intermediate declines and significance.

REFERENCES

Armour, R.A., and D.J. Teece. 1978. Organizational structure and economic performance: A test of the multidivisional hypothesis. *Bell Journal of Economics* 9: 106–22.

Bettis, R.A., and A. Chen. 1986. Organizational structure and financial market performance: preliminary test. Working paper, Southern Methodist University, Dallas.

Bettis, R.A., and V. Nahajan. 1985. Risk/return performance of diversified firms. *Management Science* 31: 785–99.

Buhner, R., and P. Moiler. 1985. The information content of corporate disclosure of divisionalization decisions. *Journal of Management Studies* 22: 309–26.

Chandler, A.D., Jr. 1962. *Strategy and Structure: Chapters in the History of American Industrial Enterprise*. Cambridge, MA: MIT Press.

Christensen, H.K., and C.A. Montgomery. 1981. Corporate economic performance: Diversification strategy versus market structure. *Strategic Management Journal* 2: 327–43.

Ezzamel, M.A., and K. Hilton. 1980. Divisionalization in British industry: A preliminary study. *Accounting and Business Research* 10: 197–211.

Fama, E.F., L. Fisher, and M.R. Roll. 1969. The adjustment of stock prices to new information. *International Economic Review* 2: 1–21.

Harrigan, K.R. 1985. Vertical integration and corporate strategy. *Academy of Management Journal* 28: 397–425.

Harris, B.C. 1983. *Organization: The Effect on Large Corporations*. Ann Arbor, MI: UMI Research Press.

Hill, C.W.L. 1985. Internal organization and enterprise performance: Some U.K. evidence. *Managerial and Decision Economics* 6: 210–16.

Hill, C.W.L., and R.E. Hoskisson. 1987. Strategy and structure in the multiproduct firm. *Academy of Management Review* 12: 331–41.

Hoskisson, R.E. 1987. Multidivisional structure and performance: The contingency of diversification strategy. *Academy of Management Journal* 30: 625–44.

Hoskisson, R.E., and C.S. Galbraith. 1985. The effect of quantum versus incremental M-form reorganization on performance: A time-series exploration of intervention dynamics. *Journal of Management* 11: 55–70.

Rumelt, R.P. 1974. *Strategy, Structure, and Economic Performance*. Cambridge, MA: Harvard University Press.

Steer, P., and J. Cable. 1978. Internal organization and profit: An empirical analysis of large U.K. companies. *Journal of Industrial Economics* 27: 13–30.

Teece, D.J. 1981. Internal organization and economic performance: An empirical analysis of the profitability of principal firms. *Journal of Industrial Economics* 30: 173–99.

———. 1982. Toward an economic theory of the multiproduct firm. *Journal of Economic Behavior and Organization* 3: 39–63.

Williamson, O.E. 1970. *Corporate Control and Business Behavior: An Inquiry into the Effects of Organization Form on Enterprise Behavior*. Englewood Cliffs, NJ: Prentice-Hall.

———. 1975. *Markers and Hierarchies: Analysis and Antitrust Implications*. New York: Free Press.

CHAPTER 15

Implementation of the M-Form Organizational Structure and Productivity of Multinational Firms

INTRODUCTION

The relationship between corporate diversification and firm performance has been at the forefront of issues relating to corporate strategy. The previous empirical research associating profitability differentials with different diversification strategies led in general to inconsistent results. They relied on accounting profit-based indicators of performance. Management discretion over the accounting profit number is assumed, however, to lead to income smoothing or income management. In addition, accounting profit is merely the proportion of wealth to be distributed to shareholders. It is not a measure of the total wealth created.

A better measure of total wealth is the value added (Belkaoui, 1992). It is the difference between the value of a firm's output and its input (material and services obtained from other firms), to be distributed to all stakeholders: shareholders, employees, bondholders, and the government. Used as a basis for productivity measures, it constitutes a more accurate measure of efficiency than the profit ratios used in prior corporate diversification studies (Hill and Snell, 1989).

With those issues in mind, we reexamine the earlier findings in the association between diversification and performance by analyzing the relationship between diversification strategy and productivity using a value-added taxed measure of performance. Our central proposition is that the implementation of the M-form structure affects productivity differently, depending upon which diversification strategy existed prior to M-form implementation. We investigate the proposition by comparing a value-added-based measure of productivity of large multinational firms before and after their reorganization.

BACKGROUND AND HYPOTHESES

The multidivisional form of structure is proposed as a response to the increasingly complex administrative problems encountered within a centralized functional structure as firm size and diversity increase (Chandler, 1962). It is also viewed as a unique structural form to overcome two problems encountered in the expansion of multiproduct firms: cumulative control, and the compounding of strategic and operating decision making, which exacerbate the risk of failure to achieve least-cost profit maximizing behavior (Williamson, 1970; 1975). Profitability as well as productivity are expected to improve following the adoption of the M-form structure.

J.R. Galbraith and D.A. Nathanson (1979) traced the growth of firms in three major categories of corporate diversification strategy: vertical integration, related business diversification, and unrelated business diversification. Each strategy results in different economic benefits or costs and implies different management objectives. The differences in economic characteristics between the strategies create a situation that may lead to different productivity for firms adopting different diversification strategies.

Vertical integration provides the firm economies due to control of its supply/ output markets. The firm's value-added margin for a chain of processing is increased due to increased control over raw materials and/or outputs (Pfeffer and Salancik, 1978). Further, market transaction costs, such as opportunistic actions by traders or the drafting and monitoring of contingent claims contracts to ensure harmonious lasting relationships, can be either eliminated or reduced (Hill and Hoskisson, 1987). Achieving the economic benefits of the implementation of the M-form structure in vertically integrated firms calls for customer divisions to buy from source divisions and for source divisions to sell to customer divisions, relying for valuation of the transactions on a fair and equitable transfer pricing system. Surveys of actual practices in transfer pricing indicate, however, less reliance on market price, and greater use of accounting-based and/ or negotiated transfer prices. Externalities of various sorts create severe problems of decentralization and an invisible-hand approach to transfer pricing, often requiring overt or covert central-office intervention for their resolution (Whinston, 1964). The invisible hand often becomes a visible ham-hand (Thomas, 1980). This may explain the results showing that the implementation of M-form structure in vertically integrated firms led to a decrease in efficiency measured by rate of return (Teece, 1980) and by risk-adjusted return derived from the capital asset pricing model.

Hypothesis 1: Implementation of an M-form structure in vertically integrated firms leads to decrease in productivity.

Firms adopting a strategy of related diversification can realize synergistic economies of scope through the joint use of inputs (Teece, 1980). Exploration of this synergy is achieved through both tangible and intangible interrelationships (Porter, 1988). Tangible relationships are created by such devices as joint procurement of raw materials, joint development of shared technologies or production processes, joint sales forces, and joint physical distribution systems. Intangible interrelationships arise from the sharing of know-how and capabilities. An intermediate group of strategic business or strategic business unit (SBU) structures may be used to centralize information flows necessary to achieve economies of scope and to create an internal capital market to achieve certain efficiencies. As a result, allocative efficiency should be better than with vertically integrated firms.

Hypothesis 2: Implementation of an M-form structure in related diversified firms leads to an increase in productivity.

Firms pursuing a strategy of unrelated diversification can realize financial economies. They may be able to apply portfolio management concepts as well as pool cash flows and then reallocate them, especially according to detailed strategic criteria, if it will not overload the information processing ability of a small central head office (Bettis and Hall, 1982b). There is the potential of achieving optimal allocation of resources as well as monitoring the divisions better than the capital markets if the divisions were independent units. Basically, unrelated diversification may overcome external capital market failures (Teece, 1980). The success of unrelated diversification rests on successfully exposing the unrelated acquisitions to the control and monitoring of an efficient internal capital market.

Hypothesis 3: Implementation of the M-form structure in unrelated diversified firms leads to an increase in productivity.

The previous discussion suggests that there is differential productivity among firms adopting different diversification strategies with higher productivity produced by related diversifiers than by vertical integrators or unrelated diversifiers. Therefore, we hypothesize that the different diversification strategies employed by firms lead to cross-sectional differences in productivity between diversification strategies. And, more specifically, that:

Hypothesis 4: Firms using related diversification strategies have higher productivity than unrelated diversifiers or vertically integrated firms.

SAMPLE AND DATA COLLECTION

Previous research has identified sixty-two firms that adopted the M-form during the period 1950–78. Our sample included all these firms. Each firm was diversified at the time of its restructuring and is classified by Rumelt's (1974) method as having been in one of three diversification classes: unrelated (sixteen firms), related (twenty-two firms), or vertical (twenty-four firms). Table 15.1 lists the firms, their classification, and the year in which the restructuring occurred.

A longitudinal design is used to capture the effects over time of the implementation of a decentralized multidivisional structure. Data for the measure of productivity we collected for year −5 through year +5 (relative to the year of restructuring). In addition, one covariate (annual asset growth) and two control variables (early/late adoption of the M-form and industry membership) were collected.

Dependent Variable

Value added represents the wealth an organization creates by its own and its employees' efforts. Many multinational firms disclose these aspects of wealth creation in a value-added statement. As a supplement to the income statement, the value-added statement is viewed as a report on the income earned by a larger group of "stakeholders"—all providers of capital, plus employees and government. It can be obtained by the following rearrangement of the income statement:

$$S - B = W + I + DP + DD + T + R \tag{1}$$

or

$$S - B - DP = W + I + DD + T + R \tag{2}$$

where

R = Retained earnings

S = Sales revenue

B = Bought-in material and services

DP = Depreciation

W = Wages

I = Interest

DD = Dividends

T = Taxes

Equation (1) expresses the gross value-added method, while equation (2) expresses the net value added. In both equations, the left side (the subtractive side) shows the value added (gross or net), and the right side (the additive side) shows the disposal of value added among the stakeholders. The additive side is used

Table 15.1
Companies and Years Studied

Companies	Year of Restructuring
Vertically Integrated Firms	
Aluminum Co. of America	1968
B.F. Goodrich	1953
Burlington Industries	1962
City Service	1967
Continental Can	1950
Crown Zellerbach	1968
Getty Oil	1959
Goodyear	1976
George A. Hormel and Co.	1966
International Paper	1973
Kaiser Aluminum	1958
Kennecott Corp.	1966
Marathon Oil	1963
Mobil Oil	1960
Occidental Petroleum	1972
Phillips Petroleum	1975
Shell Oil	1961
Standard Oil (California)	1955
Standard Oil of Ohio	1962
Standard Oil (Indiana)	1961
St. Regis Paper	1969
Sun Co., Inc.	1971
Unocal Corp.	1964
Uniroyal	1960
Related Diversified Firms	
Allied Chemical	1972
Ashland Oil	1970
Bendix	1965
Borden. Inc.	1968
Burroughs	1966
Celanese	1963
Coca-Cola	1968
CPC International, Inc.	1967
Dow Chemical Co.	1963
General Foods	1952
H.J. Heinz Co.	1967
Honeywell Co.	1962

Table 15.1 cont'd

Exhibit 15.1 (continued)	
Companies and Years Studied	
Companies	**Year of Restructuring**
IBM	1965
Ingersoll-Rand Co.	1964
Monsanto Co.	1971
Philip Morris	1967
Proctor & Gamble	1966
Quaker Oats Co.	1971
Ralston Purina Co.	1968
R.J. Reynolds	1970
J.P. Stevens and Co.	1971
White Motor Co.	1969
Unrelated Diversified Firms	
AMF	1958
Borg Warner	1970
Brunswick	1969
Colt Industries	1968
Dart Industries	1962
DAYCO	1966
Esmark	1970
FMC	1961
Gulf + Western	1967
ITT	1968
Lear Siegler	1962
Ogden Corp.	1969
Texton Inc.	1960
U.S. Industries	1969
Raytheon	1959
SCM	1962

in this study to derive the dependent variable of productive efficiency. It is computed as:

$$\frac{\text{Net Value Added}}{\text{Costs of the Inputs}}$$

The cost of the inputs is computed in this study as net value added minus sales. The productive efficiency ratio used in this study is viewed as a good measure of managerial efficiency. The rationale is that efficiency measures are conceived with the interrelationship between inputs and outputs, and the work done by the firm is best measured by the value added rather than profit or sales.

Control Variables and Covariates

The control variables (early/late adoption of the M-form and industry membership) and one covariate (annual asset growth in total assets) are included to control for possible intervening effects.

The control factor (early/late adoption of the M-form) is motivated by the belief that late movers team from the experience of early movers and are thus able to restructure faster and more efficiently (Mansfield, 1985). Early/late adoption is measured by the year of restructuring relative to the sample median. Hence, firms adopting the M-form prior to 1967 are classified as early movers and those adopting in 1967 or later are late movers.

To control the factor for a direct industry effect, all the firms were classified into two-digit Standard Industrial Classification (SIC) codes. The industrial codes obtained were used as a control variable.

Annual growth in assets was used as a covariate to control for variability in return in capital. Table 15.2 gives the means of the variables used in the study. Table 15.3 breaks the results by strategic type.

DATA ANALYSIS AND RESULTS

To test the overall relationship between (1) organizational structure and productivity, and (2) diversification strategy and productivity, an analysis of covariance is used. Early/late adoption and industry membership are control variables. Annual asset growth is a covariate. An F test is used to determine the difference between the dependent variable of net value-added input, after controlling for the control and covariate variables.

Table 15.4 presents the results of the analysis of covariance for the sixty-two firms in the sample. The results of the overall analysis of covariance are significant [F (9, 543) = 13.18, p = 0.0001, and R^2 = 18.17%]. The results suggest that the relationships between strategy and productive efficiency and between strategy-structure interaction and productive efficiency are significant, but the relationship between structure and productive efficiency is not statistically significant. These results show that implementation of the M-form leads to a different productive efficiency, and that it has a different effect on productive efficiency depending on strategy.

The impact of the M-form implementation in productive efficiency is further investigated by performing mean comparisons before and after the M-form by strategic type. Table 15.5 presents these results. The exhibit indicates that following the implementation of the M-form: (a) vertically integrated firms experienced statistically significant decrease in productive efficiency as asserted in Hypothesis 1, (b) related diversified firms experienced a statistically significant increase in productive efficiency as stated in Hypothesis 2, and (c) unrelated diversified firms experienced moderate, yet statistically insignificant, increase in productive efficiency as suggested in Hypothesis 3.

Table 15.2
Overall Means

Variables	Means	
	Before M-Form	After M-Form
1. Net Value Added/Input	0.39472	0.41322
2. Annual asset growth	3.27422	3.21342

Table 15.3
Means and Standard Deviations, by Strategic Type and Stage of the M-Form Implementation

Variables	Means	
	Before M-Form	After M-Form
(a) Vertically Integrated Firms		
1. Net Value Added/Input	0.374 (0.210)	0.344 (0.167)
2. Annual Asset Growth	1.78 (1.65)	1.78 (1.65)
(b) Related Diversified Firms		
1. Net Value Added/Input	0.484 (0.349)	0.564 (0.467)
2. Annual Asset Growth	2.22 (1.48)	2.22 (1.48)
(c) Unrelated Diversified Firms		
1. Net Value Added/Input	0.301 (0.139)	0.308 (0.155)
2. Annual Asset Growth	5.81 (6.309)	5.63 (6.205)

Standard deviations are between parentheses.

The significant impact of diversification strategy on productive efficiency is further investigated by performing mean comparisons between diversification strategy types. Table 15.6 presents the results. As suggested by Hypothesis 4, firms using related diversification strategies have a higher productive efficiency than unrelated diversifiers or vertically integrated firms. These differences were significant. The difference between vertically integrated firms and unrelated diversified firms was not significant.

DISCUSSION

The central proposition of this study was that the implementation of a multidivisional structure leads to different productive efficiency in firms that employ

Table 15.4
Results of the Overall Analysis of Covariance for Net Value Added/Input

Sources	F	P
Diversification Strategy	32.25	0.0001
M-Form Implementation (before/after)	0.82	0.3648
M-Form x ' Diversification Strategy	5.48	0.0156
Control Variables		
Industry (SIC codes)	0.05	0.8266
Early/late mover	40.03	0.0001
Covariates		
Annual asset growth rate (%)	3.64	0.0568
Overall F	13.18	0.0001

Table 15.5
F Tests and Variable Means and Standard Deviations by Strategy Type before and after M-Form Implementation

Measures	Before M-Form	After M-Form	F
1. Vertically Integrated Firms			
a. Net Value Added/Input	0.374	0.344	2.089
	(0.210)	(0.167)	
2. Vertically Integrated Firms			
a. Net Value Added/Input	0.484	0.564	2.609
	(0.349)	(0.467)	
3. Vertically Integrated Firms			
a. Net Value Added/Input	0.301	0.308	1.005
	(0.139)	(0.155)	

Standard deviations are between parentheses.

Table 15.6

Mean Comparison of Productivity Ratios by Strategic Type before and after Implementation of the Multidivisional Structure

		M-Form			Pr. > t	
Variable	Vertical Insignificance	Related Diversifiers	Unrelated Diversifiers	V vs R	V vs U	R vs U
a. Net Value Added/Input	0.35912	0.52464	0.30469	0.003***	0.623	0.001***

***Significant at $\alpha=0.01$.

the different strategic diversification approaches of unrelated diversifications, vertical integration, and related diversification. The results of this study support the contingency view of the relationship between productive efficiency and the implementation of this M-form.

Hypothesis 1 was confirmed, suggesting that the implementation of M-form controls tends to lead to a decrease in productive efficiency for vertically integrated firms. These results may be due to the different problems of coordinating the activities of interdependent divisions and the resort to a visible ham-hand. The results parallel most of the earlier work supporting a decrease in rate of return for vertically integrated firms.

Hypothesis 2 was also confirmed, suggesting that the implementation of the M-form controls tends to lead to an increase in productive efficiency for related diversified firms. The M-form appears as an efficient structure for related diversified firms. The synergistic economies of scope added to the M-form controls create a good environment for productivity. Those results do not parallel earlier work supporting a decrease in rate of return for vertically integrated firms. One explanation may be related to the respective problems of measuring the accounting profit and the assets allocated to each division.

Hypothesis 3 was confirmed. Like related diversified firms, unrelated diversifiers demonstrated an increase in productivity, although it was not significant. One explanation may be the difficulty in successfully exposing the unrelated acquisitions to the control and monitoring of an efficient internal capital market.

Hypothesis 4 was confirmed. Firms using related diversification strategies had a higher productive efficiency than unrelated or vertically integrated firms, following the implementation of the M-form structure. The M-form appears as a more efficient structure for related diversified firms than firms adopting other diversification strategies for the improvement of productive efficiency.

CONCLUSIONS

This chapter examined the relationship between multidivisional structure and productive efficiency. The relationship is hypothesized to vary with diversification strategy. Findings based on longitudinal analysis of productive efficiency data from sixty-two firms indicate that following the M-form implementation, productive efficiency decreased for vertically integrated firms and increased for related diversified firms. For unrelated diversifiers, the moderate increase in productive efficiency was not significant. In addition, firms using related diversification strategies had a higher productive efficiency than unrelated or vertically integrated firms.

REFERENCES

Armour, R.A., and D.J. Teece. 1987. Organizational structure and economic performance: A test of the multidivisional hypothesis. *Bell Journal of Economics* 9: 106–22.

Beattie, D.M. 1970. Value added and return on capital as measures of managerial efficiency. *Journal of Business Finance and Accounting* (Summer): 20–22.

Belkaoui, A. 1988. *The New Environment in International Accounting*. Westport, CT: Greenwood Press.

———. 1992. *Value Added Reporting: The Lessons for the U.S.* Westport, CT: Greenwood Press.

Bettis, R.A., and Hall. 1982a. Diversification strategy and accounting determined return. *Academy of Management Journal* 25: 254–64.

———. 1982b. Strategic portfolio management in the multidivisional firm. *California Management Review* 23: 24–38.

Chandler, A.D., Jr. 1962. *Strategy and Structure: Chapters in the History of American Industrial Enterprise*. Cambridge, MA: MIT Press.

Choi, F.D.S., and G.G. Mueller. 1992. *International Accounting*. New York: John Wiley.

Chua, K.C. 1977. The use of value added in productivity measurement. In *Productivity Measurement and Achievement*. Proceedings of Accounting, Victoria, New Zealand: University of Wellington.

Dye, R. 1988. Earnings management in an overlapping generation model. *Journal of Accounting Research* (Autumn): 195–235.

Galbraith, J.R., and D.A. Nathanson. 1979. Role of organizational structure and process in strategy implementation. In *Strategic Management: A New View of Business Policy and Planning*, eds. D. Schendel and C. Hofer. Boston: Little, Brown, 245–83.

Grant, R.M., A.P. Jammine, and H. Thomas. 1988. Diversity, diversification, and profitability among British manufacturing companies, 1972–84. *Academy of Management Journal* 4: 771–801.

Gray, S.J. and K.T. Maunders. 1980. *Value Added Reporting: Uses and Measurement*. London: Association of Certified Accountants.

Harrigan, K.R. 1985. Vertical integration and corporate strategy. *Academy of Management Journal* 28: 397–425.

Harris, B.C. 1983. *Organization: The Effect on Large Corporations*. Ann Arbor, MI: UMI Research Press.

Hay, D.A., and D.J. Morris. 1979. *Industrial Economics: Theory and Evidence*. Oxford: Oxford University Press.

Hill, C.W.L., and R.W. Hoskisson. 1987. Strategy and structure in the multiproduct firm. *Academy of Management Review* 12:331–40.

Hill, C.W.L., and S.A. Snell. 1989. Effects of ownership structure and control on corporate productivity. *Academy of Management Journal* 32: 25–46.

Hoskisson, R.E. 1987. Multidivisional structure and performance: The contingency of diversification strategy. *Academy of Management Journal* 30: 625–44.

Mansfield, E. 1985. How rapidly does new industrial technology leak out? *Journal of Industrial Economics* 34: 217–25.

McNichols, M., and G.P. Wilson. 1988. Evidence of earnings management from the provision of bad debts. *Journal of Accounting Research* (Supplement): 1–40.

Meek, G.K., and S.J. Gray. 1988. The value added statement: An innovation for U.S. companies. *Accounting Horizons* 3: 73–81.

Morley, M.F. 1978. *The Value Added Statement.* London: Gee and Co., for the Institute of Chartered Accountants of Scotland.

Pfeffer, J., and G. Salancik. 1978. *The External Control of Organizations: A Resource Dependence Perspective.* New York: Harper and Row.

Porter, M.E. 1988. *Competitive Advantage: Creating and Sustaining Superior Performance.* New York: Free Press.

Rumelt, R.P. 1974. *Strategy, Structure, and Economic Performance.* Cambridge, MA: Harvard University Press.

Scherer, F.M. 1980. *Industrial Market Structure and Economic Performance.* Chicago: Rand McNally.

Teece, D.J. 1980. The diffusion of an administrative innovation. *Management Science* 26: 464–70.

———. 1982. Toward an economic theory of the multiproduct firm. *Journal of Economic Behavior and Organization* 3: 36–39.

Thomas, A.L.A. 1980. *Behavioral Analysis of Joint Cost Allocation and Transfer Pricing.* Chicago: Stipes Publishing Company.

Trueman, B., and S. Tilman. 1988. An explanation of accounting income smoothing. *Journal of Accounting Research* (Supplement): 127–39.

Whinston, A.B. 1964. Price guides in decentralized organizations. In *New Perspectives in Organizational Research*, eds. W.W. Cooper, H.J. Leavitt, and M.W. Shelley. New York: John Wiley, 405–48.

Williamson, O.E. 1970. *Corporate Control and Business Behavior: An Inquiry into the Effects of Organization Form on Enterprise Behavior.* Englewood Cliffs, NJ: Prentice Hall.

———. 1975. *Markets and Hierarchies: Analysis and Antitrust Implications.* New York: Free Press.

CHAPTER 16

Implementation of the M-Form Organizational Structure and Capital Structure of Multinational Firms

INTRODUCTION

This chapter employs a contingency perspective to examine the impact of the implementation of the multidivisional form (M-form) structure on a firm's capital structure given different corporate diversification strategies. Theories of corporate capital structure have often focused on the various roles of debt, including: the tax advantage of debt (Modigliani and Miller, 1963), the choice of debt level to signal firm quality (Ross, 1977), the use of debt as an antitakeover device (Hams and Raviv, 1988), the agency costs of debt (Myers, 1977), and the usefulness of debt for restricting managerial discretion (Jensen, 1986). These theories and the related empirical work on capital structure have increased our understanding of the issues. There is, however, no consensus about which of the determinants have an impact on the capital structure decision or how they affect performance. We believe that Barton and Gordon's (1987) suggestion to employ a strategy perspective will add to the understanding of the capital structure decision.

Specifically, we test whether implementation of the M-form structure is associated with a change in capital structure, and whether such changes vary over firms with different corporate diversification strategies. Williamson (1988) discusses a theory of the firm's strategy for financing projects based on the redeployability of the assets involved and the governance structure best suited to those assets. Both concepts are used in this study to motivate the differential capital structures expected from different diversification strategies. Three major categories of corporate diversification strategy are examined: vertical integration, related business diversification, and unrelated diversification (Galbraith and Nathanson, 1979). Our central proposition is that the implementation of the M-form structure affects the capital structure decision differently depending on which diversification strategy exists prior to M-form implementation. We investigate the proposition by comparing the capital structure of large multiproduct firms before and after their reorganization.

The chapter proceeds as follows: The next section discusses the multidivisional form and its relation to firm performance. Hypotheses related to the impact of M-form restructuring and diversification strategy on capital structure are presented. The third section details the sample, data collection, and the variables used in the study. Our approach and empirical results are presented in the fourth section. The final section contains a discussion of the results.

BACKGROUND AND HYPOTHESES

Implementation of the Multidivisional Form and Capital Structure

Extending Chandler's (1962) work, Williamson (1970) argues that as the size and diversity of centralized (U-form) firms increase, managers reach their limits of control and may resort to opportunism, thereby threatening efficiency and profitability. He suggests that the multidivisional form (M-form) of managerial structure can reduce such opportunism. Since M-form implementation requires the firm to be decomposed into distinct divisions, most operating decisions, and some strategic decisions, are decentralized to these divisions. With effective decentralization, middle-management opportunism can be reduced, since responsibility for operating budgets and cost management is shifted to division managers.

Although the M-form may reduce middle-management opportunism, it offers less to control top-management opportunism. One area where top management may display opportunism is in the misuse of free cash flow; namely, cash flow in excess of that required to fund all projects that have positive net present value when discounted at the relevant cost of capital. M-form implementation does not prevent top management from investing free cash flow at below the cost of capital, or wasting it on organizational inefficiencies.

M-form adopters may tend to have free cash flow. Population-ecology theory suggests that as organizations age, they reach higher levels of performance reliability and move to a state of "structural inertia" (Hannan and Freeman, 1977), which is characterized by substantial free cash flow. Fligstein (1985) uses population-ecology theory to explain the adoption of the M-form.

Management that has been retaining free cash flow may be forced to release it when seeking new financing. Jensen (1986) theorizes that the capital market may force firms to finance new capital with debt, rather than equity, to reduce management misuse of free cash flow. He argues that debt reduces the agency costs of free cash flow by reducing the cash flow available for discretionary spending by top management. Increased debt financing would act to increase the efficiency of organizations that have large cash flows but few high-return investments by forcing them to disgorge cash to investors.

Two features of M-form implementation suggest that additional financing may be needed by the firm. First, the evidence shows that the size and asset growth of firms increase after implementation of the M-form. Second, costly coordination and information-processing functions may be needed to realize the economic gains associated with the M-form. Following the implementation of the M-form, we expect that firms will seek new financing and be required to use an increased amount of debt to reduce opportunism in the use of free cash flow. Thus, we hypothesize:

H_1: The implementation of the M-form leads to an increase in the firm's debt/equity ratio.

Diversification Strategy and Capital Structure

Galbraith and Nathanson (1979) trace the growth of firms in three major categories of corporate diversification strategy: vertical integration, related business diversification, and unrelated business diversification. Each strategy results in different economic benefits or costs and implies different management objectives. Transaction cost economics (TCE) suggests that the economic characteristics of the three diversification strategies may call for different types of financing.

TCE views project financing as a choice between alternative corporate governance and cash-flow requirements. Debt financing does not allow the debtholder voting power, but it imposes mandatory cash outflows for interest and principal on the borrower. Equity financing requires shared voting power, but does not involve mandatory cash flows. Since management is assumed to desire as little dilution of its voting power as possible, it will opt for debt financing so long as the project can generate sufficient cash flow. Thus, the choice of debt or equity funding for a project is related to the project specificity of its assets. If a project's assets are redeployable (less project-specific), they can be sold or put to an alternative productive use in the firm, and the cash flow stream from these assets is less risky. Projects with redeployable (less risky) assets are thus suited to debt financing. The implications of TCE for the three diversification strategies are discussed later.

Vertical integration offers the firm economies due to control of its supply/output markets. The firm's value-added margin for a chain of processing is expanded due to increased control over raw materials and/or outlets (Harrigan, 1985). Further, market transaction costs, such as opportunistic action by traders or the drafting and monitoring of contingent claims contracts to ensure harmonious trading relationships, can be either eliminated or reduced. Because up- or downstream integration provides cost savings to the firm, redeployment of these assets could tend to reduce the value of the firm disproportionately to their individual value.

Firms pursuing a strategy of related diversification can realize synergistic economies of scope through the joint use of inputs (Teece, 1980). Exploitation of this synergy is achieved through both tangible and intangible interrelationships. Tangible interrelationships are created by such devices as joint procurement of raw materials, joint development of shared technologies or production processes, joint sales forces, and joint physical distribution systems. Intangible interrelationships arise from the sharing of know-how and capabilities. Redeployment of assets in a related diversified firm would again imply a disproportionate loss in firm value since synergistic economies could be lost.

A traditional argument for unrelated diversification suggests that the multiproduct firm can realize financial economies. The risk pooling of imperfectly correlated income streams created by unrelated diversification is, in principle, assumed to produce an asset with a superior risk/return relationship (Lewellen, 1971). The same risk diversification can, however, be more efficiently achieved by the investor with a portfolio of bond holdings (Levy and Samat, 1970). Empirical evidence is also inconsistent with the idea that unrelated diversification reduces risk. Furthermore, unrelated diversification in itself does not imply the achievement of input/output market cost savings or the existence of managerial, technological, or operational synergies. Although Williamson (1975) contends that "conglomerate" firms may benefit from improved governance after the adoption of the M-form structure, assets (divisions) of unrelated diversifiers remain highly redeployable through spin-off or outright sale with little synergistic loss to the firm.

TCE argues that as assets become more redeployable, management prefers debt financing over equity financing. The previous discussion suggests that there is differential redeployability of assets among firms that follow different diversification strategies, with unrelated diversifiers holding more redeployable assets than related diversifiers and vertical integrators. In addition, Jensen (1986) argues that firms that are generating large free cash flows (and are thus subject to the market discipline of debt financing) often diversify into unrelated areas. We hypothesize that the different diversification strategies employed by firms are associated with cross-sectional differences in capital structure between diversification strategies. More specifically:

H_2: Firms using related diversification or vertical integration strategies have lower debt/ equity ratios than firms using an unrelated diversification strategy.

SAMPLE AND DATA COLLECTION

Previous research has identified sixty-two firms that adopted the M-form during the period 1950–78. Our sample consists of these firms. Each firm was diversified at the time of its restructuring and was classified as having been in one of the three diversification classes—unrelated (sixteen firms), related (twenty-two firms), or vertical (twenty-four firms). Table 16.1 lists the firms, their classifications, and the year in which the restructuring occurred.

Dependent Variable

A longitudinal design was used to capture the effects over time of the implementation of a decentralized multidivisional structure. Data for the measure of capital structure, year-end long-term debt to common equity, was collected for years −5 through +5 (relative to the year of the restructuring). Financial statement data for each firm were collected from *Compustat* and, in cases where *Compustat* coverage was incomplete, from *Moody's Industrials Manual*. The data collected for the dependent variable were long-term liabilities (*Compustat* data item 9) and common equity (item 60).

Control Variables and Covariates

A control factor, early/late adoption of the M-form and three covariates (firm size, growth in total assets, and growth in gross national product [GNP]) are included to control for possible intervening effects. The control factor, early/late adoption of the M-form, is motivated by the belief that late movers learn from the experience of early movers and are thus able to restructure faster and more efficiently (Mansfield, 1985). Early/late adoption is measured by the year of restructuring relative to the sample median. Firms adopting the M-form prior to 1967 are classified as early movers; those adopting in 1967 or later are classified as late movers.

Firm size, asset growth rate, and GNP growth rate are included as covariates. Their use is motivated by (1) the known relationship between leverage and size, (2) the suggestion that firms may sacrifice profitability in periods of growth, and (3) the need to control for changes in capital structure related to major external shifts in aggregate demand. Firm size is measured as the natural logarithm of average total assets; asset growth rate is measured as the proportional change in total assets. Data for year-end total assets were collected from *Compustat* (data item 6), or from *Moody's Industrials Manual* when *Compustat* coverage was incomplete. GNP growth rate is measured as the proportional change in GNP. Data for GNP were collected from the National Income and Product Accounts constructed by the U.S. Department of Commerce. Each of the covariates is measured over the same period as the dependent variable. Table 16.2 gives the means, standard deviations, and correlations for the variables used in the chapter.

DATA ANALYSIS

A longitudinal design is used to capture the effects over time of the implementation of a decentralized multidivisional structure. Years −1, 0, and +1

Table 16.1
Diversified Firms Restructuring to the M-Form from the U-Form

Company Name	Diversification strategy	Year of restructuring	Company Name	Diversification strategy	Year of restructuring
Aluminum Co. of America	V	68	CPC	R	67
BF Goodrich	V	53	Dow Chemical	R	63
Burlington	V	62	General Foods	R	52
City Service	V	66	Heinz	R	67
Continental Can	V	50	Honeywell	R	62
Crown Zellerbach	V	66	IBM	R	65
Getty Oil	V	59	Ingersoll Rand	R	64
Goodyear	V	76	Monsanto	R	71
Hormel	V	66	Phillip Morris	R	67
International Paper	V	73	Proctor & Gamble	R	66
Kaiser Aluminum	V	58	Quaker Oats	R	71
Kennecott Paper	V	66	Ralston Purina	R	68
Marathon Oil	V	63	R.J. Reynolds	R	70
Mobil Oil	V	60	J.P. Stevens	R	71
Occidental Petroleum	V	72	White Motor Co.	R	69
Phillips Petroleum	V	75			
Shell Oil	V	61	AMF	U	58
Standard Oil (California)	V	55	Borg Warner	U	70
Standard Oil (Ohio)	V	62	Brunswick	U	69
Standard Oil (Indiana)	V	61	Colt Industries	U	68
St. Regis Paper	V	69	Dart Industries	U	62
Sun Oil	V	71	Dayco	U	66
Union Oil	V	64	Esmark	U	70
Uniroyal	V	60	FMC	U	61
			Gulf & Western	U	67
Allied Chemical	R	72	ITT	U	68

Company	Type	Value	Company	Type	Value
Ashland Oil	R	70	Lear Siegler	U	62
Bendix	R	65	Ogden	U	67
Borden	R	68	Textron	U	60
Burroughs	R	66	US Industries	U	69
Celanese	R	63	Raytheon	U	59
Coca-Cola	R	68	SCM	U	62

V=vertically diversified, R=related diversification, U=unrelated diversification

Table 16.2

Means, Standard Deviations, and Correlation Coefficients of Variables by Strategic Type and Strategic Type and Stage of M-Form Implementation (Three-Year Window Excluded)

Variables	Means [a]		Correlations [b]			
	Before M-Form	After M-Form	1	2	3	4
(A) *Vertically Integrated Firms*						
1. Long-term Debt/Total Equity	0.36 (0.07)	0.42 (0.07)	1.000	0.088	0.209	-0.393
2. Size[c]	6.77 (0.98)	7.32 (1.00)	0.054	1.000	0.585	0.019
3. Total Growth in GNP[d]	0.21 (0.06)	0.26 (0.07)	-0.058	0.330	1.000	0.223
4. Total asset growth[e]	0.29 (0.26)	0.28 (0.15)	0.339	0.224	0.324	1.000
(B) *Related diversified firms*						
1. Long-term Debt / Total Equity	0.25 (0.07)	0.46 (0.07)	1.000	-0.006	0.123	0.186
2. Size[c]	6.34 (0.69)	7.12 (0.67)	0.161	1.000	0.131	0.169
3. Total Growth in GNP[d]	0.22 (0.04)	0.28 (0.04)	-0.014	0.161	1.000	-0.045
4. Total Asset Growth[e]	0.30 (0.23)	0.42 (0.21)	0.145	-0.055	0.258	1.000
(C) *Unrelated diversified firms*						
1. Long-term Debt/Total Equity	0.59 (0.10)	0.70 (0.08)	1.000	0.075	-0.173	-0.030
2. Size[c]	5.19 (1.08)	6.37 (1.03)	-0.091	1.000	0.582	-0.396
3. Total Growth in GNP[d]	0.21 (0.05)	0.28 (0.05)	0.066	0.526	1.000	-0.084
4. Total Asset Grrowth[e]	0.65 (0.58)	0.62 (0.83)	-0.351	-0.471	-0.147	1.000

[a]Standard deviations are in parentheses.

[b]Correlations in the upper (lower) half of the matrices are from after (before) implementation of the M-form.

[c]Size is computed as in (Average Total Assets).

[d]Total growth in GNP is computed as (TA–TA)/TA, where B denotes the beginning of a period and E the end of a period.

[e]Total Asset Grrowth is computed as (TA–TA)/Ta, where TA=total assets, B denotes the beginning of a period and E denotes the end of a period.

relative to the year of the restructuring (year 0) were excluded from the analysis to avoid the potential confounding of capital structure measures with events during the transition. An analysis of covariance is used to test the overall relationship between (1) organizational structure and capital structure, (2) diversification strategy and capital structure, and (3) the interactive effect of organizational structure and diversification strategy on capital structure. Early/late adoption is a control variable; firm size, asset growth rate, and GNP growth rate are covariates. The effects on capital structure of M-form implementation, diversification strategy, and their interaction are first examined by an F test of the difference between variances after controlling for the effects of early/late adoption and the covariates.

Table 16.3
Results of Analysis of Covariance for Long-Term Liabilities/Total Common Equity

Sources	F-Statistic	Pr. $> F$
Diversification Strategy	6.59	0.002
M-Form implementation	2.66	0.100
M-Form × diversification strategy	0.65	0.526
Control variable		
Early/late adopter	2.85	0.094
Covariates		
Size	0.00	0.948
Total asset growth	0.17	0679
Total growth in GNP	1.09	0.299

Table 16.4
Mean Comparisons of Long-Term Liabilities/Total Common Equity by Strategy Type before versus after M-Form Implementation

Strategy type	Before the M-Form	After the M-Form	r-probability
(1) All strategies	0.4010	0.5276	0.05
(2) Unrelated diversified firms	0.5879	0.7048	0.19
(3) Vertically integrated firms	0.3607	0.4173	0.29
(4) Related diversified firms	0.2542	0.4605	0.03

[a]H_2 predicts that the debt/equity ratio increases after M-form implementation, t-probabilities are one-tailed.

Table 16.3 presents the results of the analysis of covariance for long-term debt to total common equity for the sixty-two firms in the sample. The overall analysis of covariance is statistically significant (F [9,123] = 2.70, p = 0.007, and K1 = 0.18). Further, nondirectional F tests for differences in variance indicate that (1) the implementation of the M-form leads to a different capital structure and (2) the different diversification strategies employed by the sample firms are associated with cross-sectional differences in capital structure. There is no interactive effect of organizational form and diversification strategy on capital structure. Directional tests of hypotheses related to the main effects are reported below.

Hypothesis H_1 states the implementation of the M-form is associated with an increased use of debt in the firm's capital structure. The impact of the M-form implementation on capital structure is further investigated by performing comparisons of mean debt/equity ratios before and after the M-form for the overall sample, and by strategic type. Table 16.4 presents these results. In agreement

Table 16.5

Mean Comparisons of Long-Term Liabilities/Total Common Equity by Strategy Type

Means for strategy types			t-probability [a]		
Unrelated diversifiers	Vertical integraters	Related diversifiers	U versus V	U versus R	R versus V
0.6463	0.3890	0.3574	0.0025	0.0026	0.6519

[a]U=unrelated diversifiers, V=vertical integraters, R=related diversifiers. H_2 predicts that unrelated diversifiers have higher debt/equity ratios than do related diversifiers or vertical integraters. Thus, the reported t-probabilities for U versus V and U versus R are one-tailed. H_2 makes no predictions about the relationship between R and V firm; the reported t-probability is two-tailed.

with H_1, the table indicates that following the implementation of the M-form, firms in the overall sample significantly increased their debt/equity ratios. Further, the mean debt/equity ratio for firms in each of the strategy types increased. The analysis indicates, however, that the increase is statistically significant only in the case of firms employing the strategy of related diversification.

Hypothesis H_2 states that firms employing a strategy of unrelated diversification use more debt in their capital structure than do firms employing strategies of related diversification or vertical integration. The impact of diversification strategy on capital structure is further investigated by performing mean comparisons between type of diversification strategy. Table 16.5 presents these results. As suggested by H_2, unrelated diversified firms have long-term debt/equity ratios that are significantly larger than those for vertically integrated firms and related diversified firms. Hypothesis H_2 did not make a projection about the relative use of debt and equity between vertically integrated firms and related diversified firms. A test indicates, however, that there is no significant difference in debt/equity ratios for firms following these strategies.

DISCUSSION

The central proposition of this study was that implementation of a multidivisional structure is associated with different capital structures in firms that employ the different strategic diversification approaches of unrelated diversification, vertical integration, and related diversification. The results of this study support the contingency view of the relationship between capital structure and the implementation of the M-form.

Hypothesis 1 was confirmed; the sample firms increased the level of debt used in their capital structure. Although percentage debt usage generally increased for all diversification classes, within diversification classes only related diversified firms made a statistically significant change. An explanation for the general increase in debt is that the implementation of the M-form controls its creation. The reduction of opportunism implied as one of the goals of decentralization is further enhanced by the "control" mechanism of debt creation. The increase in debt level following the implementation of the M-form points to the role of debt in reducing the agency costs of free cash flow.

Regarding the significant increase in debt usage for related diversified firms, Hill and Hoskisson (1987) suggest that, among the strategies of unrelated diversification, related diversification, and vertical integration, the strategy of related diversification requires higher costs of coordination and information processing to realize potential economic gains. A significant increase in debt level for the related diversified firms, rather than for the unrelated diversified or vertically integrated firms, supports their suggestion that extra funds may have been needed to achieve and exploit economies of scope, which require efficient interdivisional coordination.

The test hypothesis 2 also yielded statistically significant results, suggesting that, in agreement with Williamson's thesis, debt as a governance structure is more suited to projects where assets are highly redeployable and, therefore, that different diversification strategies with different asset redeployabilities are associated with different capital structures. Where the redeployability of assets is high, as in unrelated diversified firms, the use of long-term debt financing in the firm's capital structure is greater than for firms where redeployability of assets is lower, as in related diversified and vertically integrated firms. As a result, although increased costs of coordination may require a significant increase in debt for related diversified firms, the usage of debt in their capital structures after M-form implementation is still lower than in that of unrelated diversified firms.

These results show a link between diversification as a strategy, organizational structure, and capital structure. At the divisional level, diversification strategies influence capital structure strategies. These results complement and add to the strategic-group paradigm (Porter, 1985). Based on a firm's heterogeneous capabilities and resources, the strategic-group paradigm enables researchers and practitioners to map industrial firms into sets of similar competitors, the so-called strategic groups. Although a more comprehensive review of the literature is provided by McGee and Thomas (1986), Thomas and Venkatraman (1988), and Barney and Hoskisson (1990), the results of this study indicate that the strategic linkages between the divisions of the firm and the rest of the firm need to be taken into account in the formulation of strategic groups. Better strategic groups could be identified by a simultaneous consideration of corporate diversification strategy and divisional strategy.

More research is needed to verify the results of this study and to test the questions that it raises. Replication needs to consider (1) using different data and multiple measures of leverage, (2) relying on recent periods, and (3) imposing a control group of firms not adopting the M-form. Until further research is completed, the results of the leverage effects of a historical shift to an M-form framework must be interpreted with caution.

APPENDIX: CLASSIFICATION OF DIVERSIFICATION STRATEGIES

A framework for the classification categories relies on three ratios: (1) the specialization ratio, (2) the related ratio, and (3) the vertical ratio. Each is based on the proportion of revenues earned from various business activities. The specialization ratio is used to define firms into the primary categories of single business, dominant business, related business, or unrelated business. The related and vertical ratios are then used to subdivide firms into finer classifications.

The specialization ratio (SR) is defined as the proportion of the firm's revenues that is attributable to its largest discrete product-market activity. The related ratio (RR) is defined as the proportion of firm revenues that are related to one another in some way. The vertical ratio (VR) is defined as the proportion of revenues attributable to all the by-products, intermediate products, and final products of a vertically integrated sequence of manufacturing operations.

The primary diversification strategies and their subcategories are (1) single business; (2) dominant business as dominant vertical, dominant constrained, dominant linked, or dominant unrelated; (3) related business as either related constrained or related linked; and (4) unrelated business as either multibusiness or unrelated portfolio.

A specialization ratio of less than 0.7 defines a business as unrelated. If $0.7 < SR < 0.95$, then the firm is classified as a dominant business. The firm is classified as a single business if $SR \geq 0.95$. A related ratio greater than 0.7 defines a related business. A vertical ratio greater than 0.7 defines a vertically integrated business.

A reduced classification system for the sample firms is used in this study. Each firm is classified as being in one of the three following categories:

1. *Primary dominant vertical firms.* Vertically integrated firms ($VR \geq 0.7$) producing and selling different end products, no one of which contributes more than 94% of total revenues.

2. *Related-constrained firms.* Firms with $0.7 \leq SR < 0.95$ and $RR \geq 0.7$, which have diversified by relating new businesses to a specific central skill or resource, wherein each business activity is related to almost all the other business activities of the firm.

3. *Unrelated business firms.* Firms with $0.7 \leq SR < 0.95$ and $RR < 0.7$ that have aggressive programs for the acquisition of new unrelated business.

REFERENCES

Barney, J.B., and R.E. Hoskisson. Untested assertions in strategic group research. *Managerial and Decision Economics* 11 (1990): 187–98.

Barton, S.L., and P.J. Gordon. 1987. Corporate strategy: Usefulness perspective for the study of capital structure. *Academy of Managerial Review* 12: 67–75.

Chandler, A. 1962. *Strategy and Structure.* Cambridge, MA: MIT Press.

Fligstein, N. 1985. The spread of the multidivisional form among large firms. *American Sociological Review* 50: 377–91.

Galbraith, J.R., and D.A. Nathanson. 1979. Role of organizational structure and process in strategy implementation. In *Strategic Management: A New View of Business Policy and Planning*, eds. D. Schandel and C. Hofer. Boston: Little, Brown & Co., 249–83.

Hams, M., and A. Raviv. 1988. Corporate control contests and capital structure. *Journal of Financial Economics* 20: 55–86.

Hannan, M., and J. Freeman. 1977. The population ecology of organizations. *American Journal of Sociology* 92: 929–64.

Harrigan, K.R. 1985. Vertical integration and corporate strategy. *Academy of Management Journal* 28: 397–425.

Hill, C.W., and R.E. Hoskisson. 1987. Multidivisional structure and performance: The contingency of diversification strategy. *Academy of Management Review* 12: 331–40.

Jensen, M.C. 1986. Agency costs of free cash flow, corporate finance, and takeovers. *American Economic Review* 76: 323–29.

Levy, H., and M. Samat. 1970. Diversification, portfolio analysis and the uneasy case for conglomerate mergers. *Journal of Finance* 25: 795–802.

Lewellen, W. 1971. A pure financial rationale for the conglomerate merger. *Journal of Finance* 26: 521–45.

Mansfield, E. 1985. How rapidly does new industrial technology leak out? *Journal of Industrial Economics* 34: 217–25.

McGee, J., and H. Thomas. 1986. Strategic groups: Theory, research and taxonomy. *Strategic Management Journal* 7: 141–60.

Modigliani, F., and M.H. Miller. 1963. Corporate income taxes and the cost of capital: A correction. *American Economic Review* 3: 433–43.

Myers, S.C. 1977. Determinants of corporate borrowing. *Journal of Financial Economics* 5: 147–76.

Porter, M. 1985. *Competitive Advantage: Creating and Sustaining Superior Performance*. New York: Free Press.

Ross, S.A. 1977. The determination of financial structure: The incentive-signaling approach. *Bell Journal of Economics* 8: 23–40.

Teece, D. 1980. Economies of scope and the scope of the enterprise. *Journal of Behavior and Organization* 1: 223–47.

Thomas, H., and N. Venkatraman. 1988. Research on strategic groups: Progress and prognosis. *Journal of Management Studies* 25: 537–55.

Williamson, O.W. 1970. *Corporate Control and Business Behavior*. Englewood Cliffs, NJ: Prentice-Hall.

———. 1975. *Markets and Hierarchies: Analysis and Antitrust Implications*. New York: Free Press.

———. 1988. Corporate finance and corporate governance. *Journal of Finance* 43: 567–91.

CHAPTER 17

Executive Compensation, Organizational Effectiveness, Social Performance, and Firm Performance: An Empirical Investigation

INTRODUCTION

The objective of this chapter is to present evidence on the determinants of executive compensations for U.S. multinational firms. Empirical research on the relationship between executive compensation and firm performance results from the thesis that such relation is expected if executives act in the interest of shareholders. Several empirical studies of executive compensation tested the relative importance of sales and as determinants of executive salaries to establish whether executive compensation encouraged sales maximization or profit maximization, under the assumption advanced by Baumol (1967) that profit maximization is preferred by the shareholders. Even after controlling for size the results are mixed, and where the relation between compensation and firm performance is significant the firm performance variables differ. Examples of such studies include: Cosh (1975), Hirschey and Pappas (1981), Lewellen and Huntsman (1970), Masson (1971), McGuire, Chiu, and Elbing (1962), Murphy (1985), Antle and Smith (1986), Fox (1980), and Rich and Larson (1984).

The main assumption in all these studies is that profit and/or sales are indicators of executive performance. By confining the examination of independent variables to size and profitability, these studies restrict the internal managerial control mechanisms at the disposal of a corporation's compensation-setting board. This results from the traditional neoclassical managerial productivity approach to wage determination where performance is the principal determinant of compensation. Examples of other determinants include (a) the management turnover decision (Coughlan and Schmidt, 1985), and (b) the personal characteristics of individual executives (Hogan and McPheters, 1980). Other forces from outside the institution can also bring pressure on the firm's compensation-setting board or committee to reassess the level of executive compensation. The perception of the managerial ability of executives by outside concerned groups is an example of such external forces. What these groups think of (a) the overall performance of managers, known as organizational effectiveness; and (b) their social performance, may affect the compensation-setting board in their executive compensation decision. In essence, this thesis is consistent with the view that in addition to the internal control mechanisms of the corporation, external perceptions, like organizational effectiveness and social performance, are taken into account in the determination of executive compensation.

This chapter provides an empirical evaluation of the impact of organizational and social performance on executive compensation. The next section develops four hypotheses about executive compensation on the one hand and organizational effectiveness, social performance, size, and profitability on the other hand. These hypotheses state that the level of executive compensation is a positive function of organizational effectiveness, social performance, size of the firm, and level of profit in a particular year. All the hypotheses, with the exception of the impact of social performance, are supported.

ALTERNATIVE HYPOTHESES

This section introduces four testable hypotheses about compensation and control of top management by a board of directors extending previous work by Coughlan and Schmidt (1985). The hypotheses concern the relationship between firm size and management compensation; firm financial performance and management compensation; organizational effectiveness and management compensation; and social performance and executive compensation.

Firm Size and Management Compensation

Most studies examining the determinants of executive compensation indicate that it is positively correlated with size. Size is generally measured as sales. This evidence shows that the compensation-setting board sets compensation on the basis of size with the rationale that higher compensation is necessary for larger firms whose management is involved in more complex and demanding tasks. Therefore, the first hypothesis is as follows:

H_1: The executive compensation decisions of boards produce a positive correlation between the sales and executive compensation in a given year.

While Murphy (1985) presents evidence linking executive compensation and sales growth, this hypothesis extends the thesis by linking the level of executive compensation in a given year to the level of sales in that particular year.

Firm Profitability and Management Compensation

There is ample evidence indicating a relationship between firm profitability and management compensation. This evidence shows that the executive compensation committee of the board of directors, in their search for incentive arrangements, which encourage management to act in the shareholders' interest, set compensation on the basis of financial performance as measured by profit or rate of return on assets. This is also consistent with the evidence provided by Smith and Watts (1984), indicating that the compensation plans approved by the boards of directors generally link pay to performance measures, which are themselves directly related to shareholder wealth. One such performance measure is the profit of the firm. Therefore, the second hypothesis is as follows:

H_2: The executive compensation decisions of boards produce a positive correlation between firm profit and executive compensation in a given year.

This hypothesis is in direct conflict with (a) Baumo 1 (1967) and Marris (1963), who assert that a CEO is more concerned with the size of growth rate of the firm than with its profitability; and with (b) Loomis (1982), who claims that there is no link between compensation and any measure of profitability or stock performance. This hypothesis, added to the first hypothesis in this study, to *both* size as measured by sales and performance as measured by profit as key variables are considered by the compensation-setting board rather than competing variables in explaining the level of executive compensation as expressed in the neoclassical managerialist debate and earlier empirical studies.

Organizational Effectiveness and Executive Compensation

Outside groups (shareholders, executives from other firms, watchdog groups, etc.) monitor the performance of managers of a given firm and organize their relationship with that firm (investing in, purchasing from, supply to, etc.) in terms of their perception of the effectiveness of the managerial ability of the firm. This perception, known as organizational effectiveness, has been also termed participant satisfaction, ecological model, or external effectiveness (Keely, 1978; Kilman and Herden, 1976; Miles, 1980; Connolly et al., 1980; and Price, 1972). There are three major schools of thought on organizational effectiveness: the goal-attainment model focusing on organizational ends as effectiveness criteria, the systems model focusing on the means necessary for assuring organizational persistence, and the ecological model, incorporating the interests of internal and external groups (Miles, 1980, 384). Unlike the two other models, which attempt to produce a single effectiveness statement to a given organization, the ecological model proposes a multiconstituency view of effectiveness, which treats organizations as systems generating differential assessments of effectiveness by different constituencies (Connolly et al., 1980, 214).

The approach, following suggestions by Scott (1981, 323) and Ullman (1985, 543) consists of (a) choosing one constituency, (b) measuring the members' satisfaction using different measures, and (c) combining the results on each measure to develop an overall index so that firms can be ranked in terms of their overall organizational effectiveness. Such a measure of overall effectiveness as viewed by one constituency will create pressure on the compensation-setting board, as it provides the perception on an important outside group on the overall performance of managers. Conscious of the impact of this outside group decision on the survival of the firm, the compensation-setting board will use the measure of overall effectiveness as an input for the setting of the level of executive compensation. Therefore, the third hypothesis is:

H_3: The executive compensation decisions of boards produce a positive correlation between organizational effectiveness and executive compensation in a given year.

Social Performance and Executive Compensation

The relationship between economic performance and social performance has been postulated to include either (a) a positive correlation implying either that economically sound firms can afford the luxury of above-average social performance or that management is responding to the multiple demands emanating from the various constituencies; or (b) a negative correlation given the high expenditures required to attain a higher level of social performance (Alexander and Buchholz, 1978; Bowman and Haire, 1985; Bragdon and Martin, 1979; Chen and Metcaff, 1980; Cochran and Wood, 1984; Fogler and Nutt, 1975; Kedia and Kuntz, 1981; Moskowitz, 1975; Parket and Eilbirt, 1975; Spicer, 1978a, 1978b; Sturdivant and Ginter, 1977; and Vance, 1975).

If the relationship between economic performance and social performance is effectively positive and the board feels it is important to respond to the multiple demands emanating from various constituencies, then compensation-setting boards would link pay to social performance measures. Therefore, the fourth hypothesis is:

H_4: The executive compensation decisions of boards produce a positive correlation between social performance and executive compensation in a given year.

A rejection of this hypothesis would indicate either (a) a negative correlation between economic and social performance, or (b) a failure or a refusal of the board to respond to social demands emanating from various concerned constituencies.

EMPIRICAL ANALYSIS

Specification and Measurement of Variables

The hypotheses focus on the relationship between executive compensation on the one hand and organizational effectiveness, social performance, size, and profitability on the other hand. Those variables are defined and measured as follows:

1. Executive compensation is measured as either (a) cash salary plus bonus compensation or (b) cash salary plus bonus, plus long-term compensation for the year 1986.
2. Organizational effectiveness of a firm is the 1986 combined score obtained by asking executives, directors, and analysts in the particular industry to rate the company on the following eight key attributes of reputation: (1) quality of management, (2) quality of products/services offered, (3) innovativeness, (4) value as a long-term investment, (5) soundness of financial position, (6) ability to attract/develop/keep talented people, (7) responsibility to the community/environment, and (8) wise use of corporate assets. The survey conducted by Endos and Morgan, Inc. covered 292 companies in thirty-one industries and involved eight thousand executives, outside directors, and financial analysts with a 50% response rate (Hutton, 1986, 16–20). Ratings were on a scale of 0 (poor) to 10 (excellent). This 1986 combined score meets the multiple-constituency ecological model view of organizational effectiveness.
3. Social performance of each company is measured by the score obtained in item 7 of the organizational effectiveness instrument, namely, responsibility to the community/environment.
4. The size factor was measured by the 1986 sales amount.
5. The profitability factor was measured by the 1986 net profit amount.

The year 1986 was chosen as the test period because of the availability of the organizational effectiveness factor in that particular year.

The Model

The structure of the model is similar to that advanced by Boyes and Schlagenhauf (1979), who indicated that the log-linear transformation of the compensation income, and other data performs as well as the generalized Box-Cox transformation. The basic model is:

$$LnP_i = \beta_0 + \beta_1 LnINC + \beta_2 OE + \beta_3 sp + \beta_4 SALES + e_i$$

P_i = Dependent Variable i = 1, 2

1 = (Cash Salary + Bonus)

2 = (Cash Salary + Bonus + Long-Term Compensation)

INC = Net Income for the Year

OE = Organizational Effectiveness

SP = Social Performance

SALES = Sales for the Year

0 = Intercept Term

β_1, β_2, β_3, β_4 = Coefficients for the INC, OE, SP, and SALES

e_i = Error Term

Ln = Natural Log

The Sample

The following data requirements were imposed on the selection process for the firms: (1) each company was rated on organizational effectiveness and social performance in 1986 (Hutton, 1986, 16–20); (2) each company was currently (in 1986) listed on *Compustat* in order to obtain sales and assets data; and (3) executives' salaries were available for each company for the year 1986 in their annual reports, 10K report, or the *Business Week* executive pay survey (Byrne, 1987, 50–94). The final sample consisted of 155 firms from twenty-eight industries (see table 17.1).

Regression Results

The results for the model are shown in table 17.2 using as dependent variables (a) either salary plus bonus or (b) salary plus bonus, plus long-term compensation. As shown in both cases, heteroscedasticity in the residuals was observed after using the Glejser test (Johnston, 1972, 220). Nevertheless, all the independent variables were found to be significant with the predicted sign with one exception—the negative coefficient obtained for the social performance factor.

To correct for heteroscedasticity, a weighted least squares was used (Abdel-Khalik, 1985; Lewellen and Huntsman, 1970). Deflating the variables of executive compensation, size, and profits by the logarithm of total assets and then applying OLS is equivalent to using a weight least square (Commons, 1985, 459–62; Neter and Wasserman, 1974, 131–36).

This transformation yielded the following model:

$$\text{Lnpi/LnA} = b_0 \left(\frac{1}{\text{LnA}}\right) + b_1\text{LnINC/LnA} + b_2\text{OE}$$
$$+ b_3\text{SP} + b_4\text{LnSALES/LnA} + u_i$$
$$\text{LnA} = \text{Logarithm of Total Assets}$$

The results of the regression using the new form of the model are presented in table 17.3. As shown, there were drastic improvements in the significance of the regression and in the adjusted R^2 values. At the same time, the independent variables were found to be significant with the correct sign, with the exception

Table 17.1
Sample of Companies Used in the Study

Name	Industry	Name	Industry
Boeing	Aerospace		
Rockwell International	Aerospace	Becton Dickinson	Measuring, Scientific and Photographic Equipment
General Dynamics	Aerospace	EG & G	Measuring, Scientific and Photographic Equipment
Lockheed	Aerospace		
Martin Marietta	Aerospace	Eastman Kodak	Measuring, Scientific and Photographic Equipment
McDonnell Douglas	Aerospace		
Northrop	Aerospace	General Signal	Measuring, Scientific and Photographic Equipment
Textron	Aerospace		
United Technologies	Aerospace	Perkin-Elmer	Measuring, Scientific and Photographic Equipment
		Polaroid	Measuring, Scientific and Photographic Equipment
AMAX	Mining, Crude-Oil		
Standard Oil	Mining, Crude-Oil	Textronix	Measuring, Scientific and Photographic Equipment
Freeport-McMoran	Mining, Crude-Oil		
Vulcan Materials	Mining, Crude-Oil		
		Borg- Warner	Motor Vehicles Equipment
Archer Daniels Midland	Food	Dana	Motor Vehicles Equipment
Borden	Food	Ford Motor	Motor Vehicles Equipment
CPC International	Food	General Motors	Motor Vehicles Equipment
General Mills	Food	TRW	Motor Vehicles Equipment
Ralston Purina	Food		
Sara Lee Corporation	Food	Abbott Laboratories	Pharmaceuticals
		American Home Products	Pharmaceuticals
American Brands	Tobacco	Bristol-Meyers	Pharmaceuticals
Phillip Morris	Tobacco	Johnson & Johnson	Pharmaceuticals
Armstrong World Industries	Textiles, Vinyl Flooring	Eli Lilly	Pharmaceuticals
		Pfizer	Pharmaceuticals
Burlington Industries	Textiles, Vinyl Flooring	Smithkline Beckman	Pharmaceuticals
		Warner-Lambert	Pharmaceuticals
Gulf & Western Industries	Textiles, Vinyl Flooring		
		Avon	Soap, Cosmetics
VF	Textiles, Vinyl Flooring	Clorox	Soap, Cosmetics
		Colgate-Palmolive	Soap, Cosmetics
		International Flavors & Fragrances	Soap, Cosmetics
Boise Cascade	Paper, Fiber and Wood Products	Proctor & Gamble	Soap, Cosmetics
Georgia-Pacific	Paper, Fiber and Wood Products		
International Paper	Paper, Fiber and Wood Products	Control Data	Office Equipment (including Computers)
Kimberly-Clark	Paper, Fiber and Wood Products		
Mead	Paper, Fiber and Wood Products	Digital Equipment	Office Equipment
		Honeywell	Office Equipment
Scott Paper	Paper, Fiber and Wood Products	IBM	Office Equipment
		NCR	Office Equipment
Weyerhaeuser	Paper, Fiber and Wood Products	Pitney Bowes	Office Equipment
		Wang Laboratories	Office Equipment
R.R. Donnelley & Sons	Publishing, Printing	Catepillar Tractor	Industrial and Farm Equipment
Dow Jones	Publishing, Printing	Teledyne	Industrial and Farm Equipment
Gannett	Publishing, Printing	Combustion Engineering	Industrial and Farm Equipment
		Cummins Engine	Industrial and Farm Equipment
		Deere	Industrial and Farm Equipment

Table 17.1 cont'd

Name	Industry	Name	Industry
Knight-Ridder Newspapers	Publishing, Printing	American Standard	Ship Building, Railroad and Transportation Equipment
McGraw-Hill	Publishing, Printing		
New York Times	Publishing, Printing		
Times, Inc.	Publishing, Printing	Emhart	Industrial and Farm Equipment
Times Mirror	Publishing, Printing	Ingersoll-Rand	Industrial and Farm Equipment
Washington Post	Publishing, Printing		
		Anheuser-Busch	Beverages
Allied	Chemicals	Coca-Cola	Beverages
American Cyanamid	Chemicals	General Cinema	Beverages
E. I. DuPont De Nemours	Chemicals	Pepsico	Beverages
Hercules	Chemicals		
Monsanto	Chemicals		
Union Carbide	Chemicals	CBS	Diversified Service Companies
		Fluor	Diversified Service Companies
Amoco	Petroleum Refining		
Atlantic Richfield	Petroleum Refining		
Chevron	Petroleum Refining		
Mobil	Petroleum Refining		
Phillips Petroleum	Petroleum Refining		
U.S. Steel	Petroleum Refining		
Copper Tire & Rubber	Rubber, Plastic Products		
Firestone Tire & Rubber	Rubber, Plastic Products		
Gencorp	Rubber, Plastic Products		
B.F. Goodrich	Rubber, Plastic Products		
Corning Glass Works	Glass, Concrete, Abrasives		
PPG Industries	Gypsum		
Reynolds Metals	Metal Manufacturing		
American Can	Metal Products		
Ball	Metal Products		
Gillette	Metal Products		
Parket-Hannifin	Metal Products		
Stanley-Works	Metal Products		
American Telephone & Telegraph	Electronics, Appliances		
Emerson Electric	Electronics, Appliances		
ITT	Electronics, Appliances		
Litton Industries	Electronics, Appliances		
Motorola	Electronics, Appliances		
North American Philips	Electronics, Appliances		
Texas Instruments	Electronics, Appliances		
Westinghouse Electric	Electronics, Appliances		

of social performance which had a negative sign. Based on these results, it appears that the executive compensation computed as either salary plus bonus or salary plus bonus plus long-term compensation are positively related to size, profitability, and organizational effectiveness, and negatively related to social

Table 17.2
Regression Results

Independent Variable	Dependent Variable (in logarithm)	
	(Salary + Bonus) 1986	(Salary + Bonus + Long Term Compensation) 1986
Intercept	4.3410	4.4193
	(13.659)*	(9.444)*
Ln (Profit)	0.1131	0.1082
	(2.887)**	(1.977)**
Organizational Effectiveness	0.0897	0.0875
Social Performance	(3.681)*	(2.569)*
	-0.1414	-0.1551
Ln (Sales)	(-5.457)	(-4.282)*
	0.0921	0.1353
F	(2.091)**	(2.199)*
R^2 (Adjusted)	16.372*	10.540*
Heteroscedasticity	0.2935	0.2050
	Yes ($p < 0.05$)	Yes ($p < 0.05$)

*Significant at $\alpha=0.01$.
**Significant at $\alpha=0.05$.

Table 17.3
Regression Results Using Weighted Least Squares

Independent Variable	Dependent Variable (in logarithm)	
	(Salary + Bonus) 1986	(Salary + Bonus + Long Term Compensation) 1986
Intercept	-0.0388	-0.379
	(-0.736)	(-0.605)
Ln (Profit/Total Assets)	0.2157	0.2101
	(3.641)*	(2.987)*
Organizational Effectiveness	0.0082	0.0080
	(2.318)*	(1.986)**
Social Performance	-0.0196	-0.0208
	(-5.024)*	(-4.503)*
Ln(Sales/Total Assests)	0.5299	0.5570
	(8.663)	(7.670)*
F	43.275*	32.791*
R^2 (Adjusted)	0.5333	0.4621

*Significant at $\alpha=0.01$.
**Significant at $\alpha=0.05$.

performance. In terms of the four hypotheses stated in this study, it appears that the executive compensation decision of boards produce a positive correlation between executive compensation on the one hand, and profit, size, and organizational effectiveness on the other hand. Social performance does not appear to be a major external force considered by the executive compensation committee.

DISCUSSION AND LIMITATIONS

Results of this study provide additional evidence regarding linkages between executive performance and executive compensation. Findings revealed both a significant effect of internal and external control mechanisms available to the compensation committee boards upon executive compensation. Internal control mechanisms based on profit and sales had a significant impact upon compensation. Both sales to assets and profits to assets were significantly related to compensation providing additional evidence in the ongoing debate about the relative significance of both measures of performance (Ciscel and Carroll, 1980; Lewellen and Huntsman, 1970). The significance of both measures confirms earlier findings of their joint impact upon executive compensation (Baker, 1969; Boyes and Schlagenhauf, 1979). Partially linking compensation to sales growth protects the executives from the vagaries of the stock price movements. The results also provide additional evidence pertinent to manager-shareholder incentive compatibility issues. To the extent that executive compensation is positively and significantly associated with corporate sales and earnings, shareholder and managerial interests should be better aligned.

In addition to the internal control mechanisms, executive compensation was found to be positively associated with external perceptions of industry analysts and executives, regarding firm organizational effectiveness. These results provide additional evidence that executives are rewarded for perceived performance beyond defined historical financial measures. External information signals obtained from the managerial labor market with respect to executive performance are significantly related to firm compensation decisions. Interestingly, the significant negative relationship between external perceptions of firm social performance and executive compensation suggests that executives may be penalized for such activities.

Several limitations should be noted in interpreting the results. First, due to data restrictions, as the measures of organizational effectiveness and social performance were only available for 1986, the analysis was limited to a cross-sectional approach. Assuming future availability of data on organizational effectiveness, time-series analysis may be used to verify the findings. Second, the measure of organizational effectiveness was computed in the survey as a sum of the eight key attributes of reputation. While there is no a priori justification for a differential weighing of these eight attributes, it is conceivable that an alternative weighing could yield different results. Future research should extend the findings in light of the above limitations.

REFERENCES

Abdel-Khalik, A.R. 1985. The effect of LIFO-switching and firm ownership on executives' pay. *Journal of Accounting Research* 23: 427–47.

Alexander, G.J., and R.A. Buchholz. 1978. Corporate social responsibility and stock market performance. *Academy of Management Journal* 21: 479–86.

Antle, R., and A. Smith. 1986. An empirical investigation into relative performance evaluation of corporate executives. *Journal of Accounting Research* (Spring): 1–39.

Baker, S. 1969. Executive incomes, profit and revenues: A comment on functional specification. *Southern Economic Journal* (April): 379–83.

Baumol, W.J. 1967. *Business Behavior, Value, and Growth.* New York: Harcourt, Brace & World.

Benston, G.J. 1985. The self-serving management hypothesis: Some evidence. *Journal of Accounting and Economics* (April): 67–84.

Bowman, E.H., and M. Haire. 1985. A strategic posture toward corporate social responsibility. *California Management Review* 18, no. 2: 49–58.

Boyes, W.J., and D.E. Schlagenhauf. 1979. Managerial incentives and the specification of functional forms. *Southern Economic Journal* (April): 1225–32.

Bragdon, J.H., and J.A.T. Martin. 1979. Is pollution profitable? *Risk Management* 19, no. 4: 9–18.

Byrne, J.A. 1987. Executive pay: Who got what in '86. *Business Week* (May 4): 50–94.

Chen, K.H., and R.W. Metcalf. 1980. The relationship between pollution control and financial indicators revisited. *The Accounting Review* (January): 168–77.

Ciscel, D.H., and T.M. Carroll. 1980. The determinants of executive salaries: An econometric survey. *Review of Economics and Statistics* (February): 7–13.

Cochran, P.L., and R.A. Wood. 1984. Corporate social responsibility and financial performance. *Academy of Management Journal* 27: 42–56.

Commons, M.S. 1985. *Basic Econometrics.* London: Longman.

Connolly, T., E.J. Conlon, and S.T. Deutsh. 1980. Organizational effectiveness: A multiple-constituency approach. *Academy of Management Review* 5, no. 2: 211–17.

Cosh, A. 1975. The remuneration of chief executives in the United Kingdom. *Economic Journal* 85: 75–94.

Coughlan, A.T., and R.M. Schmidt. 1985. Executive compensation, management turnover, and firm performance: An empirical investigation. *Journal of Accounting and Economics* (April): 43–66.

Fogler, H.R., and F. Nutt. 1975. A note on social responsibility and stock valuation. *Academy of Management Journal* 18: 155–60.

Fox, H. 1980. *Top executive compensation: 1978.* New York: The Conference Board.

Healy, P.M., S.-H. Kang, and K.G. Palepu. 1987. The effect of accounting procedure changes on CEO's cash salary and bonus compensation. *Journal of Accounting and Economics* (April): 7–34.

Hewley, P.M. 1985. The effect of bonus schemes on accounting decisions. *Journal of Accounting and Economics* (April): 85–108.

Hirschey, M., and J.L. Pappas. 1981. Regulatory and life cycle influences of managerial incentives. *Southern Economic Journal* 48: 327–34.

Hogan, T.D., and L.R. McPheters. 1980. Executive compensation: Performance versus personal characteristics. *Southern Economic Journal* 46: 1060–68.

Hutton, C. 1986. America's most admired corporation. *Fortune* (January 6): 16–27.

Johnston, J. 1972. *Economic Methods.* New York: McGraw Hill.

Kedia, B.L., and E.C. Kuntz. 1981. The context of social performance: An empirical study of Texas Banks. In *Research in Corporate Social Performance and Policy,* Vol. 3, ed. L.E. Preston. Greenwich, CT: JAI Press, 133–54.

Keely, M.A. 1978. Social justice approach to organizational evaluation. *Administration Science Quarterly* 23: 272–92.

Kilman, R.H., and R.P. Herden. 1976. Towards a systematic methodology for evaluating the impact of interventions on organizational effectiveness. *Academy of Management Review* 1, no. 3: 87–98.

Lewellen, W.G., and B. Huntsman. 1970. Managerial pay and corporate performance. *American Economic Review* 60: 710–20.

Loomis, C.J. 1982. The madness of executive compensation. *Fortune* (July 12): 42–52.

Marris, R. 1963. A model of the managerial enterprise. *Quarterly Journal of Economics* 27: 185–209.

Masson, R.T. 1971. Executive motivations, earnings, and consequent equity performance. *Journal of Political Economy* 79: 1278–92.

McGuire, J.W., J.S.W. Chiu, and A.O. Elbing. 1962. Executive income sales and profits. *American Economic Review* 57: 753–61.

Mecks, G., and G. Whittington. 1981. Directors' pay, growth and profitability. *Journal of Industrial Economy* 3: 22–36.

Miles, R.H. 1980. *Macro-Organizational Behavior.* Glenview, IL: Scott, Foresman.

Moskowitz, P. 1975. Choosing socially responsible stocks. *Business and Society Review* 1: 71–75.

Murphy, K.J. 1985. Corporate performance and managerial remuneration: An empirical analysis. *Journal of Accounting and Economics* (April): 11–42.

Neter, H., and W. Wasserman. 1974. *Applied Linear Statistical Methods.* Homewood, IL: Irwin.

Parket, I.R., and H. Eilbirt. 1975. Social responsibility: Underlying factors. *Business Horizons* 18, no. 4: 5–10.

Price, J.L. 1972. The study of organizational effectiveness. *Sociological Quarterly* 13: 3–15.

Ramanathan, K.V. 1976. Toward a theory of corporate social accounting. *The Accounting Review* (July).

Rich, J.T., and J.A. Larson. 1984. Why some long-term incentives fail. *Compensation Review* 16, no. 1: 26–37.

Scott, W.R. 1981. *Organizations: Rational, Natural and Operational Systems.* Englewood Cliffs, NJ: Prentice Hall.

Smith, C.W., and R. Watts. 1992. The investment opportunity set and corporate financing, dividend, and compensation policies. *Journal of Financial Economics* 263–92.

Spicer, B.H. 1978a. Investors, corporate social performance and information disclosure: An empirical study. *The Accounting Review* (January): 94–111.

———. 1978b. Market risk, accounting data and companies' pollution control records. *Journal of Business Finance & Accounting* 5, no. 1 (Spring): 67–83.

Sturdivant, F.D., and J.L. Ginter. 1977. Corporate social responsiveness, management attitudes and economic performance. *California Management Review* 19, no. 3: 30–36.

Ullman, A.A. 1985. Data in search of a theory: A critical examination of the relationship among social performance, social disclosure and economic performance of U.S. firms. *The Academy of Management Review* (July): 540–57.

Vance, S.C. 1975. Are socially responsible corporations good investment risks? *Management Review* 64, no. 8: 15–24.

CHAPTER 18

Effects of Ownership Structure, Firm Performance, Size, and Diversification Strategy on CEO Compensation in U.S. Multinational Firms: A Path Analysis

INTRODUCTION

The purpose of this chapter is to expand the nature of the evidence on the determinants of compensation to CEOs of American industrial multinational corporations. Most research to date has focused on testing the relative importance of measures of firm performance as determinants of executive salaries in general, and CEOs in particular.

This study proposes that ownership structure and diversification strategy may have an important role in the determination of CEO compensation. Drawing on unique data on stock ownership obtained from the proxy statements of Fortune 500 firms, this study addressed the question, How does ownership structure and diversification strategy affect the determination of CEO compensation?

THEORETICAL FRAMEWORK

The research model is illustrated in figure 18.1. Each line represents a research hypothesis. Stock concentration, a proposed measure of ownership structure, and firm size are shown as influencing CEO compensation both directly and indirectly through the mediators of diversification strategy, management stockholdings and firm performance. Stock concentration is the level of stockholdings of major shareholders retaining a material proportion of the outstanding shares of the firm. The material proportion is set at 5%.

Stock Concentration and Management Stockholdings

The model assumes a differentiation between managers' and stockholders' interests. The distinction is based on the premise made in the literature on man-

Figure 18.1
Research Model

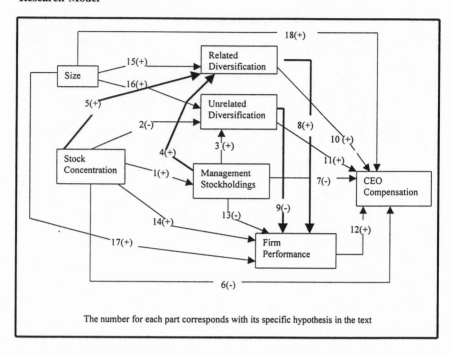

The number for each part corresponds with its specific hypothesis in the text

agerial discretion that, while stockholders are wealth maximizers requiring a maximization of efficiency, managers have a tendency to maximize a utility function which has remuneration, power, security, and status as major arguments, requiring a maximization of firm size and diversity (Aoki, 1984; Belkaoui, 1980; Gailbraith, 1961; Marris, 1964; Williamson, 1964).

The model also assumes, as Berle and Means (1932) argue, that stock concentration matters. Dispersion of stockholders' ownership allows managers holding little equity in the firm to forego shareholder wealth maximization in favor of their own interests rather than those of the stockholders. This is due to the presumed existence of information asymmetries and the inability of the shareholders to remove management in the case of diffused stock ownership (Aoki, 1984; Hill and Snell, 1989; Leech, 1987; Salancik and Pfeffer, 1980). To increase managers' holdings of stock and therefore better align the interests of owners and managers, stock-based compensation plans have been utilized (Demsetz, 1983; Lewellen, Loderer, and Rosenfeld, 1985). As stock ownership becomes more concentrated, owners are in a better position to take actions such as the implementation of stock-based compensation plans in order to align manager's interests with their own. An identical rationale was also used by Hill and Snell (1989). Therefore, we hypothesize that:

H_1: There will be a positive relationship between stock concentration and a firm's level of management stockholdings.

Ownership Structure and Diversification

The model distinguishes between two types of diversification, related and unrelated, and two types of ownership structure, stock concentration and management stockholdings. Diversification into unrelated businesses has been associated with both lower economic returns and lower risk than diversification into related businesses (Amit and Livnat, 1988; Bettis and Mahajan, 1985; Christensen and Montgomery, 1981; Rumelt, 1974, 1982). Given the divergence of interests of managers and owners, the pursuit of an unrelated diversification strategy would serve managers eager to maximize the size of the firm, which ultimately would lead to higher remuneration, power, and prestige (Marris, 1964; Mueller, 1969, 1978), while at the same time diversifying their own employment risk (Amihud and Lev, 1981). Stockholders, on the other hand, have little to gain from the risk-reducing effects of unrelated diversification (Levy and Sarnet, 1970) and will disapprove of a strategy that trades efficiency for an increase in size. Thus:

H_2: There will be a negative relationship between stock concentration and unrelated diversification.
H_3: There will be a positive relationship between the extent of management stockholdings and unrelated diversification.

Alternatively, diversification into related businesses has been associated with superior economic performance due to economies of scope resulting from skill transfers and revenue sharing (Porter, 1987; Teece, 1980). Related diversification is therefore both in the interests of stockholders and managers as their own holdings increase. Thus:

H_4: There will be a positive relationship between the extent of management stockholdings and related diversification.
H_5: There will be a positive relationship between stock concentration and related diversification.

Ownership Structure and Executive Compensation

While management is assumed to act as a surrogate for owners, the greater the separation of ownership and control indicates instead a difference between the interests of owners and management (Berle and Means, 1932; Galbraith, 1961). Various studies provide evidence supporting systematic differences between owner-controlled and management-controlled firms. Owner-controlled firms are reported to have higher profitability (McEachern, 1975) and to replace executives frequently when performance declines (Salancik and Pfeffer, 1980). Management-controlled firms are reported to show a tendency towards over-reporting of earnings (Saloman and Smith, 1979), to be more risk-adverse (Palmer, 1973), and to be more likely to engage in activities which violate antitrust laws (Blain and Kasserman, 1983). This evidence implies that for owner-controlled firms, the key determinants of the pay level of chief executives are the owners themselves. With increasing levels of stock concentration, owners are in direct competition for the correct distribution of total return of the firm and would vote a higher share for themselves. Thus:

H_6: There will be a negative relationship between stock concentration and CEO compensation.

Managers in manager-controlled firms are more likely to view other factors than performance as the key basis of their pay (Gomez-Mejia et al., 1987). Therefore, CEOs holding enough voting power to guarantee their jobs may favor pay packages which include bonuses and long-term income as opposed to base salary. Thus:

H_7: There will be a negative relationship between the extent of management stockholdings and CEO compensation.

Diversification and Performance

Empirical results on the effects of the implementation of a decentralized organizational structure on performance differentiated between the impact of related and unrelated diversification strategies on firm performance (Hoskrisson, 1987). Unrelated diversification is achieved when managers trade efficiency for an increase in firm size and decrease operating risks (Marris, 1964). In fact, empirical evidence shows that unrelated diversification is associated with lower economic return (Christensen and Montgomery, 1981; Rumelt, 1974, 1982) and lower risk (Amit and Livnat, 1988; Bettis and Mahajan, 1985) than related diversification. On the other hand, both theory and empirical results indicate an association of related diversification with superior economic performance (Bettis, 1981; Christensen and Montgomery, 1981; Rumelt, 1974, 1982). Thus:

H_8: There will be a positive relationship between performance and related diversification.
H_9: There will be a negative relationship between performance and unrelated diversification.

Executive Compensation and Diversification

Finkelstein and Hambrick (1988) suggested the interesting notion that compensation practices may drive diversification activity, and be a partial explanation for the often disappointing returns accrued. With the exception of a study by Harris (1983), there is a noticeable absence in the literature of empirical findings on the possible effects of organizational structure on executive compensation. Harris' study (1983) views executive compensation as a potential form of discretionary behavior, and that under a decentralized structure, opportunistic discretionary behavior is better controlled than under a centralized form of organization. Using time-series data for nineteen firms and a dummy variable for organizational structure, he finds evidence of a positive significant relationship between the decentralized form of organization and executive compensation. In addition, the control arrangements needed to implement decentralization are more complex and more demanding than with a centralized organization (Hill and Hoskisson, 1987). Thus:

H_{10}: There will be a positive relationship between unrelated diversification and CEO compensation.

H_{11}: There will be a positive relationship between related diversification and CEO compensation.

Firm Performance and Executive Compensation

There is ample evidence indicating a positive relationship between firm profitability and executive compensation (Antle and Smith, 1985, 1986; Ciscel and Carroll, 1980; Coughlin and Schmidt, 1985; Lambert and Larker, 1987; Larker, 1983; Lewellen and Huntsman, 1970; Masson, 1971; McGuire et al., 1962: Murphy, 1985; Watlel, 1978): This evidence shows that the executive compensation committees of the board of directors, in their search for incentive arrangements that will encourage management to act in the shareholders' interests, set compensation on the basis of financial performance. This is also consistent with the evidence provided by Smith and Watts (1982), indicating that the compensation plans approved by the boards of directors generally link pay to performance measures which are themselves related to shareholder wealth. One such performance measure is the accounting profit of the firm. Antle and Smith (1986) present two reasons why accounting measures, as opposed to market measures might be used. The first is related to the fact that stock prices impound all information relevant for evaluating the performance of the firm's management (Gjesdal, 1981). The second reason is that it is easier for the executive to hedge the risk from a contract based on stock returns than one based on accounting variables. Both accounting and market-based measures will be used in this study. Thus:

H_{12}: There will be a positive relationship between firm performance and CEO compensation.

Ownership Structure and Firm Performance

Building on Berle and Means's (1932) thesis on the deterioration in managerial efficiency associated with the separation of ownership and control characterizing the modern corporation, various theorists have examined the effects of such conflicts of interest of firm performance and the discretionary forces that may reduce managers' private returns (e.g., shirking and consumption of perquisites), i.e., the market for control (Manne, 1965), the managerial labor market (Fama, 1980), incentive contracts (Holmstrom, 1979, 1982; Shavell, 1979), and debt (Jensen, 1986). The empirical relationship between firm performance and corporate ownership structure is, however, characterized by mixed results (see, for example, Demsetz and Lehn, 1985; Morck, Shleifer, and Vishny, 1988; and Ravenscraft and Sherer, 1987). Two competing hypotheses characterize this relationship, namely: (a) the convergence-of-interest hypothesis and (b) the entrenchment hypothesis.

According to the convergence-of-interest hypothesis, market value as well as profitability increase with management ownership. Berle and Means (1932) argued that the dispersion of shareholders' ownership allows managers holding little equity in the firm to forego value maximization and use corporate assets to benefit themselves rather than their shareholders. Jensen and Meekling (1976) argued instead that the costs of deviation from value maximization decline as the manager's stake in the firm rises, as managers are less likely to squander corporate wealth when they have to pay a larger share of the costs.

According to the entrenchment hypothesis, market value as well as profitability does not rise with management ownership. Demsetz (1983) and Fama and Jensen (1983) have pointed out the offsetting costs associated with higher management stockholdings. If managers have a small stockholding, they will work towards value maximization as a result of factors including market discipline [e.g., the managerial labor market (Fama, 1980), the product market (Hart, 1983), and the market for corporate control (Jensen and Ruback, 1983)]. However, if managers hold a larger proportion of a firm's stock, giving them enough voting power to guarantee their jobs, they may opt for nonvalue maximization behavior. What the two hypotheses imply is that performance would be negatively related to increasing levels of management ownership. Thus:

H_{13}: There will be a negative relationship between a firm's financial performance and management stockholdings held at high ranges.

Stockholders are generally assumed to be wealth maximizers. As such, their view of managers' responsibility is the maximization of efficiency. With a large concentration of ownership, stockholders are in a position to coordinate action and demand information that will allow them to overcome any information asymmetries (Berle and Means, 1932). They are also in a better position to influence management's decisions and responsibility towards wealth maximization, and strategies that are in the stockholders' interest. Therefore, performance will be positively related to higher ranges of stock concentration. Thus:

H_{14}: There will be a positive relationship between a firm's performance and stock concentration held at high ranges.

The Effects of Size

The effects of firm size on diversification strategy, firm performance, and CEO compensation are well established in the literature. First, the effect of size on either related diversification or unrelated diversification strategy is positive in the sense that both strategies possibly imply a growing and expanding firm (Hoskisson, 1987). Therefore:

H_{15}: There will be a positive relationship between a firm's size and related diversification.
H_{16}: There will be a positive relationship between a firm's size and unrelated diversification.

Second, the effect of size on performance is positive in the sense that bigger firms have more resources to devote to profitable opportunities. The alternate hypothesis may be that bigger firms have more obsolete assets that hinder profitability. Therefore:

H_{17}: There will be a positive relationship between a firm's size and financial performance.

Third, the effect of size on CEO compensation is positive because of two possible rationales: (a) bigger firms tend to pay more because the CEO oversees substantial resources (Finkelstein and Hambrick, 1989), and (b) bigger firms have the ability to pay more (Ciscel and Carroll, 1980). Thus:

H_{18}: There will be a positive relationship between a firm's size and CEO compensation.

METHODS

Our hypotheses suggest that ownership structure and firm size affect CEO compensation directly. They also suggest that ownership structure and firm size affect executive compensation indirectly through the impact of stockholder and manager preferences on diversification strategy and firm performance. Given that both direct and indirect effects are postulated within the framework of the causal model, the model is a partial mediation model, and path analysis is the appropriate analytical strategy (James and Brett, 1984).

Table 18.1
Mean Values of Rate of Return on Assets and Executive Compensation for 197
Fortune 500 Companies in 1987 Grouped by Level of Management Stockholdings
(MSH)

MSH%	Number of Firms	Mean Rate of Return on Assets	Standard Error of Mean Rate of Return	Mean Executive Compensation	Standard Error of Compensation
0-5	133	.0729	.449	894.02	288.94
5-10	23	.0643	.0737	844.96	360.97
10-15	15	.0605	.0592	797.33	309.52
15-20	6	.0909	.0278	693.66	194.56
20-25	7	.0073	.1400	582.71	261.67
25-30	4	.0872	.0285	884.00	139.99
30-35	2	.1124	.0270	845.50	456.50
35-40	2	.0735	.0986	474.50	81.50
40-45	1	.0782	n/a	688.50	n/a
45-50	2	.0933	.0067	702.50	66.50
50-55	0	n/a	n/a	n/a	n/a
55-60	0	n/a	n/a	n/a	n/a
60-65	1	.0848	n/a	928.00	n/a
65-70	0	n/a	n/a	n/a	n/a
80-85	1	.1563	n/a	684.00	n/a

Dependent Variable

Cash compensation for the year 1987 (i.e., salary plus annual bonus) is used
as a measure of executive compensation. As discussions of the issues involved
in various compensation studies indicate, salary plus bonus is almost always a
significant portion of total compensation (salary plus bonus, long-term bonuses,
perquisites, pensions, grants of stock options) (Antle and Smith, 1986; Lambert
and Larker, 1987). In addition, evidence shows that salary plus bonus represents
between 80% and 90% of total compensation (Benston, 1985; Boot, Alien, and
Hamilton, 1988; Hay Associates, 1985). Finally, Jensen and Murphy (1987) also
provide evidence that indicates the slope coefficient relating salary plus bonus
to changes in performance is not statistically different from the slope coefficient
that relates total compensation to changes in performance.

Ownership Structure

This study avoided the weaknesses of previous studies that relied on a single
dichotomous variable, contrasting owner control and management control de-

Table 18.2
Mean Values of Rate of Return on Assets and Executive Compensation for 197
Fortune 500 Companies in 1987 Grouped by Level of Stock Concentration (STC)

STC%	Number of Firms	Mean Rate of Return on Assets	Standard Error of Mean of Rate of Return	Mean Executive Compensation	Standard Error of Mean of Executive Compensation
0-5	84	.0851	.0823	941.55	306.36
5-10	43	.0705	.0383	883.14	305.92
10-15	12	.0543	.0603	708.75	130.57
15-20	14	.0789	.0409	746.14	217.88
20-25	7	.0433	.0679	720.29	323.47
25-30	13	.0558	.0584	818.38	276.83
30-35	5	-.0044	.1158	563.60	166.26
35-40	5	.0011	.1207	591.00	312.55
40-45	3	.0388	.0499	760.33	262.44
45-50	2	.1089	.0645	1079.50	141.50
50-55	2	.1189	.0532	677.50	121.50
55-60	2	.0657	.0143	848.00	152.00
60-75	0	n/a	n/a	n/a	n/a
75-80	1	.0718	n/a	776.00	n/a
80-85	2	.0176	.0245	911.50	188.50
85-90	2	.0454	.0162	430.50	12.50

fined on the basis of some arbitrary statistical criteria for size of controlling stockholders. It also did not rely on the 1980 data assembled one time only by Corporate Data Exchange and used by most contemporary studies on ownership structure. Instead, the data were collected from the 1988 proxy statements of the firms. The stock concentration was computed as the share of ownership by outside stockholders owning more than 5% of the common voting stock in 1987. Management stockholdings were measured by the percentage of common voting stock held by management in 1987.

Diversification

The product count method, used in industrial organization literature, was used to determine the extent of related and unrelated diversification. The extent of unrelated diversification was measured by the number of two-digit SIC industries outside the primary two-digit industry that a firm was active in during 1987. The extent of related diversification was measured by the number of four-digit

Table 18.3
Pearson Correlations for All Variables

Variables	1	2	3	4	5	6	7
1. Executive Compensation							
2. Management Stockholdings Stock	-.206***						
3. Stock Concentration	-.251***	.178***					
4. Related Diversification	.158**	-.096	-.109				
5. Unrelated Diversification	.073	-.029	-.006	-.486***			
6. Profits over Assets	.162***	.203***	-.116	-.007	-.280***		
7. Market Value over Assets	.087	.161***	-.091	.052	-.293***	.711***	
8. Assets	.264***	-.174**	-.173***	-.027	1.72**	-.167**	-.262***

*p<.10   **p<.05   ***p<.01

SIC industries within its main two-digit industry that a firm was active in during 1987. Dunn and Bradstreet's *Reference Book of Corporate Management* was used to collect the data. The rationale used for the choice is that although not all of a firm's diversification outside of its primary two-digit industry is necessarily unrelated to its core skills, the greater the extent of a firm's involvement in activities outside its primary two-digit industry, the more likely it is that some are unrelated to its core skills. These SIC-based measures compared to the categorical measures devised by Rumelt (1974) were found to be both continuous measures of diversification that reflect more accurately the diversification differences between firms, and at the same time less subjective measures (Montgomery, 1982).

Firm Performance and Size

Firm performance was measured as profit over total assets for the year 1987. To assess the sensitivity of the results to alternative measures of firm performance, the study was replicated using other measures such as net assets after taxes for the year 1987 and Tobin's Q, defined as market value/historical cost of the assets in 1987. The results for the alternative measures were found to be similar to those based on the rate of return on total assets in terms of sign and significance of coefficients. Firm size was measured by total assets for the year 1987.

Table 18.4
Results of the Regression Analysis[a]

Independent Variables	Regression # 1[b]	Regression # 2[c]
Related Diversification	0.17553 (2.146)**	0.23331 (3.032)*
Unrelated Diversification	.22952 (2.738)**	0.23610 (2.989)*
Management Stockholdings	-0.09707 (1.392)***	-0.14239 (-2.127)**
Stock Concentration	-0.15998 (-2.281)**	-0.13307 (-1.979)**
Profits over Assets (log)	0.23161 (3.200)*	——
Market Value over Total Assets (log)	——	0.22019 (3.156)*
Total Assets	0.27559 (3.925)*	0.26471 (30854)*
R^2 (Adjusted)	18.11%	19.39%
F	7.78*	8.859*

[a]Standardized betas are reported. t-statistics are in the parentheses. The significance levels are indicated as follows: * for <.01, ** for <.05, and *** for <.10.
[b]Regression 1 is where performance is measured as logarithm of profit over assets.
[c]Regression 2 is where performance is measured as logarithm of market value over total assets.

Sample

To insure the greatest sample of firms for which data will be available for ownership structure, diversification strategy, size, performance, and CEO compensation, the initial sample chosen was the Fortune 500 industrial corporations. The next step was to collect the needed information from the *Compustat* tape, the proxy statements, the 1988 *Business Week* compensation survey, and other sources.

The final sample included 216 companies from twenty-eight different industries. Tables 18.1 and 18.2 present relevant statistics on ownership structure,

Table 18.5
Initial Path Coefficients

Variables	1	2	3	4	5	6
1. Related Diversification			-0.04950	-0.1278		-0.8433
2. Unrelated Diversification			0.05390	0.6579		0.0862
3. Management Stockholdings				0.1433**		
4. Stock Concentration						
5. Profit over assets, log.	-0.18397**	-0.32083*	0.20307*	-0.13102***		-0.20626*
6. Total Assets						
7. CEO Compensation, Log.	0.17553**	0.22952*	-0.09707***	-0.15998**	0.23161*	0.27559*

$*p<0.01$ $**p<0.05$ $***p<0.10$

performance, and CEO compensation based upon available data for the firms included in the sample.

RESULTS

The logarithm of executive compensation and of return on assets was used in the analysis. Both variables, before transformation, were skewed to the right. If the distribution of the variables is skewed to the right, using a logarithmic transformation helps to normalize them. Table 18.3 gives the correlation for all the variables. The analysis proceeded in two steps: The first was the use of regression analysis to test the effects of all the independent variables on executive compensation, and the second relied on path analysis to test for the direct and indirect effects of ownership structure and firm size on executive compensation.

Regression Model

Table 18.4 reports the results of the tests for the determinants of executive compensation differences between firms. The results of two regression equations are reported, one with performance measured as the logarithm of profit over assets, and one for performance measured as the logarithm of market value over book value of total assets.

The results of both equations were significant and explained an adequate amount of variance. The signs in both equations were as expected. In what follows, the results of the path analysis will be shown with performance measured as the logarithm of profits over assets. The results of the path analysis using performance as the logarithm of market value over book value of assets,

Figure 18.2
Final Path Model and Coefficients

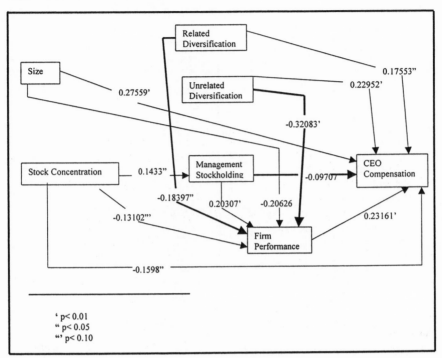

and other measures of performance are similar in terms of sign and significance
to the reported results in the study.

Path Analysis

Path analysis was used to test the partial mediation model set out in figure
18.1. The initial path coefficients were derived by regressing each variable on
all prior variables in the model. The initial path coefficients are shown in Table
18.5.

In accordance with the theory-trimming approach to path analysis suggested
by James and Brett (1984) the coefficients not significant at the 10% acceptance
level or better are assumed to be zero and are excluded from the final estimation
of path coefficients. The final estimates are reported in figure 18.2. The decomposition of the causal relationships shown in figure 18.2 is reported in table
18.6.

Mixed support is shown for the path model described in figure 18.1. All paths
emanating from diversification strategy to ownership structure and size were
found to be insignificant. Significant evidence was, however, found for all the

Table 18.6
Decomposition Table for the Final Path Model

	Causal Path		
Bivariate Relationships	Direct	Indirect	Total
1. CEO Compensation and Related Diversification	0.17553	(0.18397)(0.23161)=0.04261	0.21814
2. CEO Compensation and Unrelated Diversification	0.22952	(0.32083)(0.23161)=0.07431	0.30383
3. CEO Compensation and Firm Performance	0.2316		0.23161
4. CEO Compensation and Management	-0.09707	(0.20307)(0.23161)=0.04703	0.14410
5. CEO Compensation and Size	0.27559	(0.20626)(0.23161)=0.04777	0.32366
6. CEO Compensation Stock Concentration	-0.15998	(0.1433)(0.09707)+(0.1433) (0.20307)(0.23161)+(0.13102) (0.23161)=0.05099	0.21097
7. Firm Performance and Related Diversification	-0.18397		0.1837
8. Firm Performance and Unrelated Diversification	-0.32083		0.32083
9. Firm Performance and Size	0.20626		0.20626
10. Firm Performance and Mngt. Stockholdings	0.20307		0.20307
11. Firm Performance and Stock Concentration	0.13102	(0.1433)(0.20307)=0.02910	0.16012
12. Stock Concentration and Management Stockholdings	0.1433		0.1433

other hypothesized paths. Basically, the results suggest that ownership structure, firm size, and diversification strategy affect CEO compensation directly and indirectly through the mediator of firm performance. Table 18.6 shows that (a) 75.84% of the effect of stock concentration on CEO compensation was direct and 24.16% was mediated by firm performance and management stockholdings, (b) 67.36% of the effect of management stockholdings on executive compensation was direct and 32.64% was mediated by firm performance, (c) 80.47% of the effect of related diversification was direct and 19.53% was mediated by firm performance, (d) 75.54% of the effect of unrelated diversification was direct and 24.46% was mediated by firm performance, and (e) 85.23% of the effect of size was direct and 14.77% was mediated by firm performance.

DISCUSSION AND CONCLUSIONS

This study shows the importance of size, management stockholdings, stock concentration, related diversification, unrelated diversification, and firm performance on compensation. The negative relationship observed between stock concentration and management stockholdings on one hand, and CEO compensation on the other, lend support to the view that powerful stockholders may vote a higher share of the resources to themselves rather than to the executives, and to the view that powerful managers may prefer pay packages favoring bonuses and long-term income rather than base salary (Gomez-Mejia et al., 1987).

The negative relationship between stock concentration and firm performance indicates that the low levels of stock concentration in our sample did not allow the stockholders to overcome the information asymmetries and force management to act in the stockholders' interest. Similarly, the positive relationship between management stockholdings and firm performance indicates that the managers do not own enough voting power to focus on nonvalue maximization behavior as indicated by the entrenchment hypothesis. On the contrary, managers in our sample own a sufficient share of the firm to justify a convergence of interest with the shareholders on profit.

The negative relationship between the two types of diversification strategy and firm performance is consistent with the theory and other studies in the case of unrelated diversification and different in the case of related diversification. The evidence presented in this study is that related diversification is not associated with superior economic return. The same phenomena was observed by Hoskisson (1987) with the rationale that the decline in performance may be due to the lack of ability to allocate resources between interdependent divisions.

The positive relationship between the two types of diversification strategy and CEO compensation is inconsistent with the view that the control arrangements under the M-form of organization are more demanding than under the U-form, dictating the need for higher pay for executives in companies adopting a related or unrelated diversification strategy.

The insignificant results between ownership structure and diversification strategy may be due to the realization by stockholders and managers alike of the formidable implementation problems created by related and unrelated diversification strategies (Hill and Hoskisson, 1987).

The most important results confirm that in addition to a direct effect, size, ownership structure, and diversification strategy have an indirect effect on CEO compensation through the impact and/or influence of firm performance. The mediating relationships support the contention that (a) economic performance can be used as the key justification by owners and managers in the final determination of CEO compensation, and (b) size and the extent of related and/or unrelated diversification can be used as determinants of CEO compensation when associated with the right economic performance.

In conclusion, from a management perspective, the study underlies the importance of size, ownership structure, diversification strategy, and firm performance in the determination of CEO compensation.

Three limitations, however, characterize this study and need to be addressed in future research: (1) A limitation arises from viewing the determinants of CEO compensation cross-sectionally as current pay depends on the CEO's cumulative performance during his tenure (Finkelstein and Hambrick, 1988). A multiperiod study of the determinants of CEO compensation as defined in this study may be needed to observe the "settling-up" process (Fama, 1980); (2) While this study accounts for the size of the firms, various other probable determinants of compensation need to be accounted for. Examples include industry differences between firms, credentials of CEOs, and board structure to only name a few; and (3) This study relied on product count measures of diversification. Replication may be needed to evaluate the sensitivity of the results to other measures of diversification, such as Herfindahl-type measures (Montgomery, 1982).

REFERENCES

Amihud, Y., and B. Lev. 1981. Risk reduction as a managerial motive for conglomerate mergers. *Bell Journal of Economics* 12: 605–17.

Amit, R., and J. Livnat. 1988. Diversification and the risk-return tradeoff. *Academy of Management Journal* 3: 154–65.

Antle, R., and A. Smith. 1985. Measuring executive compensation: Methods and an application. *Journal of Accounting Research*: (Spring): 296–337.

———. 1986. An empirical investigation into relative performance evaluation of corporate executives. *Journal of Accounting Research* (Spring): 1–39.

Aoki, M. 1984. *The Co-operative Game Theory of the Firm.* Oxford, U.K.: Clarendon Press.

Belkaoui, A. 1980. *Conceptual Foundations of Management Accounting.* Reading, MA: Addison Wesley.

Benston, G. 1985. The self-serving hypothesis: Some evidence. *Journal of Accounting and Economics.* (April): 67–84.

Berle, A.A., and G.C. Means. 1932. *The Modem Corporation.* New York: MacMillan.

Bettis, R.A. 1981. Performance differences in related and unrelated diversified firms. *Strategic Management Journal* 2: 379–93.

Bettis, R.A., and V. Mahajan. 1985. Risk/return performance of diversified firms. *Management Science* 31: 785–99.

Blain, R., and L. Kasserman. 1983. Ownership and control in modern organizations: Antitrust implications. *Journal of Business Research* 11: 333–44.

Boot, Alien, and Hamilton. 1988. *Executive Pay in the Eighties: Major Exposures Ahead.* New York: Boot, Alien and Hamilton.

Christensen, H.K., and C.A. Montgomery. 1981. Corporate economic performance: diversification strategy versus market structure. *Strategic Management Journal* 2: 327–43.

Ciscel, D., and T. Carroll. 1980. The determinants of executive salaries: An econometric survey. *Review of Economics and Statistics* (February): 7–13.

Coughlin, A., and R. Schmidt. 1985. Executive compensation, management turnover, and firm performance: An empirical investigation. *Journal of Accounting and Economics* (April): 43–66.

Demsetz, H. 1983. The structure of ownership and the theory of the firm. *Journal of Law and Economics* 26: 375–90.

Demsetz, H., and K. Lehn. 1985. The structure of corporate ownership: theory and consequences. *Journal of Political Economy* 93: 1155–77.

Fama, E.F. 1980. Agency problems and the theory of the firm. *Journal of Political Economy* 88: 288–307.

Fama, E.F., and M.C. Jensen. 1983. Agency problems and residual claims. *Journal of Law and Economics* 20: 327–49.

Finkelstein, S., and D. Hambrick. 1988. Chief executive compensation: A synthesis and reconciliation. *Strategic Management Journal* 9: 543–58.

———. 1989. Chief executive compensation: A study of the intersection of markets and political processes. *Strategic Management Journal* 10 (April): 121–34.

Galbraith, J.K. 1961. *The New Industrial State.* New York: New American Library.

Gjesdal, F. 1981. Accounting for stewardship. *Journal of Accounting Research* (Spring): 208–31.

Gomez-Mejia, L., H. Tosi, and T. Hinkin. 1987. Managerial control, performance and executive compensation. *Academy of Management Journal* 30: 51–70.

Gordon, R.A. . Ownership and compensation as incentives to corporate executives. *Quarterly Journal of Economics* (May).

Harris, B.C. 1983. Organization, the effect on large corporations. *Research in Business Economics and Public Policy*, no. 2. Ann Arbor, MI: UMI Research Press.

Hart, O.D. 1983. The market mechanism as an incentive scheme. *Bell Journal of Economics* 14: 366–82.

Hay Associates. 1985. Fifth annual Hay report on executive compensation. *Wharton Magazine* (April): 85–107.

Hill, C.W.L., and R.E. Hoskisson. 1987. Strategy and structure in the muitiproduct. *Academy of Management Review* 12: 331–41.

Hill, C.W.L., and S.A. Snell. 1989. Effects of ownership structure and control on corporate productivity. *Academy of Management Journal* 32: 25–46.

Holstrom, B. 1979. Moral hazard and observability. *Bell Journal of Economics* (Spring): 74–91.

———. 1982. Moral hazard in teams. *Bell Journal of Economics* (Autumn): 324–40.

Hoskisson, R.E. 1987. Multidivisional structure and performance: The contingency of diversification strategy. *Academy of Management Journal* 30, no. 4: 625–44.

James, LR., and J.M. Brett. 1984. Mediators, moderators and tests for mediation. *Journal of Applied Psychology* 69: 307–21.

Jensen, M. 1986. Agency costs of free cash flow, corporate finance, and takeover. *The American Economic Review* : 323–99.

Jensen, M., and W.H. Meekling. 1976. Theory of the firm and managerial behavior, agency costs, and ownership structure. *Journal of Financial Economics* 3: 305–60.

Jensen, M., and E. Murphy. 1987. Are executive compensation contracts structured properly? Working paper, University of Rochester.

Jensen, M., and R. Ruback. 1983. The market for corporate control: The scientific evidence. *Journal of Financial Economics* 11: 5–50.

Lambert, R.A., and D.E. Larker. 1987. An analysis of the use of accounting and market measures of performance in executive compensation contracts. *Studies in Stewardship Uses of Accounting Information, Supplement to the Journal of Accounting Research.*

Larker, D. 1983. The association between performance plan adoption and corporate capital investment. *Journal of Accounting and Economics* (April): 3–30.

Leech, D. 1987. Ownership concentration and the theory of the firm: A simple game theoretical approach. *Journal of Industrial Dynamics* 35: 225–40.

Levy, H., and M. Sarnet. 1970. Diversification: Portfolio analysis and the uneasy case for conglomerate mergers. *Journal of Finance* 25: 795–802.

Lewellen, W.G., and B. Huntsman. 1970. Managerial pay and corporate performance. *American Economic Review* (September): 710–20.

Lewellen, W.G., C. Loderer, and A. Rosenfeld. 1985. Merger decisions and executive stock ownership in acquiring firms. *Journal of Accounting and Economics* 7: 209–31.

Manne, H. 1965. Mergers and the market for corporate control. *Journal of Political Economy* 73: 110–20.

Marris, R. 1964. *The Economic Theory of Managerial Capitalism.* London: Macmillan.

Masson, R.T. 1971. Executive motivations, earnings and consequent equity performance. *Journal of Political Economy* (December): 1278–92.

McEachern, W.A. 1975. *Managerial Control and Performance.* Lexington, MA: D.C. Health Co.

McGuire, J., J. Chiu, and A. Elbing. 1962. Executive incomes, sales and profits. *American Economic Review* (September): 753–61.

Montgomery, C.A. 1982. The measurement of firm diversification: Some new empirical evidence. *Academy of Management Journal* 25: 299–307.

Morck, R.A., Shleifer, and R.W. Vishny. 1988. Management ownership and market valuation: An empirical analysis. *Journal of Financial Economics* 20: 293–315.

Mueller, D.T.C. 1969. A theory of conglomerate mergers. *Quarterly Journal of Economics* 83: 643–59.

———. 1978. The effects of conglomerate mergers. *Journal of Banking and Finance* 1: 315–47.

Murphy, K. 1985. Corporate performance and managerial remuneration: An empirical analysis. *Journal of Accounting and Economics* (April): 11–42.

Palmer, J. 1973. The profit variability effects of managerial enterprise. *Western Economic Journal* 2: 228–31.

Porter, M.E. 1987. From competitive advantage to corporate strategy. *Harvard Business Review* 3: 43–59.

Ravenscraft, D., and F.M. Sherer. 1987. Life after takeover. *The Journal of Industrial Economics* (December): 147–56.

Rumelt, R.P. 1974. *Strategy, Structure and Economic Performance*. Cambridge, MA: Harvard University Press.

————. 1982. Diversification strategy and profitability. *Strategic Management Journal* 3: 359–65.

Salancik, G.R., and J. Pfeffer. 1980. The effects of ownership and performance on executive tenure in U.S. corporations. *Academy of Management Journal* 23: 653–64.

Saloman, G.L., and E.D. Smith. 1979. Corporate control and managerial misrepresentation of firm performance. *Bell Journal of Economics* 10: 315–28.

Shavell, S. 1979. Risk sharing and incentives in the principal and agent relationship. *The Journal of Economics* (Spring): 55–73.

Smith, C., and R. Watts. 1982. Incentive and tax effects of executive compensation plans. *Australian Journal of Management* 7: 139–57.

Teece, D.J. 1980. Economics of scope and the scope of the enterprise. *Journal of Economic Behavior and Organization* 3: 223–47.

Watlel, H. 1978. Chief executive officer compensation. *Hofstra University Yearbook of Business*. New York: Hofstra University.

Williamson, O. 1964. *The Economics of Discretionary Behavior: Managerial Objectives in a Theory of the Firm*. Englewood Cliffs, NJ: Prentice-Hall.

CHAPTER 19

Determinants of Executive Tenure in Large U.S. Multinational Firms

INTRODUCTION

The purpose of this chapter is to expand on the nature of the evidence on the determinants of executive tenure of the CEOs of large American industrial corporations. Salancik and Pfeffer (1980) related executive tenure to both ownership and performance. Performance measures were found to be related to the tenure of chief executives depending on the concentration of stock ownership. Basically, tenure was unrelated to performance for owner-managed firms, positively related to profit margins in externally controlled firms, and positively related to stock market returns in management-controlled firms.

This study proposes a different way of expressing performance and ownership structure, and adds diversification strategy and CEO compensation level as important variables affecting executive tenure. Drawing on unique data on CEOs from a sample of Fortune 500 firms, the study addresses the question: How does performance, compensation level, diversification strategy, and ownership structure affect the tenure of CEOs in large U.S. firms?

DETERMINANTS OF EXECUTIVE TENURE

The research model is illustrated in Figure 19.1. Each line represents a specific research hypothesis. Related diversification, unrelated diversification, and stock concentration are shown to be negatively related to executive tenure. Management stockholdings, performance, and compensation levels are shown to be positively related to executive tenure.

Figure 19.1
Research Model

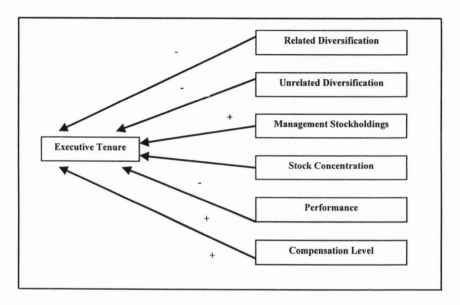

Executive Tenure and Diversification Strategy

The strategic management literature differentiates between two types of diversification strategies: related and unrelated. Firms adopting a related strategy diversify predominantly within their industries, while those adopting an unrelated strategy diversify predominantly across industries (e.g., Rumelt, 1974). To realize the benefits associated with pursuing either of the two strategies within an M-form (multidivisional) firm structure, control requirements that fit the strategies are required (Hill and Hoskisson, 1987). These controls involve determination of the degrees of decentralization of decisions to divisions, decomposition between divisions, and accountability for divisional profits.

As these controls need to be updated, revised, and adapted to new environmental characteristics, the situation calls for the use of different managerial styles to effect changes. Different executives may be needed to adopt different controls as the firms increase their diversification programs. The argument is that when an organization diversifies its activities according to a related or unrelated strategy, different executives are needed to adopt and adapt new control mechanisms that fit these strategies, and replacement of managers might be expected. From the above reasoning, the first hypothesis is derived:

Hypothesis 1: Diversification strategy affects executive tenure. Tenure will be negatively related to the level of related and unrelated diversification.

Ownership Structure and Executive Tenure

Ownership represents a source of power that can affect executive tenure. Various studies have examined the impact of ownership structure on executive tenure (Pfeffer and Salancik, 1977; Salancik and Pfeffer, 1980). Our study differentiates between managers' and stockholders' interests, and views the firm as an imperfect and unstable risk-sharing arrangement between managers, employees, and shareholders that is in flux rather than in equilibrium (Coffee, 1988). The distinction between managers' and stockholders' interests is based on the following premises made in the literature on managerial discretion: While stockholders are wealth maximizers requiring a maximization of efficiency, managers have a tendency to overemphasize a personal utility function that has remuneration, power, security, and status as major arguments, requiring a maximization of firm size and diversity (Aoki, 1984; Belkaoui, 1980; Belkaoui and Pavlik, 1992; Galbraith, 1967; Marris, 1964; Pavlik and Belkaoui, 1991; Williamson, 1964). The impact of ownership structure on executive tenure is assumed to differ depending on whether ownership structure is expressed by stock concentration or management stockholdings.

First, according to the entrenchment hypothesis, market value and profitability of a firm do not increase with management ownership. Demsetz (1983) and Fama and Jensen (1983) have pointed out the offsetting costs associated with higher management stockholdings. If managers hold a large enough proportion of the common stock, they will opt for nonvalue maximizing behavior and behavior that would increase their tenure with the firm.

Second, with concentrated ownership, stockholders are better able to both coordinate action and demand information that will allow them to overcome any information asymmetries (Berle and Means, 1932), and influence management's decisions and responsibility towards value maximization, and strategies that are in the stockholders' interests. The power, given to them by stock concentration, puts owners in more instances to oppose management's policies, even in the case of good performance. Accordingly:

Hypothesis 2: There will be a positive relationship between management stockholdings and executive tenure.
Hypothesis 3: There will be a negative relationship between stock concentration and executive tenure.

Performance and Executive Tenure

Common sense dictates that a poor firm performance will cause a manager to be replaced. Evidence, in fact, supports a positive association between performance and executive tenure. This includes findings that (a) chief executives are more likely to quit after a four-year or more decline in profits (McEachern, 1975); (b) executive tenure was negatively related to financial risk (Pfeffer and

Leblebici, 1973); (c) baseball managers are likely to be dismissed with declining team performance (Grusky, 1961); (d) academic department heads are likely to quit in difficult times in terms of resource acquisition; (e) hospital administrators have lower tenure when there is great competition for funding and staff (Pfeffer and Salancik, 1977); and (f) tenure is related positively to profit margins for externally controlled firms, and to stock market rates of return for management controlled firms (Salancik and Pfeffer, 1980). Accordingly:

Hypothesis 4: There will be a positive relationship between firm performance and executive tenure.

Executive Tenure and Level of Compensation

It is customary to use the level of executive salary as the appropriate dependent variable in the empirical estimation of the determinants of executive compensation. The rationale is that the level of executive salary is the most important reason for seeking employment with the firm and it should be set commensurate with the firm performance. There are, of course, transaction costs to the firm of hiring a new executive and to the departing executive upon leaving the firm. Consequently, these transaction costs define a bargaining range within which the executive salary may vary without creating an incentive for the firm to let an executive go and without motivating the executive to leave (Masson, 1971). If the level of salary is below this range, or if a competing firm offers a level of salary beyond this range, an executive may be tempted to leave. Therefore, executive tenure is a positive function of the level of compensation.

Hypothesis 5: There will be a positive relationship between executive tenure and the level of executive compensation. The higher the level of executive compensation, the longer the tenure.

METHODS

Model and Measurement of Variables

The five hypotheses state that executive tenure is negatively connected to related and unrelated diversification and stock concentration, and positively related to firm performance, management stockholdings, and level of compensation. The linear regression model follows:

$$ET_i = a_1 + a_2 + a_3 UTD_i + a_4 MSH_i + a_5 STC_i + a_6 PERF_i + a_7 COMP_i + \mu_i$$

where:

ET_i = Executive tenure

RTD_i = Related diversification

UTD_i = Unrelated diversification

MSH_i = Management stockholdings

STC_i = Stock concentration

$PERF_i$ = Firm performance

$COMP_i$ = Level of compensation

The variables were measured as follows:

1. The dependent variable of executive tenure was measured according to the number of years as CEO up to 1987.

2. The product-count method was used to determine the extent of related and unrelated diversification. The extent of unrelated diversification was measured by the number of two-digit SIC industries outside the primary two-digit industry in which the firm was active during 1987. The extent of related diversification was measured by the number of four-digit SIC industries within the main two-digit industry in which the firm was active during 1987. Dunn and Bradstreet's *Reference Book of Corporate Management* was used to collect the data.

3. Ownership structure was measured by both management stockholdings and stock concentration. The data were collected from 1988 proxy statements. Stock concentration was computed as the share of ownership by outside stockholders owning more than 5% of the common voting stock in 1987. Management stockholdings were measured by the percentage of common voting stock held by officers and directors in 1987.

4. Firm performance was measured by the 1987 profit deflated by the 1987 level of executive compensation.

Sample

To ensure a large sample size with readily available data, the initial sample chosen was the Fortune 500 industrial corporations; the information needed was gathered from both the *Compustat* tape and the 1988 *Business Week* survey of executive compensation. The final sample for which information on all variables was available included 196 companies from twenty-eight different industries.

RESULTS AND DISCUSSION

Table 19.1 presents the results of the regression model which relates executive tenure in large U.S. corporations and related diversification, unrelated diversification, management stockholdings, stock concentration, firm performance, and level of compensation for the year 1987. As predicted in the five hypotheses, executive tenure in large U.S. corporations is negatively connected to unrelated and related diversification, and to stock concentration, and positively related to management stockholdings, firm performance, and the level of compensation.

Table 19.1
1987 Cross-Section Estimates [1]

Dependent Variables: Executive Tenure		
Intercept	-22.301	(-2.336)**
Related Diversification	-1.326	(-3.137)*
Unrelated Diversification	-1.348	(-2.704)*
Management Stockholdings	0.146	(3.143)*
Stock Concentration	-0.0617	(-2.076)**
Profit/Compensation	2.539	(2.041)**
Compensation	5.111	(3.555)*

[1]Value of t-statistic in parentheses
*Significant at $\alpha=0.01$.
**Significant at $\alpha=0.05$.

It appears as if tenure with a firm depends on the manager's actions, which include (a) holding enough voting power via the acquisition of enough stock; (b) ensuring an adequate firm performance through a judicious allocation of resources and value-maximization behavior; and (c) negotiating an adequate level of executive compensation within a broad acceptable range. Furthermore, it seems that tenure is also affected by the actions of others, namely the shareholders that can (a) hold enough voting power through acquisition of stock; and (b) call for policies of diversification that demand the constant upgrading of control mechanisms and consequently the turnover of executives.

Executive tenure appears to be a complex phenomenon that depends on a host of important environmental factors. Other factors that have not been included in this study need to be investigated. Future research should also investigate the relationship examined here for other contracts and time periods.

REFERENCES

Aoki, M. 1984. *The Cooperative Game Theory of the Firm*. Oxford: Clarendon Press.

Belkaoui, A. 1980. *Conceptual Foundations of Management Accounting*. Reading, MA: Addison Wesley.

Belkaoui, A., and E. Pavlik. 1992. The effects of ownership structure and diversification strategy on performance. *Managerial and Decision Economics* 13: 343–52.

Berle, A.A., and G.C. Means. 1932. *The Modern Corporation*. New York: Macmillan.

Coffee, J.C. 1988. Shareholders versus managers: The strain in the corporate web. In J.C. Coffee et al., *Knights, Raiders and Targets: The Impact of the Hostile Takeover*. New York: Oxford University Press.

Demsetz, H. 1983. The structure of ownership and the theory of the firm. *Journal of Law and Economics* 26: 375–90.

Fama, E.F., and M.C. Jensen. 1983. Agency problems and residual claims. *Journal of Law and Economics* 20: 327–45.

Galbraith, J.K. 1967. *The New Industrial State*. New York: New American Library.

Grusky, O. 1961. Managerial succession and organizational effectiveness. *American Journal of Sociology* 67: 263–69.

Hill, C.W.L., and R.E. Hoskisson. 1987. Strategy and structure in the multiproduct firm. *Academy of Management Review* 12: 331–41.

Marris, R. 1964. *The Economic Theory of Managerial Capitalism*. New York: Free Press.

Masson, R.T. 1971. Executive motivation, earnings and consequent equity performance. *Journal of Political Economy* 75: 1278–92.

McEachern, W.K. 1975. *Managerial Control and Performance*. Lexington, MA: Lexington Books.

Pavlik, E., and A. Belkaoui. 1991. *Determinants of Executive Compensation*. Westport, CT: Quorum Books.

Pfeffer, J., and H. Leblebici. 1973. Executive recruitment and the development of interfirm organizations. *Administrative Science Quarterly* 18: 449–61.

Pfeffer, J., and G.R. Salancik. 1977. Organizational context and the characteristics and tenure of hospital administrators. *Academy of Management Journal* 20: 74–88.

Rumelt, R.P. 1974. *Strategy, Structure and Economic Performance*. Cambridge, MA: Harvard University Press.

Salancik, G.R., and J. Pfeffer. 1980. Effects of ownership and performance on executive tenure in U.S. corporations. *Academy of Management Journal* 23: 653–64.

Williamson, O.E. 1964. *The Economics of Discretionary Behavior: Managerial Objectives in a Theory of the Firm*. Englewood Cliffs, NJ: Prentice Hall.

CHAPTER 20

An Analysis of the Use of Accounting and Market Measures of Performance, CEO Experience, and Nature of the Deviation from the Analysts' Forecasts in CEO Compensation Contracts of Multinational Firms

INTRODUCTION

The purpose of this chapter is to expand the nature of the evidence on the determinants of compensation for CEOs of American industrial multinational corporations. Most research to date has focused on measures of performance as determinants of executive salaries in general, and CEOs in particular. This study proposes that such measures of performance are not the sole determinants of compensation. It is held that personal characteristics of CEOs, as well as measures of organizational effectiveness, may have an important role in the determination of CEO compensation. More explicitly, this study posits that CEO experience—as one salient measure of the personal characteristics of CEOs—and the nature of the financial analysts' forecast of earnings-per-share—as one salient measure of organizational effectiveness—are important determinants of CEO compensation. In what follows, the theoretical framework, the methods used, the empirical results, and a discussion of the findings are presented.

THEORETICAL FRAMEWORK

Figure 20.1 illustrates the model. Each line represents a research hypothesis. The CEO experience, the nature of the deviation from the analysts' forecasts, and both the accounting and market measures of performance are shown as directly influencing executive compensation. The main hypotheses are presented below.

Figure 20.1
A Model of the Determinants of CEO Compensation

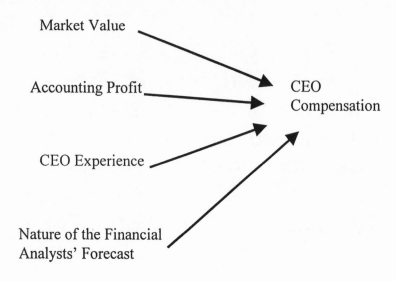

CEO Experience and Executive Compensation

Most studies dealing with the determinants of executive compensation rely on the traditional marginal productivity approach to wage determination. That approach considers performance as the principal determinant of compensation. With one exception, little attention has been directed to the broader determinants of executive compensation, such as the personal characteristics of the individual executives (Hogan and McPheters, 1980). In contrast, this study assumes that CEO experience—in terms of the number of years as CEO in the firm—can be identified as an explicit determinant in two alternative views of wage determination: the screening hypothesis (Arrow, 1973; Stiglitz, 1975; Taubman and Wales, 1973; Wolpin, 1977) and the job competition hypothesis (Thurow, 1975).

The *screening hypothesis* suggests that in a world of imperfect information, such personal characteristics as the number of years as CEO (i.e., CEO experience) are indicators of qualities conducive to successful performance. Thus, a compensation board is likely to take that variable into account in setting executive compensations, since it will be perceived as an indicator of future performance.

The *job competition hypothesis* favors the heavy investment in employee training for a specific job and for the particular conditions of the firm (Becker, 1964). CEO experience is considered favorable because training costs incurred by the firm prepares the executive for a future productive post. It is therefore a good indicator of future performance.

The hypothesis suggests that CEO experience provides an assessment of future performance and will be related to executive compensation:

Hypothesis 1: There will be a positive relationship between CEO experience and compensation.

There is ample evidence indicating a positive relationship between firm profitability and executive compensation (Antle and Smith, 1985, 1986; Ciscel and Carroll, 1980; Coughlan and Schmidt, 1985; Larcker, 1983; Lewellen and Huntsman, 1970; Masson, 1971; Murphy, 1985; Wattel, 1978; McGuire et al., 1962; Lambert and Larcker, 1987). Those studies demonstrate that executive compensation committees of the board of directors—in their search for incentive arrangements which will encourage management to act in the shareholders' interests—set compensation on the basis of financial performance measures, which are themselves related to shareholder wealth.

One such performance measure is the accounting profit of the firm. However, various arguments suggest inclusion of a market measure of performance, in addition to the accounting measure. First, using the results of Holstrom (1979) and others—which suggest that relative weight placed on a measure in a compensation contract is an increasing function of its "signal-to-noise" ratio with respect to the agent's functions—Lambert and Larcker (1987) examined whether the relative use of security market and accounting measures of performance in executive compensation is related to the amount of "consistent noise" inherent in two signals and the "sensitivity" of these two signals to managerial actions. Their results were

consistent with the hypothesis that firms place relatively more weight on market performance (and less weight on accounting performance) in compensation contracts for situations in which (i) the variance of the accounting measure is high relative to the variance of the market measure of performance, (ii) the firm is experiencing high growth rates in assets and sales, and (iii) the value of the manager's personal holdings of his firm's stock is low. (Lambert and Larcker, 1987, 86)

Second, much of the previous empirical research (e.g., Murphy, 1985; Coughlan and Schmidt, 1985; Antle and Smith, 1986) relied on an annual stock return as a measure of performance. Such a measure impounds changes in a firm's financial condition associated with both current and anticipated actions and events. In addition, unlike accounting measures used to evaluate executives, market-based performance measures are not subject to a moral hazard. While these arguments are commonly accepted, Antle and Smith (1986) present two reasons why accounting measures can be used in addition to (or instead of) the market measures of performance. First, stock prices impound information relevant for valuing the firm, but do not necessarily impound all information relevant for evaluating the performance of the firm's management (Gjesdal, 1981). Second, it is easier for the executive to hedge the risk from a contract based on stock returns than one based on accounting variables.

Moreover, one widely held position is that stockholders' welfare—in the form of increases in stock prices or dividends paid, rather than profitability—should dictate executive pay (Poster, 1985; Rappaport, 1978). However, concern about the effect of paying out dividends on reinvestments and R&D projects, and the sensitivity of stock prices to other external events, has led various compensation consultants to discourage use of market-based performance as the primary basis for establishing a CEO's pay (Bickford, 1981; Ellig, 1984; Rich and Larrson, 1984). These arguments suggest that while market measures of performance may not always dominate accounting-based variables, they are still likely candidates for consideration in the compensation plans linking pay to performance measures. Thus:

Hypothesis 2: There is a positive relationship between accounting and market measures of financial performance and executive compensation.

Executive Compensation and Nature of the Analysts' Forecast

Outside groups (i.e., shareholders, executives from other firms, watchdog groups, financial analysts, etc.) monitor performance of managers of a given firm. Such groups then organize their relationship with that firm (i.e., investing in, purchasing from, forecasting, etc.) in terms of their perception of the effectiveness of the managerial ability of the firm. This perception, known as organizational effectiveness, has also been termed participant satisfaction, ecological model, or external effectiveness domain (Keely, 1978; Kilman and Herden, 1976; Miles, 1980; Connolly et al., 1980; Price, 1972). The ecological model of organizational effectiveness suggests a multiconstituent view of effectiveness (Miles, 1980). It treats organizations as systems penetrating differential assessments of effectiveness by different constituencies (Connolly et al., 1980, 214). The approach, following suggestions by Scott (1981, 323) and Ullman (1985, 543), consists of: (a) choosing one constituency, (b) measuring the members' satisfaction using different measures, and (c) combining the results of each measure to develop an overall index so that firms can be ranked by overall organizational effectiveness. Such a measure of overall effectiveness will create pressure on the compensation-setting board, because it represents the perception of an important outside group regarding managers' overall performance. Recognizing the impact of this outside group decision on the firm's survival, the compensation-setting board will use the measures of overall effectiveness in the setting of the level of executive compensation.

Financial analysts are seen as an outside group esteemed for the superiority of their effectiveness measure. The evidence from recent empirical tests—comparing the accuracy of financial analysts forecasts of firm earnings to the accuracy of predictions from univariate time-series forecasting models—indicate a clear superiority of the financial analysts' forecasts (see Brown et al. [1987a] and their references). In addition, the financial analysts' forecasts were found to be a better surrogate for market expectations (Fried and Givoly, 1982; Brown, Richardson, and Schwages, 1987), and firm size.

Given the superiority of the analysts' forecast of earnings, the compensation board will view the nature of the analysts' forecast—expressed as either a percentage increase or decrease from the actual earnings-per-share—as a measure of overall effectiveness. The board will then utilize it for the setting of the level of executive compensation. Thus:

Hypothesis 3: There will be a positive relationship between the nature of the analyst's forecast of earnings and executive compensation for a given year.

MEASUREMENT OF VARIABLES

a. *Executive Compensation Data.* Cash compensation (i.e., salary plus annual bonus) is used as the measure of executive compensation. As indicated in discussions of the issues involved in valuing various forms of compensation, salary plus bonus is almost always a significant portion of total compensation (i.e., salary plus bonus, long-term bonuses, perquisites, pensions, grants of stock options) (See Lambert and Larcker, 1987; Antle and Smith, 1986). In addition, evidence shows that salary plus bonus represents between 80% and 90% of total compensation (Benston, 1985; Hay Associates, 1985). Finally, evidence exists which suggests that the slope coefficient relating salary plus bonus to changes in performance is not statistically different from the slope coefficient that relates total compensation to changes in performance (Jensen and Murphy, 1987).

b. *CEO Experience.* CEO experience is defined as the number of years the person has been a CEO in the firm.

c. *Nature of the Financial Analysts' Forecast of Earnings (NFAFE).* NFAFE is measured as the difference between the analysts' estimate of the earnings-per-share of the forthcoming year and the actual earnings-per-share, divided by the actual earnings-per-share. Because various analysts' forecasts are available in the marketplace, the premise adopted is that the compensation board will be looking for a measure of consensus estimate, when setting executive compensation, rather than relying on one particular individual financial analyst's forecast.

d. *Firm Performance.* The firm's performance is defined by two measures: (1) the *accounting measure* is the net profit of the firm, and (2) the *market measure* is the end-of-the-year market value of the firm.

SAMPLE

The main sample of firms was primarily obtained from the 1988 *Business Week* compensation survey. That survey includes CEO profits and compensation for the 1,000 largest corporations in the U.S. ranked by market value. Of interest to this study, that survey included 1987 data on cash compensation and bonus, and number of years as CEO. Accordingly, this study focuses on 1987 data.

Because a consensus 1987 analysts' forecasts was sought, it was derived from the consensus estimates compiled by the *Institutional Brokers Estimate* (IBES) and reprinted in the 1987 *Business Week*'s *Investment Outlook Scoreboard*. Each IBES forecast is a consensus of as many as sixty analysts. It follows that the nature of the analysts' forecasts was computed as the difference between the 1987 IBES forecast of earnings-per-share and the actual 1986 earnings-per-share, divided by the actual 1986 earnings-per-share. The actual 1986 earnings-per-share, as well as the 1987 accounting profit, was obtained from *Compustat*.

To be encompassed in our sample, a firm had to be: (1) included in the 1988 *Business Week* compensation survey, (2) the subject of an IBES consensus estimate, and (3) included in *Compustat*. The final sample consisted of 247 firms in twenty-two industries.

EMPIRICAL TESTS

Model

The various hypotheses and variables are combined into an empirically testable model

$$CEOC_i = a_{oi} + a_{1i}PRFT_i + a_{2i}IMVF_i + a_{3i}CEOE_i + a_{4i}NFAFE_i + e_i$$

where:

$CEOC_i$ = CEO 1987 Salary and Bonus

$PRFT_i$ = 1987 net profit

MVF_i = 1987 market value of the firm

$CEOE_i$ = CEO experience in terms of number of years as CEO of the firm

$NFAFE_i$ = 1987 IBES Estimate of EPS—1987 Actual EPS

e_i = Error term

a_1, a_2, a_3, a_4 = Coefficient for the PRFT, MVF, CEOE, and NFAFE

i = Firm

Empirical Tests of the Model

Based on the model, a regression was run for the year 1987. Table 20.1 contains the overall regression results. The model appears highly significant: (F = 14.205, X = .0001, R^2 = 19.1%, and R^2 Adjusted = 17.68%).

The regression coefficients for PRFT, MVF, CEOE, and NFAFE are significant at the 0.10 level or less and have the expected signs. In other words, the CEO salary and bonus is found to be significantly associated with accounting

Table 20.1
Regression Results

Variable Definition	Intercept	Net Profit	Market Value	CEO Experience	Nature of Analyst's Forecast	Model Significance
Variable		PRFT	MVF	CEOE	NFAFE	$F A^2$
Coefficient	748.059	0.1910	0.00878	5.437	55.510	14.205 17.68%
Standardized Estimates	0	0.8018	0.1406	0.1002	0.0841	
t-Score	15.52[a]	3.194[a]	1.634[a]	1.711[b]	1.647[b]	

[a]Significant at a=0.05.
[b]Significant at a=0.10.

profit (PRFT), the market value of the firm (MVF), the CEO experience (CEOE), and the nature of the analysts' forecast of the future earnings-per-share.

Interpretations of the regression results and the individual coefficients are contingent on the aptness of the model and are affected by the presence of multicollinearity. The remainder of this section discusses such issues.

The results in table 20.2 indicate the presence of some multicollinearity. There are two pairwise correlations of independent variables, which are significant at the $P = 0.10$ level. This may adversely affect the interpretation of regression coefficients. However, there is no agreement on what constitutes a high level of multicollinearity. The method suggested by Johnston (1972) calculates the co-efficient of multiple correlation between each variable and all the others. According to Judge (1985, 459), the rule of thumb for serious multicollinearity is a multiple correlation coefficient greater than 80%. Table 20.2 shows no such value. Thus, it can be concluded that serious multicollinearity is not present.

The next issue relates to the functional form of the model's relationship between compensation and the independent variables. Linearity has been assumed, although there are some theoretical results available on the basic property of contracts—e.g., the condition under which contracts are increasing (Mirrless, 1976; Grossman and Hart, 1983; Milgram, 1981), convex (Grossman and Hart, 1983), or bang-bang (Harris and Raviv, 1979; Mirrless, 1976; Demski and Feltham, 1978). Therefore, given the lack of theoretical support for the linear contracts, and that the decision was to consider the sensitivity of the results to potential model mis-specification, two tests were used.

The first test consists of plotting the residuals for each observation against the corresponding PRFT, MVF, CEOE, and NFAFE. No systematic patterns consistent with the nonlinear contracts were apparent for the sample. The second test was to compute a Spearman rank correlation test between the dependent variable of compensation and each of the independent variables. The results in each test were significant, indicating a close match of compensation with each of the independent variables.

Table 20.2
Correlation Results

Variable	CEOC	MVF	PRFT	NFAFE	CEOE
CEOC	1.000				
	0.000				
MVF	-0.135	1.000			
	(0.0355)	(0.000)			
PRFT	-0.1070	0.7899	1.000		
	(0.0903	(0.0001)	(0.000)		
NFAFE	0.0705	0.0727	0.0537	1.000	
	(0.2595)	(0.2548)	(0.7639)	(0.000)	
CEOE	0.0549	0.3712	0.9064	0.1182	1.000
	(0.3503)	(0.0001)	(0.0001)	(0.0635)	(0.000)
R2	0.5205	0.5350	0.6333	0.0042	0.1758

DISCUSSION OF FINDINGS

This study proposed a positive model of the CEO compensation as being a function of accounting and market measures of performance, CEO experience, and the nature of the financial analysts' forecasts of earnings. The results are significant for each of the independent variables examined based on the 1987 sample. For that year and for the companies included, CEOs are compensated as if their performance is evaluated relative to the accounting profit, the market value of the firm, their experience as a CEO, and the nature of the analyst's forecasts of earnings-per-share.

The significance of CEO experience as a determinant of executive compensation verifies the underlying premises of both the screening hypothesis and the job competition hypothesis—i.e., that CEO experience is a good indicator of future performance. The significance of both the accounting profit and the market value of the firm as determinants of CEO compensation: (1) add to the existing evidence that compensation plans approved by boards of directors are generally linked to performance measures, and (2) point to the importance of both accounting and market measures of performance in the compensation decision.

The significance of the nature of the analyst's forecast suggests that compensation boards take into account external indicators as measures of overall effectiveness in their compensation-setting decisions. The financial analysts' estimate of future earnings-per-share act as a measure of overall effectiveness expressed by an important outside group.

This study has implications for the determinants of CEO compensation, pointing to the importance of both internal and external indicators of performance, as well as personal characteristics of the CEO. It raises the need to examine other external indicators and other personal characteristics of CEOs as potential determinants of compensation.

REFERENCES

Antle, R., and A. Smith. 1985. Measuring executive compensation: Methods and an application. *Journal of Accounting Research* (Spring): 237–96.

————. 1986. An empirical investigation into relative performance evaluation of corporate executives. *Journal of Accounting Research* (Spring): 1–39.

Arrow, K. 1973. Higher education as a filter. *Journal of Public Economics* (July): 193–216.

Becker, G. 1964. *Human Capital.* New York: National Bureau of Economic Research.

Benston, G. 1985. The self-serving hypothesis: Some evidence. *Journal of Accounting and Economics* (April): 76–84.

Bickford, C.C. 1981. Long-term incentives for management, part 6: Performance attainment plans. *Compensation Review* 12: 14–29.

Brown, L., P. Griffin, R. Hagerman, and M. Zmijewske. 1987a. Security analyst superiority relative to univariate time-series models in forecasting quarterly earnings. *Journal of Accounting and Economics* 5: 32–51.

————. 1987b. An evaluation of alternate proxies for the market's assessment of unexpected earnings. *Journal of Accounting and Economics.*

Brown, L.D., F.D. Richardson, and S.J. Schwages. 1987. An information interpretation of financial analyst superiority in forecasting earnings. *Journal of Accounting Research* (Spring): 49–67.

Ciscel, D., and T. Carroll. 1980. The determinants of executive salaries: An econometric survey. *Review of Economics and Statistics* (February): 7–33.

Connolly, T., E.J. Conlon, and S.J. Deutsh. 1980. Organizational effectiveness: A multiple-constituency approach. *Academy of Management Review* 2: 3–15.

Coughlan, A., and R. Schmidt. 1985. Executive compensation, management turnover, and firm performance: An empirical investigation. *Journal of Accounting and Economics* (April): 43–66.

Demski, J.S., and G.A. Feltham. 1978. Economic incentives in budgeting control systems. *The Accounting Review* (April): 336–59.

Ellig, B. 1984. Incentive plans: Over the long term. *Compensation Review* 16: 39–54.

Fried, D., and D. Givoly. 1982. Financial analysts' forecasts of earnings: A better surrogate for market expectations. *Journal of Accounting Research* (October): 85–108.

Gjesdal, F. 1981. Accounting for stewardship. *Journal of Accounting Research* (Spring): 208–31.

Grossman, S., and O. Hart. 1983. An analysis of the principal-agent problem. *Econometrica* (January): 7–46.

Harris, M., and A. Raviv. 1979. Optimal incentive contracts with imperfect information. *Journal of Economic Theory* (1979): 231–59.

Hay Associates. 1985. Fifth annual Nay report on executive compensation. *Wharton Magazine* (April): 85–107.

Hogan, T.D., and L.R. McPheters. 1980. Executive compensation: Performance versus personal characteristics. *Southern Economic Journal* 46: 1060–68.

Holstrom, B. 1979. Moral hazard and observability. *Bell Journal of Economics* (Spring): 74–91.

Jensen, M., and K. Murphy. 1987. Are executive compensation contracts structured properly? Working paper, University of Rochester.

Johnston, J. 1972. *Economeric Methods.* New York: McGraw Hill.

Judge, G. 1985. *The Theory and Practice of Econometrics.* New York: Wiley.

Keely, M.G. 1978. Social justice approach to organizational evaluation. *Administrative Science Quarterly* 23: 272–92.

Kilman, R.H., and R.P. Herden. 1976. Towards a systematic methodology for evaluating the impact of interventions on organizational effectiveness. *Academy of Management Review* 1: 87–98.

Lambert, R.G., and D.E. Larcker. 1987. An analysis of the use of compensation contracts. *Studies in Stewardship Uses of Accounting Information, Supplement to the Journal of Accounting Research* 25: 85–129.

Larcker, D.E. 1983. The association between performance plan adoption and corporate capital investment. *Journal of Accounting and Economics* (April): 3–30.

Lewellen, Q., and B. Huntsman. 1970. Managerial pay and corporate performance. *American Economic Review* (September): 710–20.

Masson, R.T. 1971. Executive motivations, earnings, and consequent equity performance. *Journal of Political Economy* (November/December): 1278–92.

McGuire, J., J. Chiu, and A. Elbing. 1962. Executive incomes, sales and profits. *American Economic Review* (September): 753–61.

Miles, R.H. 1980. *Macro-Organizational Behavior.* Glenview, IL: Scott, Foreman.

Milgram, P. 1981. Good news and bad news: Representation theorems and applications. *Bell Journal of Economics* (Autumn): 380–91.

Mirrless, J. 1976. The optimal structure of incentives and authority within an organization. *Bell Journal of Economics* (Spring): 105–71.

Murphy, I.C. 1985. Corporate performance and managerial remuneration: An empirical analysis. *Journal of Accounting and Economics* (April): 11–42.

Poster, C.Z. 1985. Executive compensation: Taking long-term incentives out of the corporate tower. *Compensation Review* 17: 30–31.

Price, J.L. 1972. The study of organizational effectiveness. *Sociological Quarterly* 13: 3–15.

Rappaport, K. 1978. Executive incentives versus corporate growth. *Harvard Business Review* 56: 81–88.

Rich, J.T., and J.A. Larrson. 1984. Why some long-term incentives fail. *Compensation Review* 16: 26–37.

Scott, W.R. 1981. *Organizations: Rational, Natural and Operational Systems.* Englewood Cliffs, NJ: Prentice Hall.

Smith, C., and R. Watts. 1982. Incentive and tax effects of executive compensation plans. *Australian Journal of Management* 7: 139–57.

Stiglitz, J.E. 1975. The theory of screening, education, and the distribution of income. *American Economic Review* (June): 283–305.

Taubman, P.J., and T. Wales. 1973. Higher education, mental ability, and screening. *Journal of Political Economy* (January/February): 28–55.

Thurow, L.C. 1975. *Generalizing Inequality.* New York: Basic Books.

Ullman, A.A. 1985. Data in search of a theory: A critical examination of the relationship among social performance, social disclosure and economic performance of U.S. firms. *The Academy of Management Review* (July): 540–47.

Wattel, H. 1978. *Chief Executive Officer Compensation—Hofstra University Yearbook of Business.* New York: Hofstra University.

Wolpin, K. 1977. Education and Screening. *American Economic Review* (December): 949–58.

CHAPTER 21

Effects of Personal Attributes and Performance on the Level of CEO Compensation in Multinational Firms: Direct and Interaction Effects

INTRODUCTION

The purpose of this chapter is to expand on the nature of the evidence on the determinants of the level of compensation to CEOs of American industrial multinational corporations. Most research to date has focused on testing the relative importance of measures of firm performance as determinants of executive salaries in general, and CEOs in particular. This study proposes that the personal attributes of CEOs may have an important role in the determination of CEO compensation either through direct or interaction effects. Drawing on unique data on the personal attributes of CEOs from a sample of Fortune 500 firms, the study addresses the question, How do the personal attributes of CEOs affect the determinants of CEO compensation?

DETERMINANTS OF THE LEVEL OF CEO COMPENSATION

The model in this chapter builds and expands on previous analyses of executive compensation that focuses on the relative importance of different measures of performance (Lewellen and Huntsman, 1970; Masson, 1971; Antle and Smith, 1985; Ciscel and Carroll, 1980; Coughlin and Schmidt, 1985; Lambert and Larcker, 1987; McGuire, Chiu, and Elbing, 1962). Three main avenues characterize our model:

1. Various studies estimated the determinants of executive incomes, with an emphasis on firm size. Size effects were consistently found (Mellow, 1982; Personick and Bar-

skey, 1982; Oi, 1983). In addition, Kostiuk (1990) found the relationship between executive income and firm size to be relatively stable over time and in different countries.

Building on these findings, this study includes both sales as a measure of size, and income as a measure of profitability as independent variables in the CEO compensation valuation model. The relationship between CEO compensation and size is expected to be positive based on the rationale that bigger firms tend to pay more because the CEO oversees substantial resources, rather than because of the firms' ability to pay more or because of their number of hierarchical pay levels (Finkelstein and Hambrick, 1989, 1988, 548). The relationship between CEO compensation and profitability is also expected to be positive based on the rationale that firms may attempt to improve gauging of the CEO's marginal product by paying for delivered performance (Finkelstein and Hambrick, 1988, 548).

2. Recent theoretical work by Rosen (1982) and Oi (1983) finds the supposed conflict between size and profitability to be misplaced, given that differences in executive ability may partially explain the presence of substantial firm size differentials. We posit that CEOs are paid in part on the basis of their personal attributes. This is congruent with a human capital argument that for many types of jobs the marginal product of a person is in part estimated to be his or her human capital, e.g., his or her investments in education and experience (Becker, 1964; Mincer, 1970). Accordingly we posit that the level of CEO compensation will be a function of the age, the number of years as a CEO, and tenure. We expect the relationship between CEO compensation and age and tenure in the organization to be negative, based on the idea that younger and "imported" CEOs will require a pay level determined by market factors, while older and "homegrown" CEOs will require a pay level that is the result of performance-linked increases to base salary. We expect, moreover, the years as a CEO in the firm to be positively related to CEO compensation based on the argument that the better the profitability of the firm, the longer he or she will be a CEO and the higher the performance-based compensation (Finkelstein and Hambrick, 1988, 1989; Kostiuk, 1990).

3. While the direct effects of CEO age, number of years as a CEO, and tenure are important, their interactions can be also an important determinant of CEO compensation level. To our knowledge, this is the first study investigating the interaction effects of personal attributes. We posit that the interaction between the tenure on one hand and CEO age and years as a CEO on the other hand is positive, based on the argument that the number of years in the organization acts as a salient factor to the importance of age and experience as a CEO. We expect, however, the interaction between age and number of years as a CEO to be negative, based on the argument that younger CEOs can still command a higher market-based salary than the internally determined salary of older CEOs.

The final model is expressed as follows:

$$\log Y = a_0 + a_1 A + a_2 T + a_3 Y + a_4 AT + a_5 AY + a_6 TY + a_8 S + E$$

where:

Y = CEO compensation

A = Age of the CEO

Y = Number of years as the CEO

T = Tenure

AY, AT, and TY = Interaction between A, Y, and T

P = Profitability of the firm

S = Size of the firm

THE DATA

Dependent Variables

Cash compensation for the year 1987 (i.e., salary plus annual bonus) is used as a measure of executive compensation. As discussions of the issues involved in various compensation studies indicate, salary plus bonus is almost always a significant position of total compensation (salary plus bonus, long-term bonuses, perquisites, pensions, grants, or stock options) (Antle and Smith, 1985; Lambert and Lacker, 1987). In addition, evidence shows that the total salary plus bonus represents between 80% and 90% of total compensation (Benston, 1985; Boot, Alien, and Hamilton, 1988; Hay Associates, 1985). Finally, Jensen and Murphy (1987) also provide evidence that indicates that the slope coefficient relating salary plus bonus to changes in performance is not statistically different from the slope coefficient that relates total compensation to changes in performance.

Independent Variables

The independent variables included firm performance, size, age, years as a CEO, and tenure. They deserve explanation:

a. Firm performance was measured as either profit or profit over total assets for the year 1987.

b. Firm size was measured by total sales for the year 1987.

Sample

To insure the greatest sample of firms for which data will be available for all the variables, the initial sample chosen was the Fortune 500 industrial corporations. The next task was to collect the needed information from the *Compustat* tape, the proxy statements, the 1988 *Business Week* compensation survey, and other sources.

The final sample included 216 companies from twenty-eight different industries. Table 21.1. lists the summary statistics for the sample. As found in previous studies by Roberts (1956), Lewellen (1968), and Kostiuk (1990), these executives have been employed for a great part of their careers by their current firm. The demographic profile of our sample is almost similar to the one used

Table 21.1
1987 Summary Statistics

Variable	Mean	Standard Deviation	Minimum	Maximum
1. CEO Compensation (1000)	852.269	369.15	178.000	3445.0
2. Sales (1000)	5247.341	10587.41	464.900	101781.9
3. Assets (1000)	4802.744	10043.30	226.000	87421.9
4. Age	56.884	5.75	42.000	74.0
5. Tenure	26.537	11.36	1000	53.0
6. Years as a CEO	9103	7.92	0.080	43.0
7. Profit	276.609	670.79	-4407.000	5258.0

by Kostiuk, with an average age of fifty-seven (also found by Kostiuk), mean tenure of twenty-six (compared to twenty-four found by Kostiuk), and mean years as a CEO of nine (compared to 7.6 found by Kostiuk). Kostiuk's data were for the 1969–1981 period.

RESULTS

The logarithms of executive compensation, profit, and sales were used in the analysis. These variables, before transformation, were skewed to the right. If the distribution of the variables is skewed to normalize it, a logarithmic transformation is necessary. Table 21.2 gives the results of the regression analysis using either profit or profit over assets as measures of performance. Various interesting results emerge:

1. The model is highly significant and explains an adequate amount of variance.

2. A non-surprising result is the irrelevancy of age.

3. The direct effects of the other personal attributes is significant and the signs are as predicted. Tenure is negatively related to CEO compensation, while years as a CEO is positively related.

4. Of the interaction effect, the surprising result is the irrelevancy of the tenure and years as a CEO interaction. The other interactions are significant and the signs are as predicted. The age-tenure interaction is positively related to CEO compensation, while the age-years as a CEO was negatively related.

5. As expected, the performance and size factors are significant and positively related to CEO compensation.

Table 21.2
1987 Cross-Section Estimates[1]

Dependent Variable: log (Salary + Bonus)		
Intercept	5.5036	3.7989
	(8.781)*	(6.653)*
Age: A	-0.00319	0.0011
	(0.283)	(0.11)
Tenure: T	-0.03951	-0.041
	(1.641)***	(1.862)***
Years as a CEO: Y	0.0675	0.0597
	(2.037)**	(2.026)**
AT	0.000597	0.00063
	(2.388)**	(2.587)**
AY	-0.0010	-0.00099
	(1.612)***	(1.758)***
TY	0.00011	0.0001
	(0.307)	(0.300)
Log (profit)	0.1656	-----
	(4.363)*	-----
Profit/Assets	-----	0.4423
	-----	(8.730)*
Log (sales)	0.0695	0.3376
	(1.708)***	(13.603)*
R^2 adjusted	35.40%	48.53%
F	14.904*	26.345*

[1]Absolute value of t-statistic in parentheses
*Significant at a=0.01.   **Significant at a=0.05.   ***Significant at a=0.10

DISCUSSION

Personal attributes significantly affect a CEO's pay in two ways: directly and in tandem.

The direct effects of personal attributes were present in the case of tenure and years as a CEO. Basically, executives with less tenure in the firm and more years as a CEO are paid more than those with high tenure and less years as a CEO. *Experience* rather than tenure appears to be a more important factor in the determination of CEO compensation.

The interaction effects of personal attributes were present in the case of the age-tenure interaction and the age-years as a CEO interaction.

First, older executives with high tenure are paid more. While tenure by itself is not rewarding, when associated with age it leads to better pay. The passage of time worked with loyalty to the same firm (in other words, the survival factor) lead to better pay.

Second, older executives with more years as a CEO are paid less than younger CEOs with less years as a CEO. While years as a CEO by itself is rewarding, when associated with age, it leads to lower pay. There is definitively a salary compression phenomenon as well as a market factor favoring younger CEOs.

REFERENCES

Antle, R., and A. Smith. 1985. Measuring executive compensation: Methods and an application. *Journal of Accounting Research*: (Spring): 296–337.

Becker, G.S. 1964. *Human Capital*. New York: Columbia University Press for National Bureau of Economic Research.

Benston, G. 1985. The self-serving hypothesis: Some evidence. *Journal of Accounting and Economics* (April): 67–84.

Booz, Alien, and Hamilton. 1988. *Executive Pay in the Eighties: Major Exposures Ahead*. New York: Boot, Alien and Hamilton.

Ciscel, D., and T. Carroll. 1980. The determinants of executive salaries: An econometric survey. *Review of Economics and Statistics* (February): 7–13.

Coughlin, A., and R. Schmidt. 1985. Executive compensation, management turnover, and firm performance: An empirical investigation. *Journal of Accounting and Economics* (April): 43–66.

Finkelstein, S., and D. Hambrick. 1988. Chief executive compensation: A synthesis and reconciliation. *Strategic Management Journal* 9: 543–58.

———. 1989. Chief executive compensation: A study of the intersection of markets and political processes. *Strategic Management Journal* 10 (April): 121–34.

Hay Associates. 1985. Fifth annual Hay report on executive compensation. *Wharton Magazine* (April): 85–107.

Jensen, M., and E. Murphy. 1987. Are executive compensation contracts structured properly? Working paper, University of Rochester.

Kostiuk, P.E. 1990. Firm size and executive compensation. *The Journal of Human Resources* 25: 90–105.

Lambert, R.A., and D.E. Larcker. 1987. An analysis of the use of accounting and market measures of performance in executive compensation contracts. *Studies in Stewardship Uses of Accounting Information, Supplement to the Journal of Accounting Research* 25: 85–129.

Lewellen, W.G. 1968. *Executive Compensation in Large Industrial Corporations*. New York: National Bureau of Economic Research.

Lewellen, W., and B. Hunstman. 1970. Managerial pay and corporate performance. *American Economic Review* (September): 710–20.

Masson, R.T. 1971. Executive motivations, earnings and consequent equity performance. *Journal of Political Economy* (December): 1278–92.

McGuire, J., J. Chiu, and A. Elbing. 1962. Executive incomes, sales and profits. *American Economic Review* (September): 753–61.

Mellow, W. 1982. Employer size and wages. *Review of Economics and Statistics* 69: 495–501.

Mincer, J. 1970. The distribution of labor incomes: A survey with special reference to the human capital approach. *Journal of Economic Literature* 8: 1–26.

Oi, W. 1983. Heterogeneous firms and the organization of production. *Economic Inquiry* 21: 147–71.

Personick, M.E., and C.B. Barsky. 1982. White-collar pay levels linked to corporate work force and size. *Monthly Labor Review* vol. no: 105.

Roberts, D. 1956. A general theory of executive compensation based on statistically tested propositions. *Quarterly Journal of Economics* 70: 270–94.

Rosen, S. 1982. Authority, control and the distribution of earnings. *Bell Journal of Economics* 13: 311–23.

CHAPTER 22

Explaining Market Returns of U.S. Multinational Firms: Earnings Versus Value-Added Data

INTRODUCTION

This chapter investigates whether the relative change in earnings and/or net value-added data are relevant for evaluating earnings/returns associations. Previous studies were limited to the association between the market return and either the level of earnings and/or the changes in the level of earnings, both divided by the beginning of the period price. (i.e., Easton and Harris, 1991). This study differs in two respects. First, it examines in addition to earnings, a known and conventional measure of accounting return, net value added, a measure of wealth created and attributable to all stakeholders, and advocated as an important European innovation worthy of inclusion in U.S. company annual reports (Meek and Gray, 1988; Karpik and Belkaoui, 1989). Second, it uses the relative changes in earnings and/or net value added as measures of accounting return rather than the level of earnings only.

The results provide evidence that the relative changes in earnings as well as the relative changes in net value added are associated with stock returns of U.S. multinational corporations. Univariate as well as multivariate cross-sectional regressions of annual market returns on the relative changes of earnings and/or net value added show the coefficients of these independent variables to be statistically significant at 1% or better in all years examined. The rationale for examining the usefulness of value-added data is presented below. The next section elaborates on the valuation models relating security returns to relative changes in earnings and/or net value added. The two following sections describe the data and sample selection procedure, and the empirical results. Finally, a summary of the results and conclusions is presented.

USEFULNESS OF VALUE-ADDED DATA

The value-added reporting issue has always been a part of the international accounting literature and a continuous subject of debate. It can be traced back to the U.S. Treasury in the eighteenth century (Cox, 1978). Suggestions for its inclusion in U.S. companies' annual reports were frequently made (Suojanen, 1954; Meek and Gray, 1988). Its popularity rose in the late 1970s in most European countries. The publication of the *Corporate Report* (Accounting Standards Steering Committee, 1975) maintained the momentum through its call for a value-added statement showing how the benefits of an enterprise's efforts are shared among employees, providers of capital, the state, and reinvestment. What followed in the United Kingdom was an increase in the use of the value-added statement by British companies, as well as an increase in interest by the professional accounting institutes (Gray and Maunders, 1980; Morley, 1978; Renshall et al., 1979). As a supplement to the income statement, the value-added statement reports on the income earned by a large group of "stakeholders," all providers of capital, plus employees and government (Gray and Maunders, 1980, 75). It can be computed by the following rearrangement of the income statement:

$$S - B = W + I + DP + D + T + R \qquad (1)$$

or

$$S - B - DP = W + I + D + T + R \qquad (2)$$

where:

R = Retained earnings
S = Sales revenue
B = Bought-in material and services
DP = Depreciation
W = Wages
I = Interest
D = Dividends
T = Taxes

Equation (1) expresses the gross value added, while expression (2) expresses the net value added. In both equations, the left side (the subtractive side) shows the value added (gross or net), and the right side (the additive side) shows how value added is divided among the stakeholders. However, given the lack of mandated uniform guidelines, variations in the treatment of some of the items do exist (Morley, 1979; Harris, 1982; McLeary, 1983; Rutherford, 1972). The alleged advantages of the value-added report include: (a) its potential use in collective bargaining (Maunders, 1985, 225); (b) its measure of the size and importance of firms (Morley, 1979); (c) its potential benefit as a ratio component in financial analysis and prediction of economic events of interest to the firm (Morley, 1978; Sinha, 1983, 130–37; Cox, 1978, 62–82); (d) its use in measuring wealth created by the company to emphasize stakeholder interdependence, to condition employees' expectations regarding pay and prospects, and for productivity incentive schemes (Meek and Gray, 1988, 77–78); and (e) its superior explanatory power in explaining the variability in market betas (Karpik and Belkaoui, 1989).

The concern in this chapter is with the relative ability of value-added concepts in explaining market return. The following arguments can be used:

First, the return/earnings research shows a limited usefulness of earnings (Lev, 1989). In addition, the extent of the return/earnings association does not increase considerably when the return window is expanded to one year (and even to two years in Collins and Kothari's 1989 study). The studies which examined the informational contribution of earnings-related data provides, however, an increase in R_2 (Bublitz, et al., 1985; Lipe, 1986; Hoskins, et al., 1986). Value-added data represent earnings-related data. Those data are typically not available to investors at the time summary earnings information is released, because earnings announcement generally precede, by several weeks, the public release of annual reports and other statements to regulatory agencies. Examining the information content of value-added variables is aimed at determining whether information beyond "bottom-line" earnings is useful, at the margin, in explaining the behavior of share prices. The basic question in need of investigation is whether the more comprehensive value-added variables contain information that is relevant to the pricing of securities.

Second, in the economic and finance models establishing relationships between firms' earnings or cash flows and their market values (e.g., Fama and Miller, 1972, ch. 2), the role of earnings or other financial variables, in most of these models, is to provide investors with information about future securities' returns (e.g., Lev and Ohlson, 1982; Lev, 1989). The quality of financial variables is then determined by their contributions to the prediction of security returns. This implies that the higher the predictive contribution of value-added variables, the higher their quality. This is in line with Lev's (1989, 180) suggestion that an operational measure of quality is the ability of the variable to facilitate the prediction of securities' outcomes or to provide for improved portfolio decisions. This is also in line with the Financial Accounting Standard Board's concept of usefulness and quality.

THE RELATION BETWEEN ACCOUNTING AND MARKET RETURNS

Returns and Earnings Associated Based on a Relative Valuation Model

The conventional earnings valuation model used by Easton and Harris (1991) is as follows:

$$(\Delta P_{jt} + D_{jt}) / P_{jt-1} = \rho_1 [\Delta A_{jt} / P_{t-1}] + U_{jt} \tag{3}$$

where:

P_{jt} = Market price of the security j at time t
D_{jt} = Dividend of firm j at time t
A_{jt} = Accounting earnings of firm j at time t

The model depicted in equation (3) implies a linear relation between the change in price and the change in earnings deflated by the beginning-of-period price over the period.

A more logical model rests on expressing a relationship between relative changes on both sides of the equation. It follows that:

$$(\Delta P_{jt} + D_{jt}) / P_{jt-1} = \rho_2 [\Delta A_{jt} / A_{jt-1}] + V_{jt} \tag{4}$$

That is, there is a linear relationship between the relative changes in security prices and the relative changes in earnings.

Returns and Earnings Association Based on a Relative Net Value-Added Valuation Model

Both equations (3) and (4) reflect still the conventional thesis that the accounting return most associated with security returns is the earnings variable. Following the arguments used earlier that net value added contain information that is relevant to the pricing of securities, the following model is proposed:

$$(\Delta P_{jt} + D_{jt}) / P_{jt-1} = \rho_2 [\Delta A_{jt} / A_{jt-1}] + V_{jt} \tag{5}$$

where: NVA = net value added. Equation (5) illustrates a linear relation between the change in price and the change in net value-added data.

Combining Both Valuation Models

Stock price may be affected by both (a) earnings that signal returns to shareholders, and (b) net value added that signals returns to all stockholders, all

Table 22.1

Regression of Annual Security Returns on Relative Annual Changes of Forms of Accounting Returns

Years	Intercept	RNVA	RCE	x_1(1983)	x_2(1982)	x_3(1981)	x_4(1980)	F	R^2
1979-1983	0.079 (4.53)*	+0.2106 (+9.167)*	----------	0.1202 (5.144)*	0.1798 (7.628)*	-0.372 (-1.685)***	0.052 (2.222)***	33.94*	0.0662
1979-1983	0.126 (7.142)*	--------	0.000002 (2.355)**	0.089 (3.826)*	0.1487 (6.338)*	-0.0511 (-2.162)**	0.0406 (1.715)***	17.74*	0.0352
1979-1983	0.079 (4.5)*	+0.21111 (+9.1)*	0.000005 (0.665)	0.1206 (5.15)*	0.1799 (7.6)*	-0.0372 (-1.684)***	0.0524 (2.223)**	28.35*	0.0664

(t statistics are provided in parentheses)

*   Significant at a=0.01

**   Significant at a=0.05

*** Significant at a=0.10

Table 22.2
**Simple Regression of Annual Security Returns on Relative Annual Changes in
Level of Earnings**

$$R_{jt} = a_{t0} + a_{t1} RCE_t + E_{jt}$$

Year	a_{t0}	a_{t1}	F	R^2
1988	0.27 (2.23)*	+0.00001 (+0.182)	0.033	0.001
1983	0.23 (11.4)*	-0.000003 (-0.311)	0.097	0.0002
1982	0.276 (15.16)*	+0.048 (+3.06)*	9.36**	0.00018
1981	0.076 (5.17*)	+0.016 (+2.203)**	4.852**	0.010
1980	0.171 (10.44)*	+0.066 (7.012)*	49.16*	0.094
1979	0.1247 (11.01)*	+0.0138 (+1.556)***	1.840	0.0039

(t-statistics are provided in parentheses)
*Significant at $\alpha = 0.01$.
**Significant at $\alpha = 0.05$.
***Significant at $\alpha = 0.10$.

providers of capital, plus employees and government. By combining an "earnings only" model similar to equation (4) and a "net value added only" model similar to equation (5), this study proposes a valuation model in which the relative change in prices are a weighted function of the relative change of earnings and net value added. It follows that:

$$(\Delta P_{jt} + D_{jt}) / P_{jt} - 1 = k \rho_4 [\Delta A_{jt}/A_{jt}] + (1 - k) \rho_5 [NVA_{jt}/NVA_{jt-1}] + W_{jt} \tag{6}$$

where k is a factor for weighing the contribution of the relative change in earnings versus the relative change in net value added in the explanation of stock returns.

DATA AND SAMPLE SELECTION

The accounting return variables used were either based on value added or earnings. They were constructed from *Computstat* data items as follows:

Table 22.3
Simple Regression of Annual Security Returns on Relative Annual Changes in Net Value Added

$$R_{jt} = a_{t0} + a_{t1} RCNVA_t + E_{jt}$$

Year	a_{t0}	a_{t1}	F	R^2
1983	0.203 (10.44)*	+0.163 (+3.19)*	10.232*	0.02
1982	0.26 (14.1)*	+0.14 (+3.16)*	9.985*	0.0281
1981	0.01 (1.53)***	+0.34 (-5.777)*	33.33*	0.0657
1980	0.094 (4.4)*	+0.426 (5.524)*	30.5*	0.096
1979	0.078 (5.734)*	0.216 (-6.83)*	36.36*	0.0733

(t-statistics are provided in parentheses)
*Significant at 0.01.
**Significant at 0.05.
***Significant at 0.10.

Net Value Added [NVA] = The sum of labor expenses, corporate taxes, dividends, interest expenses, minority shareholders in subsidiaries plus retained earnings

Earnings [E] = Income available to common equity

The firms examined in this study represent all NYSE and AMEX firms that have available NVA, A, and P data over the period 1979–83 in *Compustat*.

This selection procedure resulted in a sample of 2,398 firm-year observations.

EMPIRICAL ANALYSES

Results Based on the Relative Earnings Valuation Model

The regression model based on the relative earnings valuation model is:

$$R_{jt} = \alpha_{t0} + \alpha_{t1}RE_{jt} + \varepsilon_{jt}^1 \tag{7}$$

Table 22.4
Multiple Regression of Annual Security Returns on Relative Annual Changes in Net Value Added and Related Annual Changes in the Level of Earnings

$$R_{jt} = a_{t0} + a_{t1} RCNVA_t + a_{t2} RCE_t + E_{jt}$$

Year	a_{t0}	a_{t1}	at2	F	R^2
1983	0.20 (10.4)*	+0.16 (+3.22)*	-0.000005 -(1.611)***	5.2399*	0.0205
1982	0.26 (14.4)*	+0.12 (+2.73)*	+0.04 (+2.57)*	8.36*	0.033
1981	0.021 (1.17)	+0.355 (+5.602)*	+0.012 (+1.67)***	18.126*	0.071
1980	0.115 (5.519)*	+0.324 (+4.24)*	+0.056 (+5.864)*	33.54*	0.1261
1979	0.076 (5.58)*	+0.217 (6.07)*	+0.014 (+1.632)***	19.25*	0.0774

(t-statistics are provided in parentheses)
*Significant at 0.01.
**Significant at 0.05.
***Significant at 0.10.

where:

$$R_{jt} = (\Delta P_{jt} + d_{jt}) / P_{jt-1}$$
$$RE_{jt} = \Delta E_{jt} / E_{jt-1}$$
$$E_{jt} = current\ earnings$$

This regression model was estimated for the pooled cross-section and time-series sample, as well as for each year (t) of available data. To control for a potential year effect, the regression model on the total sample included dummy variables for each of the years examined. The results using the pooled sample of all 2,398 firm-year observations, shown in table 22.1 part 1 indicates both α_{t0} and α_{t1} are significant at the 0.01 level. The results for each year are shown in table 22.2, where both coefficients are shown to be significant. Those results indicate that, as the model in equation (4) suggests, the relative change in security price is associated with the relative change in earnings.

Results Based on the Relative Net Value-Added Model

The regression model based on the related net value-added model is:

$$R_{jt} = \alpha_{t0} + \alpha_{t1}RNVA_{jt} + \varepsilon^{2jt} \tag{8}$$

where:

$$RNVA_{jt} = \Delta\, NVA_{jt} \,/\, NVA_{jt-1}$$

The results using the pooled sample of 2,398 firm-year observations shown in table 22.1, as well as in the year-by-year regressions shown in table 22.3, indicate that both α_{t0} and α_{t1} are significant at the 0.01 level. The adjusted R^2 from the pooled sample using the relative net value-added model is 6.6% compared to the R^2 of 3.5% from the same results using the relative earnings valuation model. Similar adjusted R^2 results are observed for the year-by-year regressions. These findings show that (a) the model in equation (5) suggests that the relative change in security price is associated with the relative change in earnings, and (b) the models based with the relative net value model provide a better explanatory power than the models based on the relative earnings models.

Results Based on the Combination Model

The regression model based on the combination model is:

$$R_{jt} = \alpha_{t0} + \alpha_{t0}RNVA + \alpha_{t2}RE + \varepsilon_{jt}^3 \tag{9}$$

The results using the pooled sample, shown in table 22.1, part 3, as well as the results of the year-by-year regressions shown in table 22.4, indicate that all the coefficients are significant. The adjusted R^2 from the pooled sample using the combination model is 6.64% compared to the adjusted R^2 of 3.5% using the relative earnings valuation model and the adjusted R^2 of 6.62% using the relative net value-added valuation model. Similar results are observed for the year-by-year regressions.

These findings show that (a) as the model in equation (6) suggests, the relative change in security price is correlated with both the relative changes in earnings and net value added, and (b) the combination model shows a better explanatory power than the models based on either the net value added or the earnings.

SUMMARY AND CONCLUSIONS

This study confirms an association between both the relative changes in earnings and net value added and the relative changes in security prices. It suggests that both earnings and net value added play a role in security valuation. The policy implication of the findings is that value-added accounting information can supply important explanatory power of security valuation beyond that provided by earnings. It argues for the disclosure of the underlying data needed to compute value-added variables.

REFERENCES

Accounting Standards Steering Committee. 1975. *The Corporate Report*. London: Accounting Standards Steering Committee.

Belsley, D.A., E. Kuh, and R.E. Welsh. 1980. *Regression Diagnostics. Identifying Influential Data and Sources of Collinearity*. New York: Wiley.

Bublitz, B., T.J. Frecka, and J.C. Mckeown. 1985. Market association tests and FASB statement no. 33 disclosures: A re-examination. *Journal of Accounting Research* (Supplement): 1–23.

Cox, B. 1978. *Value Added: An Appreciation for the Accounts Concerned with Industry*. London: Heineman.

Easton, P.D., and T.S. Harris. 1991. Earnings as an explanatory variable for returns. *Journal of Accounting Research* (Spring): 19–36.

Fama, E.F., and M.H. Miller. 1972. *The Theory of Finance*. New York: Holt, Rinehart and Winston.

Financial Accounting Standards Board (FASB). 1987. *Statement of Financial Accounting Concepts No. 1: Objectives of Financial Reporting to Business Enterprises*. Stamford, CT: FASB.

Gray, S.J., and K.T. Maunders. 1980. *Value Added Reporting: Uses and Measurement*. London: Association of Certified Accountants.

Harris, G.J. 1982. Value added statements. *The Australian Accountant* (May): 261–64.

Hoskins, R.E., J.S. Hughes, and W.E. Ricks. 1986. Evidence on the international information content of additional firm disclosures made concurrently with earnings. *Journal of Accounting Research* (Supplement): 1–32.

Karpik, P., and A. Belkaoui. 1989. The relative relationship between systematic Risk and Value Added Variables. *Journal of International Financial Management and Accounting* (Autumn): 259–76.

Lev, B. 1989. On the usefulness of earnings research: Lessons and directions from two decades of empirical research. *Journal of Accounting Research: Current Studies on the Informational Content of Accounting Earnings* (Supplement): 153–92.

Lev, B., and J.A. Ohlson. 1982. Market based empirical research: A review, interpretation and extension. *Journal of Accounting Research* (Supplement): 239–322.

Lipe, R.C. 1986. The information contained in the components of earnings. *Journal of Accounting Research* (Supplement): 37–64.

Maunders, K.T. 1985. The decision relevance of value added reports. In *Frontiers of International Accounting: An Anthology*, eds. F.D. Choi and G.G. Mueller. Ann Arbor, MI: UMI Research Press, 225–45.

McLeary, S. 1983. Value added: A comparative study. *Accounting Organizations and Society* 8, no. 1: 31–56.

Meek, G.K., and S.J. Gray. 1988. The value added statement: An innovation for U.S. companies? *Accounting Horizons* (June): 73–81.

Morley, M.F. 1978. The value added statement: A british innovation. *The Chartered Accountant Magazine* (May): 31–34.

———. 1979. The value added statement in Britain. *The Accounting Review* (May): 618–89.

Renshall, M., R. Allan, and K. Nicholson. 1979. *Added Value in External Financial Reporting*. London: Institute of Chartered Accountants in England and Wales.

Rutherford, B.A. 1972. Value added as a focus of attention for financial reporting: Some conceptual problems. *Accounting and Business Research* (Summer): 215–20.

Sinha, G. 1983. *Value Added Income*. Calcutta: Book World.

Suojanen, W.W. 1954. Accounting today and the large corporation. *The Accounting Review* (July): 391–98.

White, I. 1989. A heteroscedasticity-consistent covariance matrix estimator and a direct test for heteroscedasticity. *Econometrica* (May): 817–38.

CHAPTER 23

Prediction Performance of Earnings Forecasts of U.S. Firms Active in Developed and Developing Countries

INTRODUCTION

Rivera (1991) shows that the accuracy of (consensus in) analysts' earnings forecasts of U.S. domestic companies is less than for U.S. multinational corporations. This chapter extends Rivera's analysis by investigating whether the accuracy of (consensus in) analysts' earnings forecasts differs between thirty-one U.S. multinationals with substantial operations in developed countries, and twenty-six U.S. multinationals with substantial operations in developing countries. Twenty-one U.S. firms with no international operations are also examined. The results indicate that the accuracy of analysts' earnings forecasts differs across the three groups of firms: U.S. firms with no international operations are the most accurate, while U.S. firms with significant operations in developing countries are the least accurate (difference significant at .10 level). No significant differences in consensus were noted across the three groups.

The chapter is organized as follows: The background and hypotheses are presented below. Next, the empirical research design is developed and the empirical results are reported, followed by a discussion and conclusions.

BACKGROUND AND HYPOTHESES

Prior research suggests that analysts' forecasts of earnings are associated with significant security price revisions (e.g., Beaver et al., 1979; Elton et al., 1981; Givoly and Lakonishok, 1979; Gonedes et al., 1976; Patell, 1976; Penman, 1980; Imhoff and Lobo, 1980; Waymire, 1984; Fried and Givoly, 1982. The more accurate the earnings prediction, the more information content the management forecast carries (Patell, 1976, 248). Various factors are expected to influence the accuracy of analysts' earnings forecasts, including industry, size of firm, variability of earnings, and forecasting horizon (e.g., Albrecht et al., 1977; Baginski, 1987; Baldwin, 1984; Barefield and Comiskey, 1975; Brown et al., 1985, 1987; Imhoff and Pare, 1982). Also, Rivera (1991) finds that the accuracy of analysts' earnings forecasts, and their level of consensus are significantly lower for U.S. domestic than for U.S. multinational firms.

Rivera (1991) does not distinguish between U.S. firms with significant international operations in developed countries and those with significant international operations in developing countries. This difference is important, given Markham Collins's (1990) evidence that U.S. domestic and multinationals operating in developed countries exhibit higher returns and risk than U.S. multinationals operating in developing countries. Based on these findings, errors in forecasting for developed country firms and the dispersion of these forecasts around a consensus mean would be comparatively smaller than those for a domestic firm and a developing country firm. In addition, an international firm with operations in a developing country operates in a more "demanding" environment than a domestic firm, possibly leading to higher forecast errors and dispersion of these forecasts around the mean for these firms.

Two hypotheses are tested:

Hypothesis 1: The accuracy of analysts' earnings forecasts is not significantly different between U.S. domestic firms, U.S. multinationals with operations in developed countries, and U.S. multinationals with international operations in developing countries.
Hypothesis 2: The consensus in analysts' estimates is not similar across the three groups.

RESEARCH DESIGN

Sample

Sample selection followed the same procedures as Markham Collins (1990):

1. An initial set of 230 firms, numbers 1 to 230 of the 1991 Fortune 500, was selected. Although the selection appears arbitrary, it is motivated by the need to secure firms of approximately equal size and a fairly even distribution between the three categories of international involvement (Collins, 1990, 277).

2. Given the 10% threshold set by the Statement of Financial Accounting Standard (SEAS) No. 14, firms not reporting both 10% of revenues and assets as foreign in 1988–90 were classified as domestic (group 1). Those meeting the 10% test were classified as multinationals.

3. The United States Department of Commerce classifies countries as developed or developing. Developing countries include Latin American countries, African countries (excluding South Africa), Middle Eastern countries, and Asian and Pacific countries

(excluding Japan). This distinction was used to classify subsidiaries of the multinational firms (obtained in step 2) as developed or developing. Multinational firms with at least 25% of their total foreign subsidiaries and at least eight subsidiaries in developing countries were classified as having a substantial presence in developing countries (group 3). All remaining multinationals were classified as developed-country firms (group 2).

4. The original sample was restricted to firms with available data on CRSP, IBES and *Compustat*. Absolute forecast errors in excess of 100% were deleted from the sample.

The final sample includes twenty-one group 1 firms, thirty-one group 2 firms, and twenty-six group 3 firms.

Dependant Variables

The financial analysts' predictions of annual earnings-per-share for the seventy-eight firms in the sample and the actual earnings-per-share reported by the firms were used to determine the three dependent variables: percentage of error, absolute percentage of error, and coefficient of variation. They are computed as follows:

1. Percentage of error:

$$PE_{ijt} = (FE_{ijt} - AE_{ij})/AE_{ij} \qquad (1)$$

2. Absolute percentage of error:

$$APE_{ijt} = (FE_{ijt} - AE_{ij})/AE_{ij} \qquad (2)$$

where

PE_{ijt} = Percentage of forecast error for firm i for year j for forecast horizon t

APE_{ijt} = Absolute percentage forecast error for firm i for year j for forecast horizon t

FE_{ijt} = The mean analyst earnings forecast for firm i for year j at time t

AE_{ij} = Actual annual EPS for company i for one year j

= Each of the 1988–90 years covered in the study

= Forecasting horizon, three, six, or nine months preceding the month that actual EPS is reported

3. Coefficient of variation:
The coefficient of variation is used as a measure of consensus in analysts' EPS forecasts:

$$CV^{ijt} = \sigma_{FE}/FE_{ijt}$$

Where

Table 23.1

Means, Standard Deviations, and Correlation Coefficients of Variables by Firm Group

		Correlation						
	Means (a)	*1*	*2*	*3*	*4*	*5*	*6*	*7*
a. **Developing Country Group**								
1. Percentage of Error	0.0942 (0.233)		1.000	0.2750	0.1608	-0.1469	0.1187	0.2975
2. Absolute Percentage of Error	0.3281 (0.3842)			0.2750	0.1608	-0.1469	0.1187	0.2975
3. Coefficient of Variation	0.0455 (0.0424)				0.1043	0.1843	-0.2661	0.2538
4. Systematic Risk	1.1077 (0.1090)					0.2812	0.5753	0.2276
5. Assets (in millions)	4407 (2997)						0.3439	-0.0003
6. Price/Earnings Ratio	20.8571 (10.3551)							0.2083
7. Institutional Ownership	58.7600 (16.5360)							
a. **Developed Country Group**								
1. Percentage of Error	0.1154 (0.5941)		0.6880	0.1439	0.0032	0.1245	0.2857	-0.3603
2. Absolute Percentage of Error	0.3286 (0.6282)			-0.1019	-0.0797	0.2966	0.2857	-0.0637
3. Coefficient of Variation	0.6509 (0.1296)				0.4259	-0.2074	0.0751	-0.2494
4. Systematic Risk	1.0837 (0.1595)					-0.0718	0.1846	-0.0333
5. Assets (in millions)	16816 (37808)						-0.3766	-0.2749
6. Price/Earnings Ratio	20.2258 (12.2711)							0.1787
7. Institutional Ownership	57.2619 (14.3681)							
a. **Domestic Firm Group**								
1. Percentage of Error	0.0269 (0.7029)		1.000	0.1749	-0.1227	-0.0195	0.3833	0.1142
2. Absolute Percentage of Error	0.0153 (0.2782)			0.1749	-0.1227	-0.0195	0.3833	0.1142
3. Coefficient of Variation	0.0195 (0.0781)				0.0267	-0.1870	-0.0289	0.0495
4. Systematic Risk	1.1141 0.1420					0.2140	-0.0549	0.0495
5. Assets (in millions)	19170 (34368)						-0.2644	-0.3343
6. Price/Earnings Ratio	22.3864 (10.0442)							0.2864
7. Institutional Ownership	59.8485 (11.5410)							

CV^{ijt} = Coefficient of variation of forecasts, to measure the agreement or disagreement among analysts when predicting earnings of company i for year j at time t (The smaller this coefficient, the higher the agreement among the analysts about a company's estimated future earnings)

σ_{FE} = The standard deviation of the analysts' earnings forecasts

Forecast data are derived from Institutional Brokers Estimate System (IBES), a service of Lynch, Jones and Ryan.

Table 23.2
Results of Overall Analysis of Covariance for Percentage of Error

Sources	DF	Mean Square	F Value	Pr > F
Model	6	1.334	1.88	0.0965*
Firm Group	2	1.720	2042	0.0960*
Covariates				
1. Systematic Risk	1	0.7617	1.07	0.3038
2. Price-Earning Ratio	1	1.6685	2.35	0.1258
3. Size (log of Assets)	1	2.0340	2.87	0.0950
4. Institutional Ownership		0.0994	0.14	0.7093
Error	70	0.7099		
Corrected Total	76			

*Significant at p=0.10.

Table 23.3
Results of Overall Analysis of Covariance for Absolute Percentage of Error

Sources	DF	Mean Square	F Value	Pr > F
Model	6	1.002	2.17	0.056*
Firm Group	2	1.2141	2.63	0.0791*
Covariates				
1. Systematic Risk	1	0.7077	1.53	0.2197
2. Price-Earning Ratio	1	1.683	3.65	0.0685*
3. Size (log of Assets)	1	1.163	2.52	0.1168
4. Institutional Ownership	1	0.0186	0.04	0.8412
Error	70	0.4691		
Corrected Total	76			

*Significant at p=0.10.

Covariates

Four covariates were used: size, systematic risk, price-earnings ratio, and institutional membership. Size is used as covariate because previous work has shown it to affect performance (Hall and Weiss, 1967) and variability in performance (Fisher and Hall, 1965). The natural logarithm of year-end assets is used as a proxy for firm size. Logarithm transformation is justified when values of one variable are highly skewed—as is often the case with size—because the extreme values can strongly affect correlations with other variables (Kimberly, 1976; Scherer, 1980).

One influence on prediction performance may be the differences in systematic risk across firms in the three groups. Multinational investment can be used for

Table 23.4
Results of Overall Analysis of Covariance for Coefficient of Variation

Sources	DF	Mean Square	F Value	Pr > F
Model	6	0.0009	1.35	0.2491
Firm Group	2	0.0014	2.01	0.1410
Covariates				
1. Systematic Risk	1	0.00002	0.03	0.8580
2. Price-earnings ratio	1	0.00013	0.19	0.6659
3. Size (log of sales)	1	0.0026	3.67	0.0594*
4. Institutional Ownership	1	0.00001	0.16	0.6939
Error	70	0.00071		
Corrected Total	76			

*Significant at p=0.05.

risk diversification. In addition, Barefield and Comiskey (1975) show that fore-cast errors are associated with systematic risk. For each firm in the sample, market model coefficients were estimated, examining monthly CRSP returns over the 1988–90 period.

Price-earnings ratio was used as a covariate based on Copeland and Weston's (1992) evidence that higher price/earnings ratios reflect more favorable earnings growth prospects.

Finally, institutional ownership was used as a covariate based on O'Brien and Bhushan's (1990) finding that institutional ownership is positively correlated with the number of analysts following the firm. Institutional ownership was measured by the percent of outstanding shares of stock held by banks, colleges, pension funds, insurance companies, and investment companies as calculated by Vickers Stock Research Corporation.

DATA ANALYSIS AND RESULTS

Analysis of covariance was used to test the relations between the earnings prediction performance of financial analysts and groups 1, 2, and 3. The model's covariates include systematic risk, price-earnings ratio, size, and institutional ownership.

Table 23.1 reports the means, standard deviations, and correlations by firm group for the primary variables used in the study. Tables 23.2, 23.3, and 23.4 present results for, respectively, the percentage error, the absolute percentage error, and the coefficient of variation.

The results in tables 23.2 and 23.3 suggest that the relation between firm groups and percentage of error or absolute percentage of error is significant, suggesting that the accuracy of analysts' earnings forecasts differs significantly across the three groups.

Table 23.5
Mean Comparisons of Dependent Variables for the Three Groups of Firms

	Lower confidence Unit	Difference Between Means	Upper confidence Unit	Significance (a)
1. *Percentage of Error*				
Group 3-Group 2	-0.1034	0.3468	0.7971	xxx
Group 3-Group 1	0.0327	0.5258	1.018	xxx
Group 2-Group 1	-0.2992	0.1789	0.6570	NS
2. *Absolute Percentage of Error*				
Group 3-Group 2	-0.0931	0.2699	0.6330	xxx
Group 3-Group 1	0.0513	0.4488	0.8464	xxx
Group 2-Group 1	-0.2066	0.1789	0.5644	NS
3. *Coefficient of Variation*				
Group 3-Group 2	-0.0121	0.0020	0.0163	NS
Group 3-Group 1	-0.0280	-0.0124	0.0031	NS
Group 2-Group 1	-0.0296	-0.0145	0.0006	NS

(à) xxx significant at $p = 0.05$
NS = not significant

The results in table 23.4 suggest, however, that the relation between firm groups and the coefficient of variation is not significant, suggesting similar levels of agreement in analysts' earnings forecasts for the three groups.

Table 23.5 reports a mean comparison of the dependent variables for the three groups of firms. Consistent with the multivariate results, the univariate comparisons reveal no significant differences in the dispersion of analysts' EPS forecasts.

The comparison of absolute percentage forecast errors and percentage of error shows that group 3 firms (those with significant operations in developing countries) are less accurate than those of group 2 (firms with significant international operations in developed countries) or group 1 (U.S. domestic firms).

DISCUSSION

Unlike Rivera's study (1991), our results show no differences for the earnings forecast errors for domestic and U.S. multinational firms with operations in developed countries. Rivera's study (1991) did not make the distinction between investment in developed versus developing countries. Our study shows that the earnings forecast errors of financial analysts' earnings-per-share estimates are larger for U.S. multinational firms with significant international operations in developing countries than for domestic firms or U.S. multinational firms with significant international operations in developed countries. The results point to the unique characteristics associated with investments in developing countries versus developed countries as evidenced by (a) higher returns, performance measures, and risk measures for domestic and developed-country firms relative to the developing-country firms (Markham Collins, 1990), and (b) the less than perfect correlation between equity markets across national borders, with lower correlations with developing countries and higher correlations with developed countries (Van Agtamael and Errunza, 1982; Alien, 1982; Errunza and Senbet, 1981; Errunza, 1977, 1983; Levy and Sarnat, 1970; Adler and Dumas, 1983). These characteristics translate into the higher forecasting errors of financial analysts' earnings-per-share estimates of firms with significant operations in developing countries.

CONCLUSIONS

This study investigates the accuracy and dispersion among analysts' earnings forecasts for three groups of U.S. firms: those with no significant international operations, those with significant international operations in developed countries, and those with significant international operations in developing countries. The results indicate that domestic firms and firms with significant international operations in developed countries have more accurate earnings forecasts than firms with significant international operations in developing countries. Various conclusions may be made:

1. The financial analysts' forecasts need to take into account the unique factors inherent to the developing countries' environment.
2. The similarity of the forecast errors for domestic firms and firms with international operations in developed countries points to the increasing commonality of the economic environment in the United States and the developing countries.
3. These results, coupled with those of Markham Collins (1990), suggests the need to differentiate between multinational firms operating in developed countries and those operating in developing countries.

Future research should consider the removal of two major limitations of this study. First, a classification, other than the United States Department of Commerce's classification, of developed and developing countries should be used. Some measure of per capita GNP may make more sense than a classification based on geography. Second, a classification between developed and developing country investments based on an overall percentage of revenues or assets in developing countries may be tried to test the results of this study.

REFERENCES

Adler, M., and B. Dumas. 1983. International portfolio choice and corporation finance: A synthesis. *Journal of Finance* (June): 925–84.
Albrecht, W.S., O. Johnson, L.L. Lookabill, and D.J.H. Watson. 1977. A comparison of

the accuracy of corporate and security analysts' forecasts of earnings: A comment. *The Accounting Review* (July): 736–40.

Alien, L. 1982. Return and risk in international capital markets. *Columbia Journal of World Business* (Summer): 3–23.

Baginski, S.P. 1987. Intraindustry information transfers associated with management forecasts of earnings. *Journal of Accounting Research* (Autumn): 196–216.

Baldwin, B.A. 1984. Segment earnings disclosure and the ability of security analysts to forecast earnings per share. *The Accounting Review* (July): 376–89.

Barefield, R.M., and E.E. Comiskey. 1975. The accuracy of analysts' forecasts of earnings per share. *Journal of Business Research* (July): 241–52.

Beaver, W.H., R. Clarke, and W.F. Wright. 1979. The association between unsystematic security returns and the magnitude of earnings forecast errors. *Journal of Accounting Research* 1: 316–40.

Brown, L.D., R.L. Hagerman, P.A. Griffin, and M.E. Zmijewski. 1987. Security analyst superiority relative to univariate time-series models in forecasting quarterly earnings. *Journal of Accounting and Economics* (January): 61–87.

Brown, P., G. Foster, and E. Noreen. 1985. *Security Analysts Multi-Year Earnings Forecasts and the Capitol Markets*, Studies in Accounting Research No. 21. Sarasota, FL: American Accounting Association.

Collins, J.M. 1990. A market performance comparison of U.S. firms active in domestic, developed, and developing countries. *Journal of International Business Studies* 21: 289–300.

Copeland, T.E., and J.F. Weston. 1992. *Financial Theory and Corporate Policy* (3rd edition): Reading, MA: Addjson-Wesley.

Elton, E.J., M.J. Gruber, and M. Gultekin. 1981. Expectations and share prices. *Management Science* (September): 975–87.

Errunza, V.R. 1977. 'Gains from portfolio diversification in less developed countries' securities'. *Journal of International Business Studies* (Fall/Winter): 83–99.

———. 1983. Emerging markets: A new opportunity for improving global portfolios. *Financial Analysts Journal* (September/October): 51–8.

Errunza, V.R., and L.W. Senbet. 1981. The effects of international operations on the market value of the firm: Theory and evidence. *Journal of Finance* (May): 401–17.

Fisher, N., and J.R. Hall. 1965. Risk and corporate rates of return. *Quarterly Journal of Economics* 83: 79–92.

Fried, D., and D. Givoly. 1982. Financial analysts' forecasts of earnings: A better surrogate for market expectations. *Journal of Accounting and Economics* 4: 85–108.

Givoly, D., and J. Lakonishok. 1979. The information content of financial analysts' forecasts of earnings. *Journal of Accounting and Economics* (December): 165–85.

Gonedes, N.J., N. Dopuch, and S.H. Penman. 1976. Disclosure rules, information production, and capital market equilibrium: The case of forecast disclosure rules. *Journal of Accounting Research* (Spring): 89–137.

Hall, M., and L. Weiss. 1967. Firm size and profitability. *Review of Economics and Statistics* 49: 319–31.

Imhoff, E.A. Jr. and G.J. Lobo. 1980. Information content of analysts' composite forecast revisions. *Journal of Accounting Research* (Autumn): 541–54.

Imhoff, E.A. Jr., and P.V. Pare. 1982. Analysis and comparison of earnings forecast agents. *Journal of Accounting Research* (Autumn): 429–39.

Kimberly, J.R. 1976. Organizational size and the structural perspective: A review. *Administrative Science Quarterly* 21: 571–79.

Levy, H., and M. Sarnat. 1970. International diversification of investment portfolios. *American Economic Review* (September): 668–75.

Patell, J.M. 1976. Corporate forecasts of earnings per share and stock price behaviour: Empirical tests. *Journal of Accounting Research* (Autumn): 246–76.

Penman, S.H. 1980. An empirical investigation of the voluntary disclosure of corporate earnings forecasts. *Journal of Accounting Research* (Spring): 132–60.

Rivera, J.M. 1991. Prediction performance of earnings forecasts: The case of U.S. multinationals. *Journal of International Business Studies* 22: 265–88.

Scherer, F.M. 1980. *Industrial Market Structure and Economic Performance*. Chicago: Rand McNally & Co.

Van Agtamael, A.W., and V.R. Errunza. 1982. Foreign portfolio investment in emerging securities market. *Columbia Journal of World Business* (Summer): 58–60.

Waymire, G. 1984. Additional evidence on the information content of management earnings forecasts. *Journal of Accounting Research* (Autumn): 703–18.

Index

About the Author

AHMED RIAHI-BELKAOUI is CBA Distinguished Professor of Accounting in the College of Business Administration, University of Illinois at Chicago. Author of numerous Quorum books, published and forthcoming, and coauthor of several more, he is an equally prolific contributor to the scholarly and professional journals of his field, and has served on various editorial boards that oversee them.